GLOBAL CUL1

Global Cultural Economy critically interrogates the role cultural and creative industries play in societies. By locating these industries in their broader cultural and economic contexts, Christiaan De Beukelaer and Kim-Marie Spence combine their repertoires of empirical work across four continents to define the 'cultural economy' as the system of production, distribution, and consumption of cultural goods and services, as well as the cultural, economic, social, and political contexts in which it operates.

Each chapter introduces and discusses a different theme, such as inclusion, diversity, sustainability, and ownership, highlighting the tensions around them to elicit an active engagement with possible and provisional solutions. The themes are explored through case studies including Bollywood, Ghanaian music, the Korean Wave, Jamaican Reggae, and the UN *Creative Economy Reports*.

Written with students, researchers, and policy-makers in mind, *Global Cultural Economy* is ideal for anyone interested in the creative and cultural industries, media and cultural studies, cultural policy, and development studies.

Christiaan De Beukelaer is a Lecturer in Cultural Policy at the University of Melbourne, Australia. He is the author of *Developing Cultural Industries: Learning from the Palimpsest of Practice* (2015) and the editor of *Culture, Globalization, and Development: The UNESCO Convention on Cultural Diversity* (2015, with Miikka Pyykkönen and JP Singh) as well as *Cultural Policies for Sustainable Development* (2018, with Anita Kangas and Nancy Duxbury).

Kim-Marie Spence is a Rhodes scholar and a PhD scholar at the Australian National University. She has done significant research comparing the popular culture industries of Jamaica, India, and South Korea, that is, reggae, Bollywood, K-pop, and K-drama. She is a former Jamaica Film Commissioner/Head of Creative Industries in Jamaica and also worked with UNESCO on Oral and Intangible Heritage projects.

Key Ideas in Media and Cultural Studies

The *Key Ideas in Media and Cultural Studies* series covers the main concepts, issues, debates and controversies in contemporary media and cultural studies. Titles in the series constitute authoritative, original essays rather than literary surveys, but are also written explicitly to support undergraduate teaching. The series provides students and teachers with lively and original treatments of key topics in the field.

Cultural Policy
David Bell and Kate Oakley

Reality TV
Annette Hill

Culture
Ben Highmore

Representation
Jenny Kidd

Celebrity
Sean Redmond

Global Cultural Economy
Christiaan De Beukelaer and Kim-Marie Spence

For more information about this series, please visit: https://www.routledge.com/Key-Ideas-in-Media--Cultural-Studies/book-series/KEYIDEA

GLOBAL CULTURAL ECONOMY

Christiaan De Beukelaer and
Kim-Marie Spence

Routledge
Taylor & Francis Group

LONDON AND NEW YORK

First published 2019
by Routledge
2 Park Square, Milton Park, Abingdon, Oxon OX14 4RN

and by Routledge
52 Vanderbilt Avenue, New York, NY 10017

Routledge is an imprint of the Taylor & Francis Group, an informa business

British Library Cataloguing in Publication Data
A catalogue record for this book is available from the British Library

Library of Congress Cataloging in Publication Data
Names: De Beukelaer, Christiaan, 1986- author. | Spence, Kim-Marie, author.
Title: Global cultural economy / Christiaan De Beukelaer and Kim-Marie Spence.
Description: Abingdon, Oxon; New York, NY: Routledge, 2019. | Series: Key ideas in media and cultural studies | Includes bibliographical references and index.
Identifiers: LCCN 2018021134 | ISBN 9781138670082 (hardback: alk. paper) | ISBN 9781138670099 (pbk.: alk. paper) | ISBN 9781315617800 (ebook: alk. paper)
Subjects: LCSH: Cultural industries. | Culture–Economic aspects.
Classification: LCC HD9999.C9472 D42 2019 | DDC 384--dc23
LC record available at https://lccn.loc.gov/2018021134

ISBN: 978-1-138-67008-2 (hbk)
ISBN: 978-1-138-67009-9 (pbk)
ISBN: 978-1-315-61780-0 (ebk)

Typeset in Times New Roman
by Sunrise Setting Ltd., Brixham, UK

For everyone around the world struggling to make
a living in the cultural economy

CONTENTS

FIGURES

TABLES

PREFACE

This book explicitly claims to be global. And its global scope aligns with our intentions. But it can in no way explain the cultural economy of *the entire world*. So how is it global while being strongly rooted in very particular contexts?

First, it is global in its approach. We position this book in contrast to the models, critiques, policies, and textbooks concerning the cultural and 'creative industries' primarily based on practices in a handful of 'developed', 'Western' countries. Many of these books have proven very useful to conceptualise and theorise a range of issues around these industries. But given the well-documented diversity of cultural practices, there is increasing certainty that the cultural economy comes in many forms and shapes – even if it may look superficially the same: don't Bollywood, Nollywood, and Hollywood all produce movies? We don't contest at all that they do. But we start from the premise that existing models of cultural and 'creative industries' emerged from 'Western' contexts. And as they are taken up, adapted, and used around the world, they collide with existing practices that do not map onto these 'textbook models'.

Whereas existing models were predominantly meant as analytical tools to help understand the cultural economy, they have come to be used as a prescriptive mould in many places. We frame this book in a 'global' way because we want to make this tension explicit by stressing that – rather than taking these models for granted – there is a need to allow other models, objectives, and priorities to gain greater visibility within the cultural economy.

Second, we take the work of intergovernmental organisations such as UNESCO and UNCTAD as primary data. These organisations have been more influential beyond the West than they have been in Western countries. This is in large part because their policy-oriented reports are freely available, unlike the bulk of academic research. Moreover, their *Creative Economy Reports* bring together quantitative data, 'best practice' case studies, and policy recommendations, which provides a helpful narrative for both politicians, policy-makers, activists, consultants, and artists. But in doing so, these organisations fuelled the 'aspirational' perspective on the cultural economy as discussed above. This is why we triangulated our interviews with policy analysis and use of existing quantitative datasets. In as much as we refer to the UN's *Creative Economy Reports* or datasets, we treat them as primary data, not as academic sources.

Third, though this book is global in approach, it is not as vast in its empirical scope. It does after all build on our respective empirical work, which we conducted in a variety of places, during which we conducted interviews with people working in the cultural economy, be it as artists, managers, policy-makers, activists, producers, event promotors, media workers, or union organisers. Christiaan conducted the bulk of his research in West Africa, where he looked into music industries and support mechanisms that were set up specifically to support the music business as a 'cultural' or 'creative' industry, in Ouagadougou (Burkina Faso) and Accra (Ghana), respectively. This fieldwork took place in 2013, with follow-up visits to Burkina Faso (2014, 2015, and 2016). Afterwards, he did work on some minor projects with a similar focus in Central Asia (Kazakhstan, 2016) and South East Asia (Indonesia 2016–2017). Kim-Marie conducted her research in Kingston (Jamaica) and Seoul (South Korea), where she also looked into the music industries of reggae and K-pop and the policy mechanisms established to support them. She also did fieldwork in the film and television industries respectively of Bollywood and K-drama in Mumbai (India) and in Seoul (South Korea). This fieldwork took place in 2016. She also conducted some follow-up Skype interviews, as part of her thesis write-up in 2017 and 2018.

We both benefitted from the insight and analysis of our informants. We realise that they continue to work in the global cultural economy making it a reality. In a spirit of gratitude and awareness, we have anonymised many of our informants in order that they continue contributing to the global cultural economy. However, we have included their profiles, so that their positionality and perspectives are understood.

When writing this book, we took these particular contexts as a basis to open up a discussion, draw connections, and articulate general observations. With this book, we aim to open up our findings in a way that may inform a more general discussion about what the cultural economy is, how it manifests around the world, and how we can imagine different (and often conflicting) perspectives on its futures. We do however think there is a need to clarify where we have actually conducted empirical research, how we analysed the resulting data, and how we combined our separate projects when writing this book. We would also like to thank Jan Baetens for his careful comments on the proofs.

But this book remains of course a mere attempt at opening up the debate. For the world is big, and our knowledge, time, and experience limited; we realise we're merely scratching the surface. When commenting on his own *Moby Dick*, Herman Melville said it better: '*This book is but a draught – nay, but the draught of a draught. Oh, Time, Strength, Cash, and Patience!*'

Acknowledgements

This book has benefited tremendously from the kindness of colleagues with whom we've had great conversations and feisty disagreements. We have also greatly benefited from the time and effort colleagues have put into crafting their arguments in writing. And we remain thoroughly indebted to the many interviewees who kindly agreed to meet with us during the course of our research. There are however so many people to thank for these direct and indirect contributions to this book, that we cannot even start to think about listing them all. We would however like to specifically and individually thank the following people for their direct engagement with the text presented in this book.

Above all, we would like to thank Justin O'Connor, with whom Christiaan started working on this book in 2015. A good while and a book contract later, Justin unfortunately had to pull out of the project for lack of time and due to commitments to other research and publication projects. While writing had, at that point, not yet started in earnest, Justin contributed to the book in a several crucial ways. He was integral to initial discussions about the general idea behind the book and the structure of its contents. He played a significant part in drafting the book proposal and getting a contract with the publisher. On top of this, his on-going work on the 'cultural economy' (in contrast with the 'creative economy') helped framing our argument as part of a long history of intellectual engagement with the political economy of 'cultural industries'. Surely, this is not the book Justin and Christiaan would have written, but he did make his mark on its focus and orientation. We are therefore very grateful for both his contributions to the early stages of this book and for his contributions to the literature on which we were able to build.

In the process of writing this book, we did also turn to a good number of close colleagues working in a range of disciplines for comments and feedback. We believe the book benefited greatly from the time and effort these colleagues volunteered to comment on drafts of individual chapters. Justin O'Connor commented on the Introduction. Jonathan Vickery and Natalia Grincheva commented on Cultural economy.

Anamik Saha and Dave O'Brien commented on Inclusion. Antonios Vlassis, Aleysia Whitmore, and JP Singh commented on Diversity. Carol Simpson, Erin MacLeod, and Sarah Hsia-Hall commented on Ownership. Robin Jeffrey and Dinah Hippolyte commented on Public/private. Avril Joffe and Yudhishthir Raj Isar commented on Human development. Anita Kangas, Katelijn Verstraete, and Jordi Baltà Portolés commented on Sustainability. We would also like to thank Jan Baetens for his careful comments on the proofs.

While we're grateful for their time, and welcomed many of their comments, we are also stubborn. So at times we thought it appropriate to ignore their advice. We would like to apologise for this audacity, and at once acknowledge that any and all mistakes that remain in the text are entirely our own. Indeed, despite their helpful comments, this book does not necessarily represent their views. After all, the book remains imperfect, *despite* – and not *because of* – their kind comments and suggestions.

LIST OF ABBREVIATIONS

AMC	short for AMC Theatres, cinema chain in the USA
AWS	African Writers' Series
CMO	Collective Management Organisation
COP21	2015 UN Climate Change Conference ('Conference of the Parties')
COP23	2017 UN Climate Change Conference ('Conference of the Parties')
DCMS	UK Department of Culture, Media and Sport
GATT	General Agreement on Tariffs and Trade
GDP	Gross domestic product
HBO	Home Box Office, American cable television channel
IPR	Intellectual Property Rights
JACAP	Jamaica Association of Composers and Authors
JAMMS	Jamaica Music Society
NCC	National Carnival Commission of Trinidad and Tobago
NDTV	New Delhi Television Limited, Indian television channel,
OHCHR	Office of the High Commissioner for Human Rights
SARFT	State Administration of Radio, Film and Television (Chinese government agency)
SDGs	Sustainable Development Goals, the successor to the UN Millennium Development Goals
TRIPS	Agreement on Trade-Related Aspects of Intellectual Property Rights
TTIP	Transatlantic Trade and Investment Partnership
UCLA	University of California Los Angeles
UN	United Nations
UNCTAD	United Nations Conference on Trade and Development
UNCTADstat	UNCTAD's internet-based data service
UNdata	UN's internet-based data service
UNDP	United Nations Development Programme

UNESCO	United Nations Educational, Scientific and Cultural Organisation
USTR	(Office of) US Trade Representative
WIPO	World Intellectual Property Organisation
WTO	World Trade Organisation

INTRODUCTION

Park Geun-hye was the President of South Korea between 2013 and 2017.[1] During her tenure, on January 27, 2015, to be precise, she gave a speech in Gwangju, one of the country's largest cities. During this talk at the opening of the *Gwangju Center for Creative Economy and Innovation*, she argued that automobiles (yes indeed, cars) will be at the centre of the creative economy of the city.

Car manufacturing, she claimed, connects IT, design, and environmentally friendly energy, which, she implies, are key parts of the creative economy, as reported by Yoon (2015) in *Inside Korea*. The focus on 'creative industries' in South Korea is in many ways a sensible one. The country has had significant successes in gaming, music, and film throughout the region (see e.g. Fuhr 2016). And the massive K-Pop hit song Gangnam Style released by PSY in 2012 brought that success to a global level – even if the global appeal of K-Pop remains limited. But how can anyone include car manufacturing in the set of activities we call the '*creative* economy'?

Claims about the scope and importance of the creative economy have inflated considerably since the cultural and 'creative industries' became part of global policy discourses (see Chapter one). Also in South Korea, the appeal of the creative is in large part aspirational: it conveys the hope and aspiration that culture and creativity will generate wealth for society and international regard. Given the significant economic importance of *chaebol*, very large corporations,[2] in the South Korean economy, Mundy (2015) reports for the *Financial Times*, that there is much hope that Small and Medium Enterprises (or SMEs) will diversify the economy. During the tenure of Park Chung Hee (from the May 16 coup in 1961 until 1979), the promotion of *chaebol* was central to South Korea's economic policy (see Chapter four). Currently, the reliance on these gigantic firms and their stifling hierarchies have paved the way for the creative economy ideas President Park Geun-hye (who happens to be Park Chung Hee's daughter) has promoted until her impeachment in 2017.

South Korea's engagement with the creative economy is strongly connected with its political culture. The agenda, which conservative President Park Geun-hye promoted, depoliticises culture, focused on creativity as a driver of economic growth, and subdued criticism or alternative narratives on what a creative Korean society might look like (Lee 2016). This discourse broke with earlier attention to the role of culture in society and its place in the nation's economy. Under authoritarian military rule (1962–1993), cultural expressions served to cement a national identity, while *chaebol* served to secure economic growth. Under President Kim Young-sam (1993–1997), cultural policy shifted towards economic instrumentalism through the *Cultural Industries Directorate* set up in 1994. In parallel with the rise of *Hallyu* (the Korean Wave), President Kim Dae-jung (1998–2002) further expanded policy support for the sector, while renaming them *content industries*. This focus and support further expanded under the presidencies of Roh Moo-hyun (2003–2007) and Lee Myung-bak (2008–2012) (Kwon and Kim 2014; Lee 2016). The last shift heralded by President Park Geun-hye (2013–2016) was towards the creative economy in a way that was detached from cultural activity that it forms a great example of how all-encompassing and ultimately meaningless the *creative economy* has become as a concept (see Chapter one).

Why do we start a book called *Global Cultural Economy* with a story about the *creative* economy? The irony is not lost on us. We deliberately focus on an excessively (and rather exceptionally) broad use of the creative economy to make a point about why we see flaws in the current policy – and to a great extent also academic – discourse about art, culture, and creativity in societies around the world.

CULTURAL OR CREATIVE?

President Park Geun-hye's mention of cars as central to the creative economy is quite a stretch, but she is not the first to make this argument. Daniel Mato, an Argentinian scholar made a similar point in the provocative paper *All Industries are Cultural* (Mato 2009). While Park's argument is based on the creativity that goes into making cars, Mato's argument builds on the meaning cars have in people's lives:

> Consumers do not choose cars only on the basis of their functional properties, but also, and very significantly, based on their symbolic characteristics. Every car is 'different,' and also a significant object that becomes a resource for the owner's personal imagination and desires, including his/her personal 'needs' not only of mobility but also of personal identity and group belonging.
>
> (Mato 2009, 73–74)

Daniel Mato further argues that beyond the symbolic meaning of the kind of car someone uses, they have also had an important and lasting effect on the other parts of our lives, including "work, entertainment, friendship, courtship, sexuality" and spatial planning, for example shopping malls and suburbs that would be structured very differently if cars had not existed (2009, 81). Perhaps most importantly, the car industry gave its name to a whole epoch of industrial production and labour organisation, bringing with it that whole set of socio-cultural 'structures of feeling' associated with 'Fordism'.[3]

In a reaction to Daniel Mato's article, Toby Miller argues that *Not All Industries Are Cultural, and No Industries Are Creative* (Miller 2009). His retort to Mato's argument is first, that the claim that *all* industries are cultural makes the point redundant – much like claiming that 'everything is political' does (2009, 92). More importantly, the assessment as to whether or not industries are cultural or creative depends as much on if one looks at why things are consumed (as Daniel Mato argues) or what goes into their production (as Toby Miller argues).

There is, however, an important debate that simmers underneath the discursive disagreement between Mato and Miller: the distinct political and ideological implications of their arguments.[4] The differences in interpretation also have significant implications regarding the clas-sification of these industries for policy and measurement purposes. When the UK Department of Culture Media and Sport released its 'creative industries' strategy in 1997, they deliberately used 'creative' over 'cultural' industries because its broader definition would allow them to make bigger claims about the role of these industries in the UK economy. In the next chapter, we will dissect this shift and its meaning on macro-economic thinking in further detail. But here, we want to point out why 'creative industries' are not the same as 'cultural industries', and why we prefer the latter.

Nicholas Garnham commented on the discursive shift from cultural to 'creative industries' as a strategic policy decision:

> The term "creative" was chosen so that the whole of the computer software sector could be included. Only on this basis was it possible to make the claims about size and growth stand up. [But] the pursuit of these aims, the shift from cultural to creative industries marks a return to an artist-centred, supply-side cultural support policy and away from that policy direction, which the use of the term "cultural industries" originally signalled, that focused on distribution and consumption.
>
> (Garnham 2005, 26–27)

While the shift towards creation was a welcome change for the arts lobby (Garnham 2005, 27), it was the greater economic significance of the 'creative industries' that gave the discourse its broad appeal across policy domains. This is what has allowed for an ever-expanding definition and demarcation of the creative economy. Which in turn allowed President Park Geun-hye to claim that car manufacturing is part of the creative economy.

The definition, demarcation, and scope of the cultural and 'creative industries' remains important; if only because the implications of using one term over the other is not sufficiently well understood by many activists, policy-makers, cultural workers, and academics (De Beukelaer and Vlassis 2019). What we propose here is a simultaneous expansion and contraction of the scope of the sector by introducing a relatively new term: the cultural economy. It expands the notion of the 'cultural *industries*' as it provides a framework to understand monetary *and* non-monetary transactions in the creation, dissemination, and engagement with culture. It contrasts the notion of the *'creative* industries' and economy, by reframing the sector as a *cultural* affair. This does not mean that artistic and cultural endeavours are not creative, but rather rejects that *reductio ad absurdum* as inevitable in the Korean case.

We hope it is by now clear that we prefer the reflexive *'cultural* industries' above the generally celebratory *'creative* industries' and thereby position this book as a global response to key texts in the field (Hesmondhalgh 2013; Oakley and O'Connor 2015). But why do we then focus on the cultural *economy*, and not the 'cultural *industries'*?

INDUSTRIES OR ECONOMY?

While the 'cultural *industries'* presume (or at least suggest) a certain structuration through their organisational form, these structures differ significantly (albeit often invisibly) around the world. These differences can be relatively minor in that these industries may look quite the same, in that, as noted before, films are produced in fairly similar ways in Nigeria, India, and the US. But the significance of the differences that define these different film industries is the path dependency that gave rise to their existence (De Beukelaer 2015, 2017).

We build on Alex Perullo's engagement with the 'music economy' in Tanzania (Perullo 2011). He uses the term to stress the need for a grounded understanding of how music functions as an economy, rather than evaluating whether or not 'cultural industries' in 'the rest' of the world have all the characteristics and institutions we expect them to have in 'the West'. The 'cultural economy' is thus less prescriptive than the 'cultural industries', but it is not the same as 'cultural economics':

> The cultural economy is distinct from *cultural economics*, in that it does not refer to the *economy of culture* as a distinct system underpinning the production of cultural value(s). The cultural economy rather refers to the intersection of cultural and economic values across the full range of practices and institutions involved in cultural production.
>
> (O'Connor 2016, 5)

We follow Justin O'Connor in the three characteristics of the 'cultural economy' he sketches:

> It suggests first, that culture articulates – in its production and consumption – values that cannot be reduced to economic value – that is, the monetary value of transactions – even though it produces economic value. Second, the logics and ethics of cultural production (the *kind* of economy that produces culture) impacts and influences the kind of culture that results from it. Third, somewhat more radically, the way we frame and understand cultural value, rather than having to constantly translate itself into economic value, can help imagining how the economy itself might be re-framed, and thus provide a major contribution to re-thinking the challenges facing a global society of the 21st century. As Chris Gibson put it, cultural economy 'resonates well with the imminent requirement that we question current, unsustainable economic practices – requiring, I would argue, a bolder sense of the rightness/ wrongness of forms of production and commoditisation'.
>
> (O'Connor 2016, 5)

By focusing on the cultural economy, much like Alex Perullo focuses on the music economy, we aim to open up the debate beyond the 'value chain' of the industry, but open up to the normative dimensions of the economy.

While we do embrace the 'cultural economy' as the guiding concept to explain transactions of cultural expressions in contrast to 'cultural industries', we do not use the term 'cultural ecology'. John Holden, the former head of British think-tank Demos, does however argue that:

> Culture is often discussed as an economy, but it is better to see it as an ecology, because this viewpoint offers a richer and more complete understanding of the subject. Seeing culture as an ecology is congruent with cultural value approaches that take into account a wide range of non-monetary values.
>
> (Holden 2015, 2)

His definition of the cultural ecology builds on the work of Ann Markusen, who argues that the 'cultural ecology as the complex interdependencies that shape the demand for and production of arts and cultural offerings' (Markusen 2010, 8).

We steer clear from that term because, to us, a 'cultural ecology' does not adequately reflect the dynamics that characterise the cultural economy. The term ecology suggests it is a self-contained system that can survive on its own, as long as predators and prey keep each other in balance. The sheer influence of power (through elites, counter-cultures, and the power of numbers) makes this a distorted way of looking at the complex interplay of cultural production, distribution, and consumption – particularly when moving beyond the parochialism intrinsic to local or national perspectives. Moreover, the far-reaching influence of policy and regulation (both of elites and more democratic pressures) makes it difficult to consider the cultural economy an ecology or eco-system.

The ecology metaphor raises further questions about how the sector operates. Is the cultural ecology a field where the survival of the fittest dictates the outcomes in a way that mirrors social Darwinism? Or are cultural workers conservationists of endangered cultural species and landscapes? Or is cultural policy a form of genetic engineering, where elites cross-breed their preferred cultural creations (positive eugenics) while starving off those deemed undesirable for moral or strategic reasons (negative eugenics)? While we consider these questions valid, we argue that the term 'cultural economy' better equips us to analyse the political economy of cultural production, distribution, and consumption across the world.

ANALYSIS, IDEOLOGY, STRATEGY

The debate on the definition, scope, and tensions between cultural and 'creative industries' and economies are thus subject to intense debate. These different viewpoints result in different demarcations of the field, as illustrated by the variety of models that are in use. On the one hand, there are international organisations that present models that are largely pragmatic, as they align with their institutional interests and priorities, meaning that WIPO focuses on 'copyright industries', UNESCO prioritises culture, and UNCTAD stresses goods and services that are traded (De Beukelaer and Vlassis 2019). On the other hand, academics are more concerned with the ontological side of the debate; they care far more about building an understanding of what these industries are and how they relate than how to measure and strengthen the activities that fall in these categories (Garnham 2005; Hesmondhalgh 2013; Potts and Cunningham 2008; Throsby 2008;). The cultural economy has long suffered from a blurring of analysis, ideology, and strategy in the observations and claims that drive policy and strategy debates.

Many staunch defenders of the '*creative industries*' agenda have long remained immune to criticism regarding the semantic imprecision and political flimsiness of the discourse as a whole. Two such defenders recently admitted this confusion by stating that 'the conflation of culture with 'creative industries' since 1997 has harmed both cultural policy and 'creative industries' policy in the UK', which they argue critics have done (Bakhshi and Cunningham 2016, 3). But they fail to acknowledge that critics of the 'creative industries' have made that point many times over since the '*creative industries*' became a common trope in policy and academic debates. Worse, they dismiss critics like Justin O'Connor as a naive reactionary romanticist, as if he argues that moving away from the 'creative industries' will have us 'travel to sunny uplands where we can deal with cultural value unencumbered by an untoward economism' (Bakhshi and Cunningham 2016, 6).

At the other end of the ideological spectrum, Graeme Turner argues that while a political engagement used to be at the core of research into the 'cultural industries', different interests and readings of these activities have fragmented policy and research. What got lost in this fragmentation, he stresses, is the 'critical examination of this fragmentation of the cultural, social, and political function and potential of the 'cultural industries' (Turner 2015, 536).

Fragmentation, in turn, resulted in a variety of perspectives on the cultural economy. We identify five such perspectives: Celebratory, Aspirational, Refusenik, Agnostic, Reflexive (see Figure 0.1). These are not simply pragmatic or ontological, but reveal ideological presumptions at their core. These approaches may look like distinct, apolitical 'models', but it is more important to understand what the underlying approaches towards these industries are. While they do overlap in practice, these perspectives are a helpful starting point to make the political and ideological underpinnings of the cultural economy explicit.

Celebratory	Aspirational	Refusenik	Agnostic	Reflexive
• Optimistic • Uncritical • Grand claims • Economic focus • Proselytising • Contradictions and negative effects not or under-addressed • Depoliticised	• 'Pragmatic' strategy to drive economy / employment / tourism / exports • Place branding (as soft power) • Strong reliance on 'best practices' • Politically expedient and multifunctional	• Rejection of economic focus • Questioning of economic claims • Stress on negative effects • Neo-Marxist • 'Neoliberal' as critique • Political	• Empirical • Acknowledges complexity of industries • Remains neutrally investigative • No political stance • Not depoliticising	• Focus on contradictions • *Longue durée* • Reconnects theory and policy • Stresses need to be explicit about normative positions

Figure 0.1 Five perspectives on the cultural economy

Source: The authors.

The *Celebratory* perspective provides an optimistic (and at times wilfully uncritical) account of the role of the 'creative industries' (they rarely use 'cultural industries') can play in cities, regions, countries, and the world as a whole. In this context, the global competition of cities to become 'creative' (Landry 2000; Landry and Bianchini 1995) in an attempt to attract the 'creative class' (Florida 2002) in order to build a 'creative nation' (DCMS 1998; Government of Australia 1994) that will drive the economy towards growth and prosperity. In doing so, those proselytising the celebratory perspective offer a framework for 'post-industrial' growth strategies in sync with the orthodox paradigm of neo-liberal economics. While initially formulated as a strategy rooted in the local realities of Australia and Britain (Howkins 2002; Smith 1998), the idea soon caught on as a global blueprint for economic growth and development across the world (Prince 2010; UNCTAD and UNDP 2008, 2010; Wang 2004).

The *Aspirational* perspective is most common among cities, regions, and countries that buy into the idea of the cultural economy as one a driver of their local economy, be it by increasing employment, generating exports, bringing in tourism, or to formalise existing activities (so they can be counted in official statistics). Beyond these tangible outcomes, governments often embrace this aspirational perspective as a branding exercise – where the mere claim to be a 'creative' region or 'cultural' capital may bring tourism, investment, growth, and international regard even if the proliferation of such labels (see Green 2017) makes this a game of diminishing results.

What may seem like a 'pragmatic' opportunity for politicians, policymakers, but also activists and artists, is in fact the unreflexive acceptance of the 'Celebratory' take on the cultural economy. Most often, this is not down to ill faith but rather for lack of balanced information. Many consultants and reports do after all peddle a view of the cultural economy that exaggerates the positives and downplays the negatives. As a result, these aspirations often build on the hope that successes elsewhere ('best practices') can be copied, or at least emulated. This hopeful perspective makes this particular interpretation of the cultural economy politically expedient, as its preoccupation with the positive makes it a useful tool across the political spectrum. The difficulty is that the aspirations build both on a limited understanding of local needs and the contexts in which 'best practices' emerged (resulting in uncritical and often uncritical 'policy transfer'). Most importantly, the people voicing aspirations and high hopes, often insufficiently understand the negative sides of the cultural economy, its inherent contradictions, and the nuances between different sectors and approaches.

The *Refusenik* perspective encompasses a refusal to accept what is perceived as a reduction of artistic and cultural value to the 'economy'. Such refusal can be found in the writings of many arts advocates, such as Tusa (2014) or Hewison (2014). We have sympathy with some of these approaches – trying as they are to identify a value for art beyond the econometric – but suggest they avoid dealing with the reality of contemporary culture. Equally, whilst open to discussing the workings and socio-cultural implications of these industries, the Refusenik perspective is highly aware of the ideological underpinnings of the cultural and 'creative industries' as 'neo-liberal'. The book *Politicizing Creative Economy* by Da Costa (2016), an education and development scholar, is a great example: she writes with fabulous detail about political theatre in India and produces a strong political critique of the creative economy as neoliberal, but she does so without due reference to the more agnostic and reflexive literature on the cultural economy.

The continued attention to the ideological underpinnings and concomitant power relations influencing the cultural and 'creative industries' make this approach the contemporary heir to the critical theory approach initially articulated by Theodor Adorno and Max Horkheimer (2008). In a scathing critique of Richard Florida's global copy-paste consultancy, Jim McGuigan argues that Florida's 'ideas – or, rather, buzzwords – make little in the way of an original contribution to such questionable thought and the specious arguments he repeats constantly are either seriously flawed or merely trite'.[5] McGuigan's critique suggests that 'Florida's principal concerns are not to do with cultural policy as such but instead are about the articulation of neoliberal economics with cool culture' (McGuigan 2009, 298). Many critics equate 'creative industries' with the tide of neo-liberalism, and creative cities with gentrification. However, we follow Hesmondhalgh et al. (2014) in their argument that while this agenda certainly has neoliberal roots, its critique demands more than a blanket rejection solely on the basis of its neoliberal ideology.

The *Agnostic* perspective builds on the legacy of the early empirical engagement with the 'industries culturelles' by French sociologists and media scholars (e.g. Girard 1982; Huet et al. 1978; Miège 1979, 1987) and later work of their Anglophone counterparts (Caves 2000; Fitzgerald 2011). The main tenet of this strand is that it is driven by detailed empirical work. It may lead to extrapolations and discussions of the broader political economy of the cultural and 'creative industries', but it does not start from an ideological *a priori* objection to the sector. However, this perspective tends to drop the explicit or implicit critique of these approaches in favour of a more neutral investigative stance. Work within industrial and economic geography, which has given rise to a wealth of valuable empirical studies, tends to leave aside the cultural political debates, though often keeping the implicit sense that these are benign economies.

The *Reflexive* perspective explores the contemporary conditions of cultural production and consumption, and the policy settings that shape them, through the cultural and 'creative industries'. These scholars often work in media and communications studies (Banks 2017; Hesmondhalgh 2013; Oakley and O'Connor 2015; O'Connor 2010; Saha 2018), focus on labour conditions (McRobbie 2016; Menger 2009), or develop a critique of the cultural economy through one particular industry (Brouillette 2014). Their reflexive approaches embrace the contradictions of the cultural economy as an intrinsic characteristic that requires political attention. They tend to locate current issues and challenges in the *longue durée* of cultural production, without discounting the successive layers of nuance it has acquired over time. In order to do so, it connects these layers of (contradictory) theoretical perspectives with empirical rigour. And, perhaps most importantly, this perspective maintains that we need to make the normative foundations and assumptions underlying these different approaches explicit.

Needless to say, these approaches overlap. Many researchers and commentators take on board the complexities of the cultural economy when pointing out what is worth celebrating, critiquing, explaining, and reflecting upon. The reason we advocate a reflexive approach that is informed by critical perspectives and empirical exploration is that such reflexivity is necessary to work with these concepts: 'those who join the bandwagon are increasingly both instrumentalising and instrumentalised; all too often they miss the complexities, the contradictions, and the pitfalls of this agenda, as well as the relations of cause and effect that underpin it' (Anheier and Isar 2008, 6).

BOOK OVERVIEW

This book aims to provoke debate. It aims to challenge the received wisdom by grounding our discussion in the reality of the functioning of the cultural economy in various locales the world over. Yet we do not want to suggest that a return from 'creative' to 'cultural' industries or from the 'creative' to the 'cultural' economy closes future engagement with the questions we have raised do far. But we do want to challenge the ever-expanding scope of the 'creative industries' (and economy) as an academic and policy script. We started the chapter with reference to the president of South Korea who referred to automobile manufacturing as part of the creative economy. Rather than disparaging anyone's use of these malleable concepts, we want to expose underlying normative questions.

We challenge the celebratory language (see Figure 0.1) that so often surrounds this subject by refocusing the debate. We do so in four overlapping ways. First, we shift the attention to 'cultural' as opposed to 'creative' industries. Second, we explore the role and meaning of these 'cultural industries' in their broader social, cultural, and economic context. Hence the focus on the cultural *economy*: it's about what surrounds these industries in terms of social organisation, cultural context, and political economy that matters. Third, we take an explicitly global approach to the cultural economy. Thereby we interrogate how the global discourse connects to initiatives and policies at regional, national, and urban levels. Fourth, we clarify the tension inherent tension that culture is tradition and innovation, old and new, familiar and alien. Through our own empirical work across Asia, Africa, Europe, and Australia, we provide a rich overview of examples.

We aim to re-politicise the debate by foregrounding its normative dimensions. We aim to embrace the complexity of culture and its relation to the economic. We aim to delineate the cultural economy more clearly and narrowly than the creative economy, in an attempt to provide a more precise and useful term.

In sum, through this book, we hope to defy the depoliticised pragmatism of the creative economy agenda as contradictory, by embracing the Reflexive perspective. We argue that what some proselytisers of this agenda might call pragmatism, is in fact concealing an unspoken agenda. Some criticise the creative economy for its far-fetched neoliberal overtones, we do not simply dismiss this policy discourse on these grounds. Similarly, critics of the agenda who are political but insufficiently grounded in the inherent contradictions of the discourse, equally miss the mark. We rather argue that we need to repoliticise the debate by making the normative and ideological choices more explicit. Questions around inclusion, ownership, state intervention, and sustainability can never simply be 'pragmatic', they are always deeply political. Our discussion aims to resurface such political choices in order to fuel a debate about strategic possibilities and ideological perspectives, rather than the embracing of a hegemonic discourse because of its 'pragmatic' appeal.

Throughout the following chapters, we will explore and explain the tension and contradictions that may seem paradoxical, but merely conceal normative arguments and debates. These normative arguments (which implicitly or explicitly argue what the cultural economy *should* be like) are often reduced to an opposition between neoliberal free-market economics and neo-Marxist public economics. Yet, the rise of social entrepreneurship, commons, sharing economies, decentralised distribution, and so on paint a far more complex picture. Even so, these strategies and trajectories are never neutral or merely technical choices; they are deeply rooted in both the path dependencies of practices and the ideological frameworks used to understand history and plan for the future. This book is meant as a tool to navigate these choices in order to help stakeholders in the global cultural economy make informed choices.

Chapter one, *Cultural economy* argues that naming and classifying the cultural economy is a political act. Political in this context does not mean party politics, the political implications of the choices people make about the cultural economy—whether knowingly or unknowingly. This is why organisations use their position to define and delineate the scope of the cultural economy. We focus on two such institutional perspectives to the cultural economy, first, UNCTAD, which advances measurement and advocacy, and second, UNESCO, which argues for formalisation of the existing informal practices while carefully considering competing normative options. We then discuss why it matters that different countries continue to use different terms to describe the cultural economy, often without realising the implications of their discursive choices. We conclude that the cultural economy – much like culture itself –has globalised, but it has not become homogeneous in the process.

Chapter two, *Inclusion*, highlights an important tension between policy claims and research findings. While many policy documents claim that the cultural economy will help foster social inclusion, the evidence suggests otherwise. The cultural economy systematically excludes people based on race, gender, and class and other ascriptive qualities. And often different forms of exclusion intersect. We highlight these issues through a variety of cases and argue that for people working outside the key cities of the global cultural economy, further barriers to exclusion exist.

Chapter three, *Diversity*, addresses the tension between the general commitment to cultural diversity in the global cultural economy and the difficulty to govern it. We address what the *exception culturelle* means in international trade agreements and why it matters in debates around cultural diversity. We then explain how UNESCO tries to 'protect and promote' cultural diversity through its *Convention on the Protection and Promotion of the Diversity of Cultural Expressions*. The *African Writers Series*, and 'African' literature more generally, illustrates that the global cultural economy is not neatly organised country by country. We argue this creates tensions between intergovernmental (UNESCO) regulations and individual countries that have to implement and enforce them.

Chapter four, *Public/private*, calls into question how to balance the need for governmental regulation and public support with private interests in the cultural economy. The cases of Korea, India, Trinidad and Tobago, and China illustrate the extent to which the economic expediency of culture dominates the engagement with the cultural economy. We argue that despite the high hopes of economic return, many activities in the cultural economy still need continuous support (*subsidy*) and not start-up funding (*investment*) to survive.

Chapter five, *Ownership*, explores why some people argue copyright is a precondition for the cultural economy to work, while there is ample evidence than large parts of the global cultural economy function despite a lack of legislation or ineffective enforcement. However, existing mechanisms that guarantee individual copyright are not enough to ensure that individuals are compensated if the power and knowledge is not in their favour. We therefore conclude that copyright, as presently implemented, is not an intrinsic guarantor of economic benefit, especially for the powerless in the global cultural economy. At the same time, we argue for a cultural rights-based approach beyond a methodologically individualist legal regime that fails to equitably share both the moral and material interests of the global cultural economy.

Chapter six, *Human development*, raises two key questions about how the cultural economy may foster development of societies, beyond mere economic growth. First, how does the cultural economy contribute to human development while also relying human development to function properly? Second, how do we ensure human rights are respected when talking about the cultural or creative economy, which has in many ways depoliticised the discourse about the arts, by favouring economic performance over cultural value? In response to these questions, we argue that the cultural economy is not intrinsically a driver of human development nor human rights. But it can help attaining these goals by strengthening capabilities if policy and intervention explicitly focus on attaining these specific goals.

Chapter seven, *Sustainability*, explores the tension between the use of culture as an awareness-raising force towards sustainability and as a sector that puts a strain on the planetary environment itself. How can we balance the claim that culture is a 'driver of sustainable development' and the realisation cultural production can be a serious threat to a possible transition to such sustainable futures? We explore this tension by looking at 'four strategic paths' to linking the cultural economy to sustainable development. First, by safeguarding and sustaining cultural practice; second, by 'greening' the operations of cultural organisations; third, by raising awareness about sustainability and climate change through the arts; and fourth, by fostering global citizenship to strengthen political support to tackle the global issue through global measures. We conclude that while there are many good reasons to see positive links between culture and sustainability, there is no evidence of such a self-evident positive correlation.

We start each chapter with a particular case that serves to locate the paradoxes we discuss in a particular context. We then open up to a more general discussion, while drawing on other examples. The grounded approach to the issues we highlight in this book are meant to clarify that we should always approach questions around the key issues we discuss in each chapter as intrinsically interconnected with the context in which they manifest. The 'cultural economy' is a great concept to focus the debate. But the cultural economy as a concept is more helpful as an analytical lens (which is how we try to use it) than as a prescriptive framework (which is what we try to avoid).

NOTES

1 Park Geun-hye became the first Korean President to be impeached. She was impeached on charges of corruption involving collecting millions in bribes and coercing donations to foundations connected to her advisor Choi Soon-sil. The verdict will be announced in April 2018. Interestingly, Park's impeachment was largely due to widespread public protests in favour of her removal.

2 The word *chaebol* is a contraction of *chae* ('money or property') and *bol* ('clan'), and refers to massive family controlled companies such as Samsung, Hyundai, and LG that are a central and unique feature of the South Korean economy, following the Korean War (1950–1953).

3 We think of modern labour organisation in terms of 'Fordist', referring to Henry Ford who perfected the assembly for the production of the *Ford T* in 1913. The cultural economy is organised in a more 'flexible' manner than Ford's assembly line, which inspired some to call the 'flexible specialisation' in the 'cultural industries' 'post-Fordist' – even if that term may be misleading given the remaining power of media conglomerates (Hesmondhalgh 1996).

4 See also the more comprehensive work of others who have weighed in on this throughout the history of cultural and 'creative industries' (Hesmondhalgh 2013; O'Connor 2010, 2011).

5 In his latest book, *The New Urban Crisis: How Our Cities Are Increasing Inequality, Deepening Segregation, and Failing the Middle Class – and What We Can Do About It*, Florida (2017) acknowledged (or admitted?) the negative (and allegedly unintentional) side-effects of his 'creative class' ideology at the core of creative city strategies he has promoted for over 15 years. But if some commentators interpret the book as a *mea culpa*, by claiming 'Richard Florida is sorry' (Whetherell 2017), he contests this explicitly in an interview a month later: '"I'm not sorry," [Florida] barks, sitting in a hotel lobby in Mayfair, wearing a leather jacket and black T-shirt. "I will not apologise. I do not regret anything"' (Wainwright 2017).

REFERENCES

Adorno, Theodor W., and Max Horkheimer. 2008. *Dialectic of Enlightenment*. London; New York, NY: Verso.

Anheier, Helmut K, and Yudhishthir Raj Isar. 2008. "Introducing the Cultures and Globalization Series and the Cultural Economy". In *The Cultural Economy: The Cultures and Globalization Series 2*, edited by Helmut K Anheier and Yudhishthir Raj Isar, 1–12. Los Angeles, CA; London: Sage.

Bakhshi, Hasan, and Stuart Cunningham. 2016. *Cultural Policy in the Time of the Creative Industries*. London: Nesta.

Banks, Mark. 2017. *Creative Justice: Cultural Industries, Work and Inequality*. London; New York, NY: Rowman & Littlefield International.

Brouillette, Sarah. 2014. *Literature and the Creative Economy*. Stanford, CA: Stanford University Press.

Caves, Richard. 2000. *Creative Industries: Contracts between Art and Commerce*. Cambridge, MA: Harvard University Press.

Da Costa, Dia. 2016. *Politicizing Creative Economy: Activism and a Hunger Called Theater*. Dissident Feminisms. Urbana, IL: University of Illinois Press.

DCMS. 1998. *Creative Industries Mapping Document*. London: DCMS.

De Beukelaer, Christiaan. 2015. *Developing Cultural Industries: Learning from the Palimpsest of Practice*. Amsterdam: European Cultural Foundation.

De Beukelaer, Christiaan. 2017. "Toward an 'African' Take on the Cultural and Creative Industries?" *Media, Culture & Society* 39 (4): 582–91.

De Beukelaer, Christiaan, and Antonios Vlassis. 2019. "Creative Economy and International Development: Institutional Perspectives". In *The Cultural Turn in International Aid*, edited by Sophia Labadi. London: Routledge.

Fitzgerald, Scott W. 2011. *Corporations and Cultural Industries: Time Warner, Bertelsmann, and News Corporation*. Lanham, MD: Lexington Books.

Florida, Richard. 2002. *The Rise of the Creative Class*. New York, NY: Basic Books.

Florida, Richard. 2017. *The New Urban Crisis: How Our Cities Are Increasing Inequality, Deepening Segregation, and Failing the Middle Class – and What We Can Do about It*. New York, NY: Basic Books.

Fuhr, Michael. 2016. *Globalization and Popular Music in South Korea: Sounding out K-Pop*. Routledge Studies in Popular Music 7. New York, NY: Routledge.

Garnham, Nicholas. 2005. "From Cultural to Creative Industries: An Analysis of the Implications of the 'Creative Industries' Approach to Arts and Media Policy Making in the United Kingdom". *International Journal of Cultural Policy* 11 (1): 15–29.

Girard, Augustin. 1982. "Cultural Industries: A Handicap or a New Opportunity for Cultural Development?" In *Cultural Industries: A Challenge for the Future of Culture*, edited by UNESCO, 24–39. Paris: UNESCO.

Government of Australia. 1994. *Creative Nation: Commonwealth Cultural Policy*. Canberra: Government of Australia. www.pandora.nla.gov.au/pan/21336/20031011-0000/www.nla.gov.au/creative.nation/contents.html.

Green, Steve. 2017. "Capitals of Culture: An Introductory Survey of a Worldwide Activity". Prasino. www.prasino.eu/wp-content/uploads/2017/10/Capitals-of-Culture-An-introductory-survey-Steve-Green-October-2017.pdf.

Hesmondhalgh, David. 1996. "Flexibility, Post-Fordism and the Music Industries". *Media, Culture & Society* 18 (3): 469–88.

Hesmondhalgh, David. 2013. *The Cultural Industries*. 3rd ed. London: Sage.

Hesmondhalgh, David, Melissa Nisbett, Kate Oakley, and David Lee. 2014. "Were New Labour's Cultural Policies Neo-Liberal?" *International Journal of Cultural Policy* 21 (1): 97–114.

Hewison, Robert. 2014. *Cultural Capital: The Rise and Fall of Creative Britain*. London; New York, NY: Verso.

Holden, John. 2015. *The Ecology of Culture: A Report Commissioned by the Arts and Humanities Research Council's Cultural Value Project*. Swindon: Arts and Humanities Research Council.

Howkins, John. 2002. *The Creative Economy: How People Make Money from Ideas*. London: Penguin.

Huet, Armel, Jacques Ion, Alain Lefebvre, René Peron, and Bernard Miège. 1978. *Capitalisme et Industries Culturelles*. Actualités Recherches: Sociologie, Grenoble: Presses Universitaires de Grenoble.

Kwon, Seung-Ho, and Joseph Kim. 2014. "The Cultural Industry Policies of the Korean Government and the Korean Wave". *International Journal of Cultural Policy* 20 (4): 422–39.

Landry, Charles. 2000. *The Creative City: A Toolkit for Urban Innovators*. London: Earthscan Publications.

Landry, Charles, and Franco Bianchini. 1995. *The Creative City*. London: Demos.

Lee, Hye-Kyung. 2016. "Politics of the 'Creative Industries' Discourse and Its Variants". *International Journal of Cultural Policy* 22 (3): 438–55.

Markusen, Ann. 2010. *California's Arts and Cultural Ecology*. San Francisco, CA: James Irvine Foundation.

Mato, Daniel. 2009. "All Industries Are Cultural". *Cultural Studies* 23 (1): 70–87.

McGuigan, Jim. 2009. "Doing a Florida Thing: The Creative Class Thesis and Cultural Policy". *International Journal of Cultural Policy* 15 (3): 291–300.

McRobbie, Angela. 2016. *Be Creative Making a Living in the New Culture Industries*. Chichester: Wiley. www.public.eblib.com/choice/PublicFullRecord.aspx?p=4353616.

Menger, Pierre-Michel. 2009. *Le Travail Créateur: S'accomplir Dans l'incertain*. Paris: Gallimard.

Miège, Bernard. 1979. "The Cultural Commodity". *Media, Culture & Society* 1 (3): 297–311.

Miège, Bernard. 1987. "The Logics at Work in the New Cultural Industries". *Media, Culture & Society* 9 (3): 273–89.

Miller, Toby. 2009. "From Cultural to Creative Industries: Not All Industries Are Cultural, and No Industries Are Creative". *Cultural Studies* 23 (1): 88–99.

Mundy, Simon. 2015. "South Korea Aims for Creative Economy to End Reliance on Chaebol". *Financial Times*. June 24, 2015. www.ft.com/intl/cms/s/0/9203e38c-odab-11e5-9a65-00144feabdco.html#axzz45Zq6wxg8.

Oakley, Kate, and Justin O'Connor, eds. 2015. *The Routledge Companion to the Cultural Industries*. London: Routledge.

O'Connor, Justin. 2010. *The Cultural and Creative Industries: A Literature Review*. 2nd ed. Newcastle upon Tyne: Creativity Culture and Education.

O'Connor, Justin. 2011. "The Cultural and Creative Industries: A Critical History". *Ekonomiaz* 78 (3): 24–45.

O'Connor, Justin. 2016. "After the Creative Industries: Cultural Policy in Crisis". *Law, Social Justice & Global Development* 1: 1–18.

Perullo, Alex. 2011. *Live from Dar Es Salaam: Popular Music and Tanzania's Music Economy*. Bloomington, IN: Indiana University Press.

Potts, Jason, and Stuart Cunningham. 2008. "Four Models of the Creative Industries". *International Journal of Cultural Policy* 14 (3): 233–47.

Prince, Russell. 2010. "Globalizing the Creative Industries Concept: Travelling Policy and Transnational Policy Communities". *The Journal of Arts Management, Law, and Society* 40 (2): 119–39.

Saha, Anamik. 2018. *Race and the Cultural Industries*. Malden, MA: Polity Press.

Smith, Chris. 1998. *Creative Britain*. London: Faber and Faber.

Throsby, David. 2008. "The Concentric Circles Model of the Cultural Industries". *Cultural Trends* 17 (3): 147–64.

Turner, Graeme. 2015. "Culture, Politics and the Cultural Industries: Reviving a Critical Agenda". In *The Routledge Companion to the Cultural Industries*, edited by Kate Oakley and Justin O'Connor, 535–44. London: Routledge.

Tusa, John. 2014. *Pain in the Arts*. London: I. B. Tauris.

UNCTAD, and UNDP. 2008. *Creative Economy Report 2008: The Challenge of Assessing the Creative Economy: Towards Informed Policy-Making*. UNCTAD/DITC/2008/2. Geneva: United Nations.

UNCTAD, and UNDP. 2010. *Creative Economy Report 2010: Creative Economy: A Feasible Development Option*. UNCTAD/DITC/TAB/2010/3. Geneva: United Nations.

Wainwright, Oliver. 2017. "'Everything Is Gentrification Now': But Richard Florida Isn't Sorry". *The Guardian*. www.theguardian.com/cities/2017/oct/26/gentrification-richard-florida-interview-creative-class-new-urban-crisis.

Wang, Jing. 2004. "The Global Reach of a New Discourse: How Far Can 'Creative Industries' Travel?" *International Journal of Cultural Studies* 7 (1): 9–19.

Whetherell, Sam. 2017. "Richard Florida Is Sorry". *Jacobin*. www.jacobinmag.com/2017/08/new-urban-crisis-review-richard-florida.

Yoon, Sojung. 2015. "Autos Are Core of Creative Economy: President Park Geun-Hye". *Inside Korea*. January 28, 2015. www.theinsidekorea.com/2015/01/autos-core-creative-economy-president-park-geun-hye/.

1

CULTURAL ECONOMY

The way we talk about music in Africa is full of clichés. One such cliché is that the continent's music has *potential*. Take for example UNCTAD's *Creative Economy Report*, which claims that in Africa 'despite the abundance of creative talents, the creative *potential* remains highly underutilized' (UNCTAD and UNDP 2008, iv), or a chapter on the World Bank's *Africa Music Project*, that makes the opening claim that 'African music has significant business potential' (Penna et al. 2004, 95). We do not contest the existence of such potential throughout Africa. But if music across Africa is primarily characterised by its mere potential, how can we understand the successes of 'African' musicians, both locally, across the continent, and throughout the world? We do however contest the strong focus on 'potential'. First, talking about potential diverts attention from the incredibly rich musical history of the continent. Second, potential suggests we overlook what has already been realised in terms of music industries. And finally, the focus on potential makes assumptions about what is lacking, without asking the question of how the music economy on the continent could or should evolve.

The underlying issue is not what does or doesn't exist, but what we do and don't know about what exists. Take urban transport, for example.

In Melbourne, public transport is messy but formalised. Different trains, trams, and buses connect residents and visitors throughout a large network. In Nairobi, a similarly messy and largely effective network exists. The major difference between the transport systems in both cities is that most visitors will recognise that Melbourne formally has a public transport network with clearly indicated stops, route maps, timetables, and apps. In contrast, many visitors to Nairobi will see that there are plenty of *Matatus* (minibuses), but they may be less confident than when they would visit Melbourne to use this form of shared transport as a reliable, cost-effective, and largely efficient manner to move through the city. Stops are not clearly indicated, maps are absent, pricing is not transparent, and timetables are not advertised. But does this mean that Melbourne has a public transport network and Nairobi doesn't?

Both Melbourne and Nairobi are equipped with a system that transports commuters to work and students to school, like virtually any city in the world. The major difference is transparency about how the system works, and thus what the system actually is. It would be easy (and misleading) to argue that Nairobi has a deficient public transport, just because a formal system with indicated stops, route maps, timetables, and apps needs to be established in order to develop a system that is transparent and functional. Such a proposal would be misleading as it ignores the context, the existing mechanisms, and the real needs. The more probable solution is certainly more difficult, but also more likely to be effective. A team of researchers has explored the routes and stops of *Matatus* in Nairobi, which resulted in a colour-coded map that provides an effective and user-friendly overview of existing solutions. The same team also explored the possibility of using the resulting data to develop cellphone-based navigation tools (Williams et al. 2015). A similar network of semi-formal *Marshrutkas* (minibuses) exists in Bishkek. In that context, an app (*bus.kg*) exists to guide travellers through the opaque transport system.

What these transport systems have in common is that they are reasonably effective, but also perpetually imperfect. Recognising that people in Melbourne and Nairobi, or São Paulo and Bishkek, all complain about the timeliness, comfort, connections, and coverage of their transport systems is crucial in thinking about possibly improving them. What sets apart these different systems is that aspirational approaches to public transport often eclipse agnostic or reflexive approaches, because the former may look more straightforward, easy, and even elegant than the latter options, which will reveal that there is most likely not an easy way to solve the ever-changing challenges of urban transport. Our underlying argument is that the same goes for the music economy.

Music creation is widespread and wildly popular across the world. But the business of producing, distributing, and consuming music is very diverse in different parts of the world. This is why ethnomusicologist Alex Perullo argues that there's too much of an attempt to see the particular music business of Tanzania (and those across Africa) as part of a single Western paradigm with global validity. Looking for formal bodies dealing with recording music, administering performing rights, supplying record stores, and drawing up sales ranks is a bit like looking for a formal bus stop on a *Matatu* line. There are mechanisms in place, much like *Matatus* having their regular stopping points, but if you don't know where they are, you're unlikely to recognise them. This is partly because what may sound like a neatly organised system ('music industry') is in fact 'characterised by disorganisation, fragmentation, unevenness, and variability', as Chris Gibson and Lily Kong remark about the cultural economy in general (Gibson and Kong 2005, 553).

The significant difference between public transport and the global cultural economy, which includes music, is that the former remains thoroughly embedded in the physical fabric of the city, whereas the latter is simultaneously global (for music and other cultural expressions circulate around the world) and local (in that its production, circulation, and consumption relies on both central nodes such as New York, London, Paris, and Tokyo, as well as regional hubs such as Johannesburg, Seoul, Miami, Abidjan, Lisbon, Nairobi, and Cairo).

Alex Perullo further argues that some of the formal components that do exist in the UK, France, Japan, the US, or smaller countries like Sweden may be lacking in Tanzania (and by extension in most countries outside the 'West'). But there are still many people who work in the music economy and try to make a living in every corner of the world. This is why he prefers to use the term '*music economy*, [which] usefully captures this commercialization of music without relying on preconceptions and customs associated with a music industry' (Perullo 2011, xv, emphasis in original). It is the same engagement with the

interplay between the economic and the cultural beyond fixed preconceptions that informs our approach here.

The cultural economy exists through the ways in which we discuss
it. Rather than being a thing that exists independently from the discourse that aims to describe it, it is in fact *discourse* that makes it. The
recent 'discovery' of the cultural and 'creative industries' is a great
illustration of this: these activities have existed well before we started
calling them 'industries', and what we try to do in this book is both
critically analyse and reframe what we are in fact looking at.

The key way through which the discursive formation of the cultural
economy emerged beyond the handful of countries with a very active
research agenda on the subject are the United Nations' *Creative Economy
Reports*. These reports helped frame global debates, national policies,
and local meanings, by synthesising initiatives, studies, and advocacy
into an optimistic narrative. Though rather than taking this narrative
at face value, we aim to expose the dynamics and tensions between
global, national, and local levels of governance, which differ significantly
across countries.

The remainder of this chapter first explores whether the cultural
economy is a drain on, or a contributor to, the economy as a whole.
We then continue exploring two different institutional perspectives of
UNCTAD and UNESCO to the cultural economy, that of UNESCO
and UNCTAD. UNESCO advocates for the formalisation of informal
practices while UNCTAD focuses on measurement and advocacy. After
discussing these intergovernmental approaches, we discuss why it matters that different countries continue to use different terms to describe
the cultural economy, often without realising the implications of their
discursive choices. In conclusion, we argue that the cultural economy –
much like culture itself – has globalised, but it has not become homogeneous in the process.

CULTURAL ECONOMY: DRAIN OR CONTRIBUTOR?

The success of the cultural economy hinges on a key premise: that it
drives economic growth (at a higher rate than other parts of the economy), it creates jobs, increases exports, and improves well-being
(UNCTAD and UNDP 2008, 2010). Moreover, the creativity at the
core of the cultural economy is said to be the 'true wealth of nations

in the 21st century' (UNESCO and UNDP 2013, 15). In sum: it is a contributor to the economy. And yet, a major issue for artistic and cultural activities has long been that they do not generate sufficient revenue ('earned income') from sales to cover the costs, let alone make a profit. How can we understand this paradox?

One way of looking at this is by presenting a teleological reading of the cultural economy. Jason Potts and Stuart Cunningham present such an approach by outlining four different models of the 'creative industries' (Potts and Cunningham 2008). First, the 'welfare model' presumes market failure (where market prices do not cover cost). Second, the 'competition model' assumes that the sector is not really different from others (some businesses will succeed, and others won't, but this is not down to a structural deficiency of the sector). Third, the 'growth model' means that the cultural economy outperforms the rest of the economy. Fourth, the 'innovation model' results in significant economic gains too, but they derive from the influence innovation has on the economy as a whole (now often called 'disruption'), rather than on the immediate products and services of the sector.

While their celebratory approach that presumes the cultural economy can shift from being a drain to being a contributor may look appealing, we think it does not hold up. A key issue is that it does not sufficiently distinguish between different kinds of cultural and creative expressions across the cultural economy. While they argue a shift to a normative endpoint (the authors herald models three and four as the best options), we question this underlying idea of teleological progression, because such an approach favours the function the cultural economy serves, rather than building an understanding of how it came to be. We therefore argue that all four models will continue to exist simultaneously. Potts and Cunningham's celebratory thinking results in conceptual and political confusion, which makes policy for the cultural economy difficult. This is because the cultural economy consists of vastly different activities, but their argument fails to reflect the parallel existence of different industries that each have components of several of the models.

We'll try to move beyond this teleological approach because it takes the social democratic political economy of Western countries as the starting point of the discussion. To a certain extent this makes sense because this is the context where public support for the arts emerged – most notably in the UK and France (Upchurch 2016; Urfalino 2011). But it does raise the question of how this normative view on change in the cultural economy maps onto the rest of the world. Nollywood, for example, emerged as a significant centre for movie production on the African continent – or rather, it emerged through multiple centres across Nigeria (Larkin 2008; Witt 2017). In this context, there was initially no active support, including no enforcement of regulation in terms of copyright (Lobato 2010).

But rather than providing a definitive answer to the question of whether the cultural economy is a drain or a contributor, we argue that this deliberation greatly depends on the way we frame and interpret data, how to balance formal and informal activities, and how the language we use may further challenge the size and shape of the cultural economy. These three ways of looking at the cultural economy in turn raise questions about what we want to use as a measure of 'contribution': what do we value?

UNCTAD: MEASUREMENT AND ADVOCACY

The United Nations Conference on Trade and Development (UNCTAD) published the first two Creative Economy Reports, under the leadership of Edna Dos Santos-Duisenberg, in 2008 and 2010. These reports articulate explicit policy recommendations concerning the 'creative industries' in societies around the world, and provide a statistical overview of international trade in creative goods and services – the full datasets that UNCTAD compiles are updated annually and available on their website.[1] In order to provide these data, UNCTAD needed to come up with a definition of the 'creative economy' that would allow them to compile data on the industries that together form this economy (see Figure 1.1).

While this classification, and the data they have compiled, provide a useful and necessary quantitative understanding of the cultural economy, we take issue with how UNCTAD present the data at three levels.

First, the large scope of the 'creative' economy inflates the economic importance of the sector. This inflation is not unique to UNCTAD, as the UK Department of Media Culture and Sport (DCMS) also included sectors in their initial mapping document (DCMS 1998) that

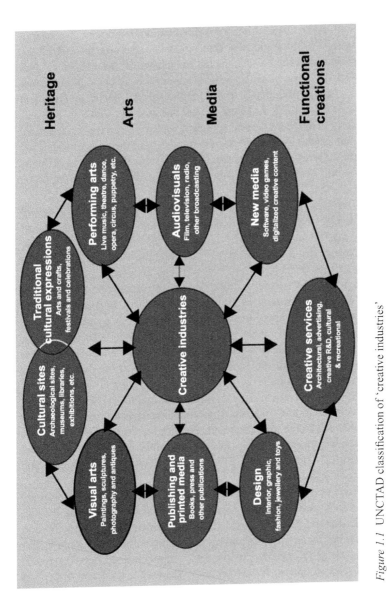

Figure 1.1 UNCTAD classification of 'creative industries'

Source: UNCTAD and UNDP 2008, 14.

were both economically very sizable and not previously considered to be 'cultural industries', most notably computer software and design. Garnham (2005) argues that this expansion of scope ties in with the increased importance of information science in the 1990s. Though through this expansion, the political significance of the 'cultural industries' as a way of critically looking at the cultural, social, and political sides of the cultural economy greatly diminished (Turner 2015), particularly in the 'celebratory' approach we outlined in the introduction. The diminished political engagement with, and the broader definition of, the cultural economy go hand in hand: the inflated claims about its role could not have been made without silently expanding the scope of the sector.

Tremblay (2011) empirically discusses the claims UNCTAD (as well as the UK's DCMS) make in the paper *Creative Statistics to Support Creative Economy Politics*. He argues that the 'cultural industries' represent only a small share of the economic value of the 'creative industries' (Tremblay 2011, 295–96). The inclusion of software and design meant that the 'cultural industries' initially felt included in the optimistic framing of the 'creative economy' and welcomed the greater visibility in political and policy contexts as a result. The arts, which are for some at the 'core' of these industries (Throsby 2008), remain formally important to the 'creative industries', but have all but 'disappeared' from the equation when looking at the data about the sector (Oakley 2009).

In this context, while the shift from cultural to 'creative industries' suggests continuity in terms of sector characteristics, it also signals a clear break in the definition and scope of the sector. This is also the reason why some academics prefer to continue using the term 'cultural industries' (De Beukelaer 2015; Hesmondhalgh 2013; Oakley and O'Connor 2015).

Second, UNCTAD data is organised through the trade *between* countries. This approach is rooted in the history of the organisation, as their mandate is to improve the 'development' of countries through trade, particularly by making trade conditions for 'developing' countries easier (Karshenas 2016). This approach does however reveal that some countries are net exporters (where the total sum of exports is greater than the total sum of imports) of 'creative goods and services' (this is the language UNCTAD use, and they have the best data

Table 1.1 Creative goods trade between Kazakhstan and the rest of the world, in millions (US$)

Year	Exports	Imports	Net exports
2002	3.4	129.4	−126
2003	7.3	162.6	−155.3
2004	12.5	259.2	−246.7
2005	26.2	329.6	−303.4
2006	21.4	463	−441.6
2007	17.2	690.2	−673
2008	11.6	600	−588.4
2009	13.1	654.7	−641.6
2010	6.5	623.2	−616.7
2011	38.1	1,074.80	−1,036.70
2012	26.5	1,068.60	−1,042.10
2013	26.7	1,181.20	−1,154.60
2014	92	1,149.60	−1,057.60
2015	48.2	473.4	−425.2

Source: UNCTADStat (2018).

on these international transactions), while others are net importers (where the total sum of imports is greater than the total sum of exports). Kazakhstan is such a net importer in the global cultural economy. Table 1.1 shows that the country's exports have grown significantly, from US$3.4 million in 2002 to US$92.0 million in 2014, which amounts to an average annual growth rate of 31.63%; even if exports drop off again to US$48.2 million in 2015. Over the same period, imports did however increase from US$129.4 million to US$1,057.6 million, at an average annual growth rate of 19.13%; again, with exports diminishing significantly to US$424.2 million in 2015.

De Beukelaer and Koretskaya (2016) argue that while this trade deficit shows that the country is not performing very well internationally, demand within the country has increased significantly. In line with Tremblay's critique, in 2015, 'design' accounts for the majority of imports (US$343.43 million of a total of US$473.40 million, or 72.5%) and exports (US$46.29 million of a total of US$48.22 million, or 96.0%) (see Table 1.2). Notwithstanding the growth of exports, Kazakhstan's balance of trade is negative for all sectors every single

Table 1.2 Kazakhstan's creative goods net exports (total exports minus total imports), in millions (US$), per sector

	Art crafts	Audio-visuals	Design	New media	Performing arts	Publishing	Visual arts	Total
2002	−7.73	−8.76	−71.42	−2.51	−0.79	−33.37	−1.41	−125.99
2003	−9.43	−10.33	−88.83	−8.82	−0.47	−35.84	−1.56	−155.29
2004	−5.93	−17.40	−140.76	−29.40	−0.73	−49.92	−2.56	−246.71
2005	−7.33	−32.75	−172.19	−11.83	−1.97	−70.57	−6.77	−303.41
2006	−11.22	−23.41	−286.43	−9.75	−1.75	−103.39	−5.67	−441.61
2007	−16.24	−69.95	−445.16	−11.06	−2.57	−120.81	−7.23	−673.03
2008	−18.95	−6.12	−410.97	−3.07	−2.35	−131.06	−15.89	−588.42
2009	−18.01	−121.63	−343.93	−33.20	−1.87	−99.31	−23.67	−641.61
2010	−31.34	−63.80	−370.97	−47.74	−4.02	−80.27	−18.54	−616.68
2011	−57.17	−135.40	−583.02	−74.25	−5.29	−98.04	−83.52	−1036.68
2012	−76.16	−63.20	−715.57	−44.73	−4.62	−104.65	−33.21	−1042.14
2013	−84.69	−61.18	−809.98	−50.12	−7.29	−122.47	−18.78	−1154.51
2014	−64.89	−0.84	−813.55	−43.13	−6.68	−104.12	−24.35	−1057.55
2015	−41.56	−20.47	−297.14	−24.04	−3.00	−28.82	−10.14	−425.18

Source: UNCTADStat (2018).

year between 2002 and 2015. This raises the question of which countries benefit from this global flow of creative goods (see also Chapter six on human development, where we discuss the balance of trade in relation to the African continent). Kazakhstan is perhaps an extreme case, but questions about the balance of trade are common in many countries. The main appeal, for many around the world, was the claim that the 'creative industries' generated economic growth at a rate above the average of the economy as a whole.

Some academics quip that one of the major exports of the UK in the early years of 'creative industries' policies was in fact the discourse itself (Oakley 2009, 404; Ross 2007, 14). This discourse did not simply travel on its own, but was propagated through the work of UK consultants and the British Council.

Third, UNCTAD presents a clear narrative that 'developing' countries have increased their relative share of creative goods exports in the global cultural economy (UNCTAD and UNDP 2008, 2010). Table 1.3 illustrates this shift, as 'developing economies' increased their creative goods exports by more than trebling them from US$84.37 billion (40.5% of total global exports) in 2002 to US$265.08 billion (52.0%) in 2015, with a peak of US$331.55 billion (57.4%) in 2014. Over the same period, 'developed economies' saw their exports grow more slowly, resulting in an almost-doubling from US$122.91 billion (59.0%) in 2002 to US$241.62 billion (47.4%) in 2015. Transition economies, including Kazakhstan, did see their exports more than double from US$1.22 billion in 2002 to US$3.05 billion, but their relative share remained stable at 0.6%.

What do these numbers tell us? One could think that this means that 'developing' countries are 'catching up' with 'developed' countries in their creative goods exports. But the story is more complex, as UNCTAD does not define which countries count as 'developing' or 'developed', or on what basis they make this firm classification. They do acknowledge that the overview is skewed, but argue they are bound by the classification of countries as used by the United Nations' statistical office (UNdata). But UNdata explains that they have no rationale for this distinction either: 'there is no established convention for the designation of "developed" and "developing" countries or areas in the United Nations system' (cited in De Beukelaer 2014a, 239). To make this issue more palpable: the only two countries in Asia that count as 'developed' in the UNCTAD/UNdata classification are Israel and Japan.

Table 1.3 Creative goods exports from country groups (UNCTAD classification) to the rest of the world, in billions (US$)

	World	Developing economies		Transition economies		Developed economies	
2002	208.49	84.37	40.5%	1.22	0.6%	122.91	59.0%
2003	232.03	94.89	40.9%	1.32	0.6%	135.81	58.5%
2004	263.19	109.28	41.5%	1.80	0.7%	152.11	57.8%
2005	291.59	125.05	42.9%	2.02	0.7%	164.53	56.4%
2006	317.41	135.93	42.8%	2.30	0.7%	179.18	56.4%
2007	400.62	170.89	42.7%	2.75	0.7%	226.98	56.7%
2008	439.17	192.93	43.9%	3.33	0.8%	242.91	55.3%
2009	377.28	180.40	47.8%	2.63	0.7%	194.26	51.5%
2010	419.77	210.08	50.0%	2.66	0.6%	207.03	49.3%
2011	491.54	255.77	52.0%	3.24	0.7%	232.53	47.3%
2012	519.89	292.75	56.3%	3.55	0.7%	223.59	43.0%
2013	531.79	297.89	56.0%	4.24	0.8%	229.66	43.2%
2014	577.19	331.55	57.4%	4.36	0.8%	241.28	41.8%
2015	509.75	265.08	52.0%	3.05	0.6%	241.62	47.4%

Source: UNCTADStat (2018).

While the data on international trade in the cultural economy is useful and necessary, it does raise questions about its meaning, scope, and classification. This does not change the validity of the data when observed at face value (the numbers UNCTAD presents are not incorrect), but it does pose problems when considering the political implications of collecting and presenting the data in a particular way.

These questions reflect the long-standing questions about how we can measure and value the cultural economy. While some people see the need to use economic data to make a political case for public support for arts and culture (see Throsby 2010), many others have contributed to the debate about what cultural value is and how we can measure it. Before considering these perspectives later in this chapter, we discuss the way in which UNESCO has opted to approach the cultural economy.

UNESCO: FORMALISATION AND NORMATIVE OPTIONS

In 2013, the United Nations Educational, Scientific, and Cultural Organisation (UNESCO) published a 'special edition' of the Creative Economy Report (UNESCO and UNDP 2013), which focused on *local* government challenges and existing strategies. It differs from UNCTAD editions both in its focus on smaller units of governance (cities and regions, as opposed to countries) and its qualitative engagement with the variety of practices in the cultural economy (rather than quantitative data on international trade).

This version of the report was lauded for its engagement with the various ways in which the cultural economy actually exists around the world and for its more nuanced approach to claims about the impact of the sector (De Beukelaer 2014b; O'Connor 2013; Sternberg 2016; Vickery 2015). The UNESCO edition could easily be referred to as the *Cultural Economy Report*, as this would better reflect its message. Yudhishthir Raj Isar, who served as the principal investigator and lead writer of the report, indicates that he would have preferred that term, even if UNESCO decided to stick to the established 'brand' of the creative economy (Isar 2015, 447). Though at the same time, UNESCO did maintain the 'creative economy' label for its special edition of the report, for reasons of continuity and familiarity, despite its lead author

Yudhishthir Raj Isar preferring the 'cultural economy' as it would better reflect what the Report tried to do:

> Although UNESCO chose prudently to stick with the existing 'creative economy' brand, my conceptual preference went to the more inclusive notion of 'cultural economy'. That is the term I would have used.
>
> (Isar 2015, 477)

What is then the difference between the 'creative' and the 'cultural' economy? We argue that despite its imperfections (De Beukelaer 2014b; Sternberg 2016), UNESCO's report gets a few nuances right.

First, the report stresses the need to counter existing imbalances between and within countries. This ties in with UNESCO's aims and objectives as articulated in its *Convention on the Protection and Promotion of the Diversity of Cultural Expressions* (UNESCO 2005), which we address in greater detail in the chapter on diversity (De Beukelaer et al. 2015; Pyykkönen 2012; Richieri Hanania 2014; Vlassis 2015).

Second, UNESCO illustrates the high degree to which activities in the global cultural economy remain in the informal sector (see Lobato and Thomas 2015). This means that workers (including artists) often lack social protection, businesses lack access to opportunities and funding, and contracts are difficult to enforce. But it also means that much of the activity in the cultural economy is not reported, as a result of which it does not count in official statistics. The report thus proposes that while formalising the informal is necessary, the informal will remain present for the time being, which means that 'informal creative activities require a different kind of policy thinking' (UNESCO and UNDP 2013, 28).

Finally, UNESCO opens up a debate about how to value the cultural economy in two ways: by rethinking what we measure and stressing the need to be strategic about objectives. This approach recognises that there is a need to measure the cultural economy beyond growth, jobs, and exports, by exploring the 22 dimensions of the *Culture for Development Indicators* (CDIS), as developed by UNESCO (2014). By identifying the variety of issues that *can* be measured, there is attention to the diversity of objectives that can be pursued, as chapter six of the report (*Towards Indicators of Effectiveness and Success*) highlights.

The tensions between countries that emerge from UNNCTAD's data, and the diversity of practices that is clear from UNESCO's report, make it clear that the cultural economy exists around the globe. But this does raise the question of how we can locate what is 'global' about the cultural economy while looking at particular instances in various parts of the world.

LOCATING CULTURE: TRANSLATING THE CULTURAL ECONOMY?

A few decades ago, the Indian-American anthropologist Arjun Appadurai (1990) published *Disjuncture and Difference in the Global Cultural Economy*. This influential article later became a key chapter of his seminal book *Modernity at Large: Cultural Dimensions of Globalization* (1996). His central argument in this article is that technological change that facilitated changes in mobility and communication has given rise to profound changes in the way we think of the place and meaning of culture in the world. While he does not argue we are living in a 'global village' as Marshall McLuhan predicted we would, decades earlier (McLuhan 1962), he does stress that we now live in a world that is at once profoundly global and unequivocally local, even if 'local' often refers to the deterritorialised imagined communities of migrants, guest workers, refugees, expats, third culture kids, and otherwise mobile humans.

While Appadurai's theoretical work has proven influential in the analysis of the politics and economics of cultural expressions' global flows, his analysis does not empirically engage with the everyday functioning of the 'cultural industries' he refers to. This is the major point of difference with this book; we combine an engagement with the dynamics of globalisation with a close analysis of the cultural, political, economic, and social workings of the 'cultural industries'. The *global cultural economy*, as an analytical framework, forms the basis in exploring existing diversities of cultural consumption, circulation, and consumption, without presuming the primacy of one model over another. In doing so, we build on Appadurai's work in moving away (or rather beyond) the Eurocentric framing of debates, as we incorporate post-colonial critiques of power relations and gatekeepers in global and regional markets. Moreover, while we acknowledge the continued importance of London, Paris, Tokyo, and New York in the global cultural economy, we do stress that smaller regional hubs now play significant roles – both in cultural and economic terms – as well.

When we talk about a 'global' perspective, we aim to provide a globally rooted engagement with concepts and practices. We hence look at cities, countries, and regions as instances where these global dynamics materialise, mutate, and challenge the cultural and 'creative industries' script. While we may refer to countries as a way to locate these practices, we do not suggest that the examples we discuss are typical examples of practices in those countries, nor that they can be extrapolated to essentialise the 'cultural industries' there. This takes us well beyond the 'celebratory' literature that remains centred on Western concepts and paradigms, which is then applied to non-Western locales without detailed primary research (see, for example, Flew 2013) or 'refusenik' literature that is grounded in a thorough understanding of cultural and artistic practice, but which misses the nuance of contradiction to the cultural economy (see for example Da Costa 2016).

We stress that the cultural economy exists and has existed across the world; but it comes in different guises. Indeed, as Raj Isar argues:

> In the global South these forms are not mirror images of those in the North, nor do they need to be. Everywhere they are contingent and path-dependent, with structures and modes of functioning that vary considerably.
>
> (Isar 2015, 480)

The 'global' angle primarily serves as a reminder that the West (which serves as the empirical basis for most analyses and publications on the way the 'cultural industries' work) constitutes the most overrepresented numerical minority in the world – it is 'the rest' of the world that conceals the variety of experiences of the majority of the global population. Even so, the discourse of the cultural economy, in its many guises, has travelled the world in the past two decades (e.g. Cunningham 2009; Poettschacher 2010; Prince 2012; Quarles 2006; Rindzevičiūtė et al. 2016; Wang 2004), but this does not mean that different terms (such as 'cultural industries', 'creative industries', creative economy', 'cultural economy') mean the same things in different places. How do we make sense of this language that is global in scope but incredibly varied in its political, social, and cultural meanings? How do we bridge the variety of terms to the variety of practices in a way that allows us to talk to each other, make comparisons, and simply talk about the same things? The answer is not straightforward, but a better understanding of differences and their genealogy may help find a common language.

International and intergovernmental organisations (such as UNCTAD and UNESCO, but also the British Council, and WIPO) have played significant roles in the spread and uptake of key policy terms across a range of issues, including cultural and 'creative industries' (De Beukelaer and Vlassis 2019). Political scientist Pertti Alasuutari describes this process in his book *The Synchronisation of National Policies* (Alasuutari 2016), by pointing out that a 'tribe of moderns', who are often part of the same social and cultural network, but employed by different organisations and governments, have tremendous influence over global policy discourse. But despite 'synchronisation' of policy discourses across individual countries in relation to the 'creative economy', there are clear differences in the terms used by differences around the world. He points out that,

> This shift from seeing cultural policy servicing democratic access to art and social cohesion of the people to conceiving of culture as a tourist attraction and as a means to enhance 'creative economy' has swept throughout the advanced economies, and the creative city is now a standard catchword that can be found in the strategy documents of almost any city in the world.
>
> (Alasuutari 2016, 154–55)

The central tenet of the uptake of the 'creative economy' in virtually all its guises is that 'cultural policy, which has traditionally been justified by art as valuable in its own right, is now commonly justified by the claim that it is beneficial for business and economy' (Alasuutari 2016, 156). While he is certainly right that the 'creative economy' discourse has permeated policies across the globe, there are important differences in the exact terms used. While many policy-makers, activists, artists, and academics are often unaware of the significant implications of using one term over another, we will clarify how in the contexts where we've done research, these differences do have political implications.

Many French-speaking countries continue to use 'industries cul-turelles' ('cultural industries'), while embracing the same connotation and predictive optimism about its impact as the 'creative industries'.[2] The resulting tension between the term used ('industries culturelles') and the strong influence of another term ('creative industries') on its meaning has prompted the question of how exactly terms like 'creative industries' and 'creative economy' ought to be translated in the Franco-phone context (Bouquillion 2012; Bouquillion et al. 2009). These ten-sions are central to academic debates in the cultural economy *in* France, but in many Francophone African countries such as Burkina Faso where we have done research, the tensions between 'cultural' and 'creative' remain in the background (De Beukelaer 2013). Other locales where we have conducted research similarly illustrate this conceptual complexity.

In Russia, the term 'industry' was met with scepticism, as it 'invokes factories and mass production' not a general idea of economic activity (O'Connor 2005, 51). At the same time, the term also carried promise of technical expertise and access to international markets, but not without simultaneously strengthening binary oppositions: 'global and Russian, commercial and artistic, superficial and spiritual' (O'Connor 2005, 52). More recently, these debates have become more sophisti-cated, but also more complex. Our research in Central Asia (where Russian is the dominant *lingua franca*), reveals that three terms exist concurrently: 'культурные индустрии' ('kulturni industrii', 'cultural industries'), 'креативные индустрии' ('kreativnye industrii', 'creative industries'), and 'творческие индустрии' ('tvorcheskie industrii', which is difficult to translate). In Kazakhstan, these terms have signifi-cantly different connotations and appeal to different parts of the cul-tural economy. While 'креативные индустрии' ('creative industries') is most common, largely because of British influence, it does not quite capture the full scope of the sector, because 'креативные' (creative) is not actually a Russian word. Christiaan De Beukelaer and Galina Koretskaya point out that 'creative industries' commonly refers to more modern practices, while the 'cultural industries' tend to map onto 'older' expressions, such as heritage and traditional practices (De Beukelaer and Koretskaya 2016, 15–16), this is quite similar to the way the terms are used in Indonesia (Fahmi et al. 2016). These conceptual debates across Russia and Central Asia, as well as Indonesia, share a concern for both consumption (what expressions mean to buyers influences whether they are part of 'cultural' or 'creative' industries) and production (whether producers are located in 'traditional' or 'modern' parts of the economy, will define whether their activities are respectively 'cultural' or 'creative').

In Korea, the use of 'cultural industries', 'content industries', and 'creative economy' tie in with the shifting political climate in the country (Kwon and Kim 2014; Lee 2016). Building on the idea that the discourse could be a 'Trojan horse' or a Rorschach blot' as Stuart Cunningham posits (2009), she argues that in the Korean context it is both:

> [I]t acts as a Trojan horse in the sense that it has paved a way for 'depoliticising' as well as marketising culture and, at the same time, it can be seen as a Rorschach blot because of its 'encompassing' nature.
> (Lee 2016, 438)

In the 1990s, the term 'cultural industries' was used in conjunction with the early economic success of Korean popular culture thanks to a decline in censorship under the presidency of Kim Yong Sam. In the early 2000s, the language shifted to the 'content industries' because its meaning was 'inclusive and flexible enough to include non-commercial arts and cultural activities without facing serious resistance' (Lee 2016, 446). Even if this shift raised suspicion in the arts community, it was reluctantly accepted for its potential to increase public funds for the sector. In 2012, then presidential candidate Park Guen Hye shifted the language to the 'creative economy' which became a vague and all-encompassing term, as we discussed in the Introduction of this book. Much like elsewhere, the choice of one term over the other was both a choice that served economic purposes (as it increased the size of the sector, and thus the claims that could be made about its economic importance) and political ends (as it helped reimagine the ideological connotations, in line with shifts in the Korean government).

In Spanish-speaking contexts, particularly in Latin America, the term 'economia naranja' (orange economy) is central to policy discourses that engage with the 'creative economy'. Felipe Buitrago Restrepo and Iván Duque Márquez, authors of the report *The Orange Economy: An Infinite Opportunity*, published by the Inter-American Development Bank, argue that the creative economy combines the perspectives of

UNCTAD, UNESCO, WIPO, DCMS, and ECLAC (Economic Commission for Latin America and the Caribbean), because in their overlaps, they share three key characteristics: first, it takes 'creativity, arts, and culture as productive endeavours'; second, the sector includes 'products strongly related to intellectual property rights, in particular copyright'; and third, it comprises 'activities with a direct role in the value chain transforming ideas into products' (Buitrago et al. 2013). Their suggestion that the 'orange economy' combines the perspectives of five different institutions raises the question of how these institutions play a role in promoting the idea of the 'creative economy' as a generic term that leads to the synchronisation of approaches, while maintaining very different views of what the sector is and what role it plays in societies.

CONCLUSIONS

Arjun Appadurai argues that 'the globalization of culture is not the same as its homogenization', but stresses that it does rely on 'instruments of homogenization' that include 'language hegemonies' (Appadurai 1996, 42). Much like the cultural expressions he discusses, the 'cultural economy' has globalised with homogenising.

As we have outlined in the Introduction, the politics of the cultural economy are very significant. The five perspectives we propose (celebratory, aspirational, refusenik, agnostic, reflexive) reflect the ways in which many artists, academics, consultants, policy-makers, and activists draw from multiple perspectives in their strategies and arguments. But these different uses are not neutral or mutually exclusive; but they are not equally valid either. These perspectives do however remain abstract interpretations of the different ways in which the cultural economy serves as a discourse. This chapter has shown that its use is messy and complex, but also agenda-driven.

Naming and classifying the cultural economy is a political act. This does not mean that these choices are the result of party politics, but rather that the choices anyone makes – whether knowingly or unknowingly – have political implications. This is why organisations use their position to define and delineate the scope of the cultural economy. And it is why certain countries very deliberately do or don't change their discourse to reflect political priorities – as has happened in Korea, for example. These choices are important because of such political considerations, but also because they reflect the normative choices about what should be included and what should not. This in turn allows us to frame and reframe *what* we value, *how* we value, and *how much* we value the social, cultural, and economic impacts of the cultural economy (Belfiore and Bennett 2008; MacDowall et al. 2015; O'Brien 2014).

Despite the great variety of practices, approaches, and ways to measure the cultural economy, not everyone has the same opportunity or power to make themselves heard. This raises the question of how we can address the selective inclusion and exclusion on the basis of race, gender, and class that is systemic to the cultural economy, which we address in the following chapter.

NOTES

1 http://unctadstat.unctad.org/EN/.
2 France is where the term 'cultural industries' was embraced by critical sociologists who started studying the way these industries function (Huet et al. 1978) in an approach that emerged as part 'agnostic' part 'reflective' (See Introduction). They thereby moved beyond the 'culture industry' approaches influenced by the work of Adorno (2001), that remained predominantly within a 'refusenik' perspective (See Introduction). See the work of O'Connor (2010) and Hesmondhalgh (2013) for a more detailed discussion.

REFERENCES

Adorno, Theodor W. 2001. *The Culture Industry: Selected Essays on Mass Culture*. Routledge Classics. London; New York, NY: Routledge.

Alasuutari, Pertti. 2016. *The Synchronization of National Policies: Ethnography of the Global Tribe of Moderns*. 1st ed. London; New York, NY: Routledge.

Appadurai, Arjun. 1990. "Disjuncture and Difference in the Global Cultural Economy". *Public Culture* 2 (2): 1–24.

Appadurai, Arjun. 1996. *Modernity at Large: Cultural Dimensions of Globalization*. Minneapolis, MN: University of Minnesota Press.

Belfiore, Eleonora, and Oliver Bennett. 2008. *The Social Impact of the Arts: An Intellectual History*. New York, NY: Palgrave Macmillan.

Bouquillion, Philippe, ed. 2012. *Creative Economy, Creative Industries. Des notions à traduire*. Paris: PU Vincennes.

Bouquillion, Philippe, Bernard Miège, and Pierre Mœglin. 2009. "La Question Des Industries Créatives En France". *Rivista Trimestrale Dell'Associazione per l'Economia Della Cultura* 1: 37–47.

Buitrago Restrepo, Pedro Felipe, and Iván Duque Márquez. 2013. *The Orange Economy: An Infinite Opportunity*. Washington, DC: Inter-American Development Bank.

Cunningham, Stuart. 2009. "Trojan Horse or Rorschach Blot? Creative Industries Discourse Around the World". *International Journal of Cultural Policy* 15 (4): 375–86.

Da Costa, Dia. 2016. *Politicizing Creative Economy: Activism and a Hunger Called Theater*. Dissident Feminisms. Urbana, IL: University of Illinois Press.

DCMS. 1998. *Creative Industries Mapping Document*. London: DCMS.

De Beukelaer, Christiaan. 2013. "Culture and Development in Burkina Faso: Social and Economic Impacts Explored". *Cultural Trends* 22 (3–4): 250–58.

De Beukelaer, Christiaan. 2014a. "Creative Industries in 'Developing' Countries: Questioning Country Classifications in the UNCTAD Creative Economy Reports". *Cultural Trends* 23 (4): 232–51.

De Beukelaer, Christiaan. 2014b. "The UNESCO/UNDP 2013 Creative Economy Report: Perks and Perils of an Evolving Agenda". *The Journal of Arts Management, Law, and Society* 44 (2): 90–100.

De Beukelaer, Christiaan. 2015. *Developing Cultural Industries: Learning from the Palimpsest of Practice*. Amsterdam: European Cultural Foundation.

De Beukelaer, Christiaan, and Galina Koretskaya. 2016. *Cultural Industries in Kazakhstan: Models, Challenges, and Strategies; Қазақстандағы Мәдени Индустриялар: Модельдері, Мәселелері, Стратегиялары; Культурные Индустрии В Казахстане: Модели, Проблемы, Стратегии*. Almaty: British Council.

De Beukelaer, Christiaan, Miikka Pyykkönen, and J. P. Singh, eds. 2015. *Globalization, Culture and Development: The UNESCO Convention on Cultural Diversity*. Basingstoke: Palgrave Macmillan.

De Beukelaer, Christiaan, and Antonios Vlassis. 2019. "Creative Economy and International Development: Institutional Perspectives". In *The Cultural Turn in International Aid*, edited by Sophia Labadi. London: Routledge.

Fahmi, Fikri Zul, Sierdjan Koster, and Jouke van Dijk. 2016. "The Location of Creative Industries in a Developing Country: The Case of Indonesia". *Cities* 59 (November): 66–79.

Flew, Terry. 2013. *Global Creative Industries*. Cambridge; Malden, MA: Polity Press.

Garnham, Nicholas. 2005. "From Cultural to Creative Industries: An Analysis of the Implications of the 'Creative Industries' Approach to Arts and Media Policy Making in the United Kingdom". *International Journal of Cultural Policy* 11 (1): 15–29.

Gibson, Chris, and Lily Kong. 2005. "Cultural Economy: A Critical Review". *Progress in Human Geography* 29 (5): 541–61.

Hesmondhalgh, David. 2013. *The Cultural Industries*. 3rd ed. London: Sage.

Huet, Armel, Jacques Ion, Alain Lefebvre, René Peron, and Bernard Miège. 1978. *Capitalisme et Industries Culturelles*. Actualités Recherches : Sociologie, Grenoble: Presses Universitaires de Grenoble.

Isar, Yudhishthir Raj. 2015. "Widening Development Pathways: Transformative Visions of Cultural Economy". In *The Routledge Companion to the 'Cultural*

Industries', edited by Kate Oakley and Justin O'Connor, 477–87. London: Routledge.

Karshenas, Massoud. 2016. "Power, Ideology and Global Development: On the Origins, Evolution and Achievements of UNCTAD: Focus: The Origins, Evolution and Achievements of UNCTAD". *Development and Change* 47 (4): 664–85.

Kwon, Seung-Ho, and Joseph Kim. 2014. "The Cultural Industry Policies of the Korean Government and the Korean Wave". *International Journal of Cultural Policy* 20 (4): 422–39.

Larkin, Brian. 2008. *Signal and Noise: Media, Infrastructure, and Urban Culture in Nigeria*. Durham, NC: Duke University Press.

Lee, Hye-Kyung. 2016. "Politics of the 'Creative Industries' Discourse and Its Variants". *International Journal of Cultural Policy* 22 (3): 438–55.

Lobato, Ramon. 2010. "Creative Industries and Informal Economies: Lessons from Nollywood". *International Journal of Cultural Studies* 13 (4): 337–54.

Lobato, Ramon, and Julian Thomas. 2015. *The Informal Media Economy*. Cambridge; Malden, MA: Polity.

MacDowall, Lachlan, Marnie Badham, Emma Blomkamp, and Kim Frances Dunphy, eds. 2015. *Making Culture Count: The Politics of Cultural Measurement*. New Directions in Cultural Policy Research. Houndmills, Basingstoke; New York, NY: Palgrave Macmillan.

McLuhan, Marshall. 1962. *The Gutenberg Galaxy: The Making of Typographic Man*. Toronto, ON: University of Toronto Press.

Oakley, Kate. 2009. "The Disappearing Arts: Creativity and Innovation after the Creative Industries". *International Journal of Cultural Policy* 15 (4): 403–13.

Oakley, Kate, and Justin O'Connor, eds. 2015. *The Routledge Companion to the 'Cultural Industries'*. London: Routledge.

O'Brien, Dave. 2014. *Cultural Policy: Management, Value and Modernity in the Creative Industries*. London: Routledge.

O'Connor, Justin. 2005. "Creative Exports: Taking Cultural Industries to St Petersburg". *International Journal of Cultural Policy* 11 (1): 45–60.

O'Connor, Justin. 2010. *The Cultural and Creative Industries: A Literature Review*. 2nd ed. Newcastle upon Tyne: Creativity Culture and Education.

O'Connor, Justin. 2013. "UNESCO Leads the Way on a Truly Global Approach to Cultural Economy". *The Conversation*. November 22, 2013. www.theconversation.com/unesco-leads-the-way-on-a-truly-global-approach-to-cultural-economy-19595.

Penna, Frank J., Monique Thormann, and J. Michael Finger. 2004. "The Africa Music Project". In *Poor People's Knowledge: Promoting Intellectual Property in Developing Countries*, edited by J. Michael Finger and Philip Schuler, 95–112. Trade and Development Series. Washington, DC: World Bank and Oxford University Press.

Perullo, Alex. 2011. *Live from Dar Es Salaam: Popular Music and Tanzania's Music Economy*. Bloomington, IN: Indiana University Press.

Poettschacher, Erich. 2010. "The Rise of the Trojan Horses in the Creative Industries". *International Journal of Cultural Policy* 16 (3): 355–66.

Potts, Jason, and Stuart Cunningham. 2008. "Four Models of the Creative Industries". *International Journal of Cultural Policy* 14 (3): 233–47.

Prince, R. 2012. "Policy Transfer, Consultants and the Geographies of Governance". *Progress in Human Geography* 36 (2): 188–203.

Pyykkönen, Miikka. 2012. "UNESCO and Cultural Diversity: Democratisation, Commodification or Governmentalisation of Culture?" *International Journal of Cultural Policy* 18 (5): 545–62.

Quarles, Jan. 2006. "Cultural Industries on the Global Stage: The Evolution of a Global Discourse, Its Key Players and Its Impact in the Asian Region". *Media Asia* 33 (1–2): 58–64.

Richieri Hanania, Lilian, ed. 2014. *Cultural Diversity in International Law: The Effectiveness of the UNESCO Convention on the Protection and Promotion of the Diversity of Cultural Expressions*. Routledge Research in International Law. London; New York, NY: Routledge.

Rindzevičiūtė, Eglė, Jenny Svensson, and Klara Tomson. 2016. "The International Transfer of Creative Industries as a Policy Idea". *International Journal of Cultural Policy* 22 (4): 594–610.

Ross, Andrew. 2007. "Nice Work If You Can Get It: The Mercurial Career of Creative Industries Policy". *Work Organisation, Labour & Globalisation* 1 (1): 13–30.

Sternberg, Rolf. 2016. "Creativity Support Policies as a Means of Development Policy for the Global South? A Critical Appraisal of the UNESCO Creative Economy Report 2013". *Regional Studies*, 51 (2) 336–45.

Throsby, David. 2008. "The Concentric Circles Model of the Cultural Industries". *Cultural Trends* 17 (3): 147–64.

Throsby, David. 2010. *The Economics of Cultural Policy*. Cambridge: Cambridge University Press.

Tremblay, Gaëtan. 2011. "Creative Statistics to Support Creative Economy Politics". *Media, Culture & Society* 33 (2): 289–98.

Turner, Graeme. 2015. "Culture, Politics and the Cultural Industries: Reviving a Critical Agenda". In *The Routledge Companion to the Cultural Industries*, edited by Kate Oakley and Justin O'Connor, 535–44. London: Routledge.

UNCTAD, and UNDP. 2008. *Creative Economy Report 2008: The Challenge of Assessing the Creative Economy: Towards Informed Policy-Making*. UNCTAD/DITC/2008/2. Geneva: United Nations.

UNCTAD, and UNDP. 2010. *Creative Economy Report 2010: Creative Economy: A Feasible Development Option*. UNCTAD/DITC/TAB/2010/3. Geneva: United Nations.

UNCTADstat. 2018. "UNCTADstat". 2018. www.unctadstat.unctad.org/.

UNESCO. 2005. *Convention on the Protection and Promotion of the Diversity of Cultural Expressions*. Paris: UNESCO.

UNESCO. 2014. *Culture for Development Indicators: Methodology Manual*. Paris: UNESCO. www.en.unesco.org/creativity/sites/creativity/files/cdis_methodology_manual.pdf.

UNESCO, and UNDP. 2013. *Creative Economy Report*. Paris and New York, NY: UNESCO and UNDP.

Upchurch, Anna. 2016. *The Origins of the Arts Council Movement: Philanthropy and Policy*. London: Palgrave Macmillan.

Urfalino, Philippe. 2011. *L'invention de la politique culturelle*. Paris: Pluriel.

Vickery, Jonathan. 2015. "Creative Economy Report 2013 Special Edition: Widening Local Development Pathways". *Cultural Trends* 24 (2) 189–93.

Vlassis, Antonios. 2015. *Gouvernance mondiale et culture: de l'exception à la diversité*. Sciences politiques et sociales. Liège: Presses Universitaires de Liège.

Wang, Jing. 2004. "The Global Reach of a New Discourse: How Far Can 'Creative Industries' Travel?" *International Journal of Cultural Studies* 7 (1): 9–19.

Williams, Sarah, Adam White, Peter Waiganjo, Daniel Orwa, and Jacqueline Klopp. 2015. "The Digital Matatu Project: Using Cell Phones to Create an Open Source Data for Nairobi's Semi-Formal Bus System". *Journal of Transport Geography* 49 (December): 39–51.

Witt, Emily. 2017. *Nollywood: The Making of a Film Empire*. New York, NY: Columbia Global Reports.

2

INCLUSION

At the 2017 International Indian Film Awards (IIFA) ceremony, Karan Johar, an influential Bollywood producer, tried to make a joke about nepotism in Bollywood. *India Today* reporter Samrudhi Ghosh reported the exchange,

> The controversy began when Varun Dhawan came up on the IIFA 2017 stage to receive the Best Performance in a Comic Role award for Dishoom.
>
> Host of the evening, Saif Ali Khan, joked that the actor had made it big in the industry because of his father, director David Dhawan.
>
> Varun replied, 'And you're here because of your mummy' [the veteran actress Sharmila Tagore].
>
> Karan chimed in, 'I am here because of my papa' [the late filmmaker Yash Johar].
>
> The trio then said in unison, 'Nepotism rocks'.
>
> (Ghosh 2017)

This joke is a response to acclaimed Bollywood actress Kangana Ranaut's charge of nepotism against Karan Johar. Earlier, in February

2017, acclaimed Bollywood actress, Kangana Ranaut[1] declared Karan Johar to be the 'flagbearer of nepotism' and 'movie mafia' on his own talk show, *Koffee with Karan* (Season 5, episode 16). Karan is one of the most powerful men in Bollywood with a filmography (where he is often producer, writer, and director) including huge Bollywood blockbusters, *Kal Ho Naa Ho* (2003) and *Ae Dil Hai Mushkil* (2016), among others. Karan Johar himself is a star kid who has facilitated 'breaks' of multiple star kids. Nepotism rocks indeed, for some people.

Ranaut's comments allude to the Bollywood phenomenon of the 'star kid'. A 'star kid' is the child of a Bollywood actor, producer, or scriptwriter. In response to Ranaut's remark, many of the star kids denied being given advantages. One such was Alia Bhatt, Bollywood star and daughter of Mahesh Bhatt, who is a legendary director, producer, and scriptwriter and head of Vishesh Films, known for films such as *Saaransh* (1984) (India's entry for the Academy Awards for foreign language film).

Karan Johar notably launched Alia Bhatt by helping her get a lead role in the 2012 film *Student of the Year* (her debut). When asked if nepotism has helped her career, Bhatt responded in a Times of India article that she thinks 'A star kid can get that first film due to nepotism. But to constantly get films just because you belong to a "filmi" family is not possible' (Thakur 2017). She thus claimed that the need to eventually prove yourself in terms of box office revenues created difficulties for star kids too; and these difficulties compensated for their ease of access. Another actor, Varun Dhawan laconically commented in a March 2017 NDTV interview with Puja Talwar that 'If my father won't do this for me then who will? They [outsiders] are acting if their father hasn't even bought a pencil box for them' (NDTV 2017), thereby arguing that nepotism was expected and commonly accepted. Economists Mark Lorenzen and Florian Täube (2008) argue that nepotism is a key tenet of Bollywood's business model and organisational culture, given the importance of social networks.

This strong reliance on nepotism undermines the argument that the cultural economy is inclusive, as many reports and documents do. UNCTAD, for example, makes the following claim in its *Creative Economy Report*:

> Developing countries around the world can find ways to optimize the potential of the creative economy for generating socio-economic growth, job creation and export earnings while at the same time promoting *social inclusion*, cultural diversity and human development.
>
> (UNCTAD and UNDP 2008, 8, emphasis added)

There is however little reason to believe this celebratory approach, as the evidence points out that labour in the cultural economy is difficult to obtain, maintain, and live off (Banks 2017; Hesmondhalgh and Baker 2010; McRobbie 2016; Throsby and Zednik 2010). This raises the question of whether Bollywood is the exception or merely the illustration of a broader issue of exclusion-based genealogy.

Despite the celebratory claims that anyone can make it (more about the 'rags to riches' ideal below), we argue that exclusion is one of the sector's strategies to make sure some people have far better chances to end up on top. This is because there is a lot at stake: in the cultural economy, the winner often takes it all (Caves 2000). The variations in the system of inclusion or exclusion, depending on one's perspective, are based on the values and biases of each society. This chapter demonstrates the variety of ways in which the global cultural economy is not a universal model of rules and principles but maintains the cultural codes of particular places.

Contrary to what some people and policy documents may claim, the cultural economy is not meritocratic. In fact, the idea that the cultural economy, and society at large, is meritocratic rests on a very shallow and uncritical reading of Michael Young's dystopian book *The Rise of the Meritocracy* (1958). This book was a social critique, rather than a policy recommendation. Nevertheless, Tony Blair's New Labour government (1997–2010) in the UK popularised the term, particularly in relation to the cultural economy. (This is, unfortunately, not the first or only time that governments have translated warnings from dystopian literature into policy.)

The global cultural economy had been promoted as a socially inclusive space (UNCTAD and UNDP 2008). The importance of family background in Bollywood, one of the largest film industries in the world, raises questions. It is almost a rite of passage for a star kid to become a star him/herself, despite the many who try to get into Bollywood. However, the dynastic political and social environment of

India makes the star kid phenomenon fairly uncontroversial. But elsewhere in the world, other forms of exclusion are more controversial, as cultural production is always embedded in particular cultural contexts. The Jamaican music industry provides another perspective, when a cultural sector is confined to margins or excluded. One can exclude by being elitist or by confining groups to marginality. This point is significant given the urgency to attain parity of diversity, particularly given the underrepresentation of historically marginalised groups in the cultural economy.

In this chapter on inclusion, we explore forms of exclusion in Bollywood, Hollywood and the Jamaica music industry. Our examples, alongside recent work from other scholars, suggest that exclusion is intrinsic to the global cultural economy. Our case on Hollywood also provides examples of intersectional exclusion on the basis of gender and race through the 2017 American TV show, *Insecure*. We discuss the concept of intersectionality as we concentrate on certain bases of inclusion to make the argument, but understand the interesting nature of bases of exclusion. We end the chapter with a discussion of reggae-dancehall to show the contrast with cultural expression or product associated with marginalised people. Interestingly, even then there is exclusion, suggesting that exclusion, rather than inclusion, is characteristic of the global cultural economy. Moreover, we discuss the longevity of stereotypical representations even in the face of diversity (promotion) measures in the UK.

INTERSECTIONALITY

Exclusion comes in many shapes, styles, and forms. But issues around gender, race, and class play out in some way or another around the world. And rather than being mutually exclusive, forms of exclusion are often mutually inclusive. This means that women of colour, for example, often face multiple layers of exclusion, because they are both women and of colour. While we discuss different forms of exclusion in separate sections of this chapter, we do build on the notion that multiple forms of exclusion intersect.

Kimberlé Crenshaw initially introduced the seminal concept of intersectionality to describe the multiple and interacting exclusions of black women (Crenshaw 1989). The concept has flourished and grown beyond that to other instances of interacting exclusions. In a 2013 review of intersectionality's scholarly impact, Devon Carbado et al. (2014) argue that the term is now a useful tool to examine parallel layers of exclusion in societies, beyond the initial concern with women of colour.

Different 'individual' forms of exclusion exist in the cultural economies all around the world and can easily be studied independently from an agnostic or refusenik perspective. And given the imbalance between abundant talent and limited paid work, these exclusions come on top of a systemically precarious organisation of labour. But what matters on top of this when discussing inclusion and exclusion in the global cultural economy is that geography matters a great deal too. We try to advance a reflexive understanding that bears in mind the intersecting forms of exclusion as they exist and persist in the global cultural economy.

The importance of *ascriptive* qualities – family, race, class, gender, age – in Bollywood is not particular to India, but is a discernible (and controversial) characteristic of the global cultural economy. Global media scholar Andreas Wittel argues that given the informality of the cultural economic system, the importance of cultural capital is unsurprising: 'where social relations are not narrational but informational . . . not based on mutual experience or common history but primarily on an exchange of data and on "catching up"'(Wittel 2001, 51). Urban planning scholar Elizabeth Currid makes a similar point: 'informal collaboration, information and ideas outside the workplace proved just as important as the interactions that happened at work' (Currid 2009, 73). Both highlight the importance of socialising outside of work in the global cultural economy. People will socialise with those who have similar interests and tastes. Here we see the linkage to family background and socialisation being translated into economic and cultural capital resources required to 'break into the circle'. Our other cases demonstrate that is not just a Bollywood phenomenon. The particular attention to family background is characteristic of Bollywood and India. However, the reliance on an ascriptive characteristics in participation in the global cultural economy is widespread.

Given the importance of regional industry clusters in the global cultural economy, geography also matters. The international clustering and agglomeration phenomenon of the 'cultural industries' means that being able to live and work in a certain country, city, or even part of a city is conducive to success, even if it is not necessarily a determining factor.

There is an assumption of a fundamental divide between the North and the South, even if statistician Hans Rosling debunks this divide for its lack of evidence (Rosling 2018). We prefer the term 'majority world' to highlight the geographic differences, rather than an essentialisation of a binary. We wrote this book to explore whether the characteristics observed in our individual case studies support the developed-developing binary in relation to the global cultural economy. We cite cases from both sides of the alleged binary. US Hollywood, Indian Bollywood, and Jamaican reggae-dancehall are the three main cases in this chapter. They show that exclusion is a global phenomenon. Evidence from the cases confirms that social inclusion is not the forte of the cultural economy irrespective of whether in minority or majority world. The social network and cultural capital-oriented economic contexts does not to open doors to minorities and marginalised communities but closes them.

'NEPOTISM ROCKS!'

Bollywood, India's largest film industry produced approximately 1,966 films in 2014 and is the largest film industry in the world in terms of titles released. In comparison, Hollywood produced 707 (see Table 2.1).

Given the long lineage of film stars, the film debuts of 'star kids' are anticipated events that lend themselves as marketing ploys, which help secure returns in in the high-risk cultural economy (see Chapter

Table 2.1 Film production in India, China, the USA, and France (2010–2016)

	2010	2011	2012	2013	2014	2015	2016
India	1,274	1,255	1,602	1,724	1,966	1,845	1,903
China	526	588	745	638	618	686	944
US	795	818	728	738	707	791	789
France	261	272	279	270	258	300	283

Source: Statista (2018).

four). The Bollywood system is very producer-centric, relying on their networks and relationships. In the absence of formal contracts or signing fees, producers broker between stars, directors, and financiers to make a movie work.

As Bollywood matured as an industry in the 1950s and 1960s, it retained its reliance on small and mostly closed networks (Lorenzen and Täube 2008). The importance of social connections emerged in response to a lack of active formal industry bodies in Bollywood. The existence of political and economic dynasties in India. This gradually resulted in the normalisation of nepotism, up to the extent that key people in these networks even feel comfortable joking about it.

Lorenzen and Täube (2008) studied Bollywood's disintegrated business structure as an alternative to the Hollywood film business model of integration, with little regard to issues of social inclusion/exclusion. They argue that the 'emerging Bollywood model's combination of integrated distribution and finance, disintegrated production, and alliances, may be a viable alternative to the Hollywood model' (Lorenzen and Täube 2008, 296). The 'cultural industries' are often portrayed as meritocratic industries where talent and skill supersede all. The informality of the global cultural economy is taken to mean that educational qualifications are not barriers to success. However, as Bollywood nepotism demonstrates, informality does not always translate into access for all, particularly in an environment where there is little attention to factors of inclusion.

Kim-Marie Spence, one of the authors of this book, has conducted primary research in Mumbai and found that the system has changed little. Spence interviewed casting director Tara George who, while her family is unconnected to Bollywood, has managed to work in both Bollywood and Hollywood. She stated there is commonly no script until very late in the process as there was a fear of ideas being stolen. At the same time, there are generally no formal contracts with stars, who are contacted and contracted through social networks by way of phone calls.

While the joke we opened the chapter with suggests widespread acceptation of nepotism in Bollywood, media attention suggests otherwise. Public opinion shows an interest and possible critical opinions to the issue of nepotism in film by the public. Something that once had been seen as normal was now up for debate. Interestingly, those outside of 'filmi' family circles seem to have accepted the status quo. In a recent interview with Bollywood actor, Kay Kay Menon, a Bollywood supporting actor of some time, responded,

> What do I gain by complaining . . . These are facts of life that I can't change. It's the norm of the industry, and no point in just complaining about it. You do your best with whatever is possible and leave the rest to god.
>
> (Sur 2018)

Spence interviewed a number of Bollywood aspirants who likened their paths to a marathon. Actor Motilal Sharma is a former television drama star, who has sought to make the transition to Bollywood many times. He decided to produce his own independent film as his attempt to enter the industry. Lacking access to financiers, he set up a bar/restaurant in Mumbai to use the profits for the production budget. In the meantime, he has been doing television serials (a standard route for non-star kid male actors) for five years, while hoping for a Bollywood opportunity. Despite his efforts, he has not found distribution for the movie yet, largely due to lack of contacts within the Bollywood network of families.

Female actors in Bollywood face similar forms of exclusion. One such actress is Sara Paul, who was raised abroad by Indian parents and decided to move to India to try her luck in Bollywood, using her singing talent as her entryway. For her first Bollywood job, she received no credit. In absence of a Bollywood breakthrough, she has taken to acting in plays, doing commercials, singing, and starring in reality shows to support herself for four years, while pursuing her Bollywood opportunity.

On top of the difficulties of getting a good role, Paul also noted an earning differential in Bollywood. According to her, Star kids usually get lead roles earning at least INR 3 crores (30 million rupees or US$469,000). Despite this, she saw herself as lucky – she had gotten some roles, whether as singer or actress, and had avoided the sleazier side of the industry, where trading of sexual favours for roles is not un-common. However, she has remained hopeful of making it into Bollywood. Both Sara Paul and Tara George spoke about importance of good looks for non-star kid women. Most outsider lead Bollywood actresses, such as Aishwarya Rai, come from the beauty queen or modelling world.

The discovery stories of star kids is palpably different. Varun Dhawan assisted Karan Johar on his film *My Name is Khan* (Pathak 2017). Harshvadhan Kapoor was spotted by Rakeysh Omprakash Mehra on the set of his sister's (Sonam Kapoor) movie where he was 'chilling'. In addition, star kids get more chances to fail than the average. Kay Kay Menon has been a supporting actor for so long as the movies in which had lead roles were not popular or had not been made. Bollywood actor Abhishek Bachchan, son of legendary Bollywood/Hollywood actor Amitabh Bachchan, had lead roles in over 50 movies to date, despite not being popular (Pathak 2017).

The cultural economy parallels the structure of the society in which it is embedded rather than transforming it. Informality does not mean a lack of conventions and customs conducive to certain types of cultural, social, and economic capital. It is rather the absence of formal regulation through institutions. Contacts and information are traded at these social events. Informality can make it harder to challenge the lack of diversity, as there is no explicit imperative, such as quota, promoting inclusion.

The exclusive nature is in contrast to the myth of inclusion around Bollywood and the cultural economy (Duffy 2016). Actress Sara Paul stated that for her, Mumbai was not the 'city of dreams' as commonly touted. It is meant to distract from the reality of the continuing power of ascriptive societal constructs, in Bollywood's case one's family. One upcoming Bollywood director, Sahat Chahaun,[2] when asked about financing arrangements for his film, simply replied 'Ask Karan Johar', begging the question of what happens if you don't know Karan Johar and highlighting the importance of being enmeshed in the right networks.

Within the cultural economy, Bollywood is not an exception. The intersectionality of the exclusion is not unusual. Neither is the ascriptive nature of the exclusion. Hollywood suffers from similar issues.

INSECURE IN HOLLYWOOD

Hollywood is the most lucrative film and television market in the world, with a box office of US\$10.31 billion in 2016, accounting for little less than a third of global box office revenue (see Table 4.3 in Chapter four). The evidence points again to the importance of ascriptive qualities in the cultural industry of Hollywood. Unlike Bollywood, it is race and gender (among others), not family background, which matters. The year 2015 saw the premieres of Aziz Ansari's *Master of None* and Lee Daniel's *Empire,* part of a wave of American TV shows about people of colour that defined the end of the Obama era. These shows highlight that representation of blackness and people of colour more broadly is still an issue in Hollywood.

Critics hailed Issa Rae's television show *Insecure* as distinct in its embrace of the ordinariness of being a black woman in America (Bastien 2016; Butler 2016; Wortham 2015). *Insecure* is Issa Rae's third successful show. Her second show, *Awkward Black Girl,* a web series, was an instant hit with the first episode garnering over 2.4 million views. A number of television networks expressed interest in reworking *Awkward Black Girl* for television. However, the studios suggested changes to the format to make it more marketable. One recommendation was to cast a lighter-skinned black actress with straight hair. Issa Rae, a dark-skinned black woman with short natural hair, had starred in *Awkward Black Girl.* Another network recommended a 'pan-racial franchise' (Wortham 2015). The USP (unique selling proposition) of *Awkward Black Girl* had been its blackness and this was exactly what the television networks wanted to change. The reason for the suggested change was that blackness limited the potential audience, an example of what media scholar Timothy Havens refers to as 'industry lore' (Havens 2013; cited in Saha 2018). In the end, Issa Rae signed with HBO (Home Box Office), a US cable network that produces its own content. Her management company hired Larry Wilmore, an African-American former co-host of *The Daily Show,* to assist and guide Issa Rae through the screenwriting process. As a result of this collaboration, *Insecure* was born. But the production of the show raised some unexpected issues.

HBO required that experienced people be hired to produce the show, which posed a challenge. Issa Rae wanted to hire people of colour, but people of colour with the necessary experience were scarce, even in Los Angeles, a city with a significant minority population. As with Bollywood, experience is often required for those outside the preferred social circles. But opportunities to gain experience are often allocated through certain social networks and might require significant resources to attain, making it difficult for the economically and socially disadvantaged to gain experience. The result was that even in Los Angeles, home to large minority communities, Rae could not find people of colour with the right experience.

Issa Rae eventually hired Melina Matsoukas, known for her music videos, notably Beyoncé's *Formation*, to direct the *Insecure*'s pilot (Wortham 2015). And HBO eventually found an African-American showrunner, Prentice Perry, who *New York Times* reporter Jenna Wortham described as coaching Issa on how to be black in Hollywood. The need for such coaching is indicative of the exclusion of African-Americans in Hollywood. Perry advised Issa that 'you can't ever look like you are not on your game. As a writer of colour, be strategic, and be careful' (Wortham 2015). The reverse conversation on how to be white in Hollywood is unimaginable. White is considered the default. This very assumption speaks to the racialised systems of cultural production in Hollywood. UCLA's 2018 *Hollywood Diversity Report* noted that only 13.9% of all film leads are people of colour, while people of colour account for 40% of the US population (Hunt et al. 2018, 3). Getting experience is therefore dependent on a mix of cultural, social, and financial capital, rather than just talent.

The cultural economy of London, a major global city with a significant 'minority' community, faces similar challenges. In a joint article, Kate Oakley, Daniel Laurison, Dave O'Brien, and Sam Friedman note the scepticism towards formal credentials and education (informality) in London's 'cultural industries' as 'many employers have not been "trained" in the crafts they practice' (Oakley et al. 2017, 6). Their interviewees often referred to education as a means of socialisation within the 'creative industries', rather than an acquisition of skills. This tendency towards informality and the privileging of experience and talent has often been taken to mean that the 'creative industries' were open to all, but their findings say differently.

Kate Oakley and her colleagues found that those from privileged class backgrounds formed the majority of those in almost all cultural sectors. Moreover, women and minorities are underrepresented. Informality is therefore assumed to mean an open door to all, but it often means an open door to those who know where 'the door' is and how to enter it.

Diversity policies within the cultural economy are often based on the assumption that increased representation of minorities in the cultural economy is the answer to their systemic exclusion from both the cultural economy and society as a whole. Diversity measures usually include some sort of quota or affirmative action system. The UCLA Diversity Reports, for example, track the percentage of leads and characters of colour in film and television and applaud an increase as a sign of progress (Hunt et al. 2018). The experience of others such as Aziz Ansari (*Master of None*), Margaret Cho (*All-American Girl*), Eddie Huang (*Fresh Off the Boat*), and Mindy Kaling (*The Mindy Project*) in Hollywood point to a systemic problem with dealing with the stories of people of colour in general, even while they are represented. For example, despite Margaret Cho, a Korean-American comedian, having the lead role, the writing team consisted of no Korean-Americans. The result was the presentation of Cho as 'Asian' rather than Korean-American, conforming to 'Oriental' stereotypes, inconsistent with her culture (Park 2014).

Anamik Saha, a media scholar, points out in his book, *Race and the Cultural Industries* (2018), that even when the representation of people of colour increases, the thinking and assumptions about them, the power dynamics *vis-à-vis* majorities, and the tendency towards negative stereotypes in media representation do not necessarily improve. He argues that increasing the representation of races in media is not enough to make it less racialised as media involves the 'production of representation' as 'representations of race are consumed in the form of cultural commodities' (Saha 2018, 113). Through his examination of the television, publishing, and theatre scenes of Britain for its representation of British South Asians, he contends that increasing the numbers of minorities working off-screen, while a welcome objective, will do very little to improve the representation of minorities onscreen (Saha 2017). In response, he advocates for greater public funding of 'minority' production companies, rather than increased representation within established (and traditional) media companies.

Saha (2018) does stress the need to resist 'industry lore' in order to attain change, as it determines which images and representation are attractive to the public. He cites the work of media scholar Ross (1995) on how black filmmakers are often told which types of blackness will sell, resulting in people of colour reproducing these stereotypes. Change in representational images is what Saha advocates and suggests measures such as investing in new platforms for minority representation and supporting the creation of new audiences. He argues such innovation and the search for novelty is inbuilt within the cultural economy: 'In the production of cultural commodities, even in the most commercialised, marketised settings, there is opportunity for different, alternative, experimental, thought-provoking narratives' (Saha 2018, 141).

It is tempting to assume that exclusion is a one-way street, where the powerful exclude the powerless. And most often this is the case, but there is evidence that certain parts of the cultural economy aim to keep the cultural expressions of marginal people marginal. Reggae is one example of a cultural expression associated with marginal groups within its home society.

GHETTO PEOPLE MUSIC

Reggae-dancehall[3] emanates from the Jamaican lower class. Reggae songs tend to have anti-colonial, anti-oppression messages and became popular worldwide for this reason (see Chapter five). Reggae's message has resonated in newly independent countries (see, for example, Alpha Blondy and Tiken Jah Fakoly in Côte d'Ivoire), those still persisting with independence movements (for example, the anti-apartheid lyrics of Lucky Dube in South Africa), and Black Power.

In Jamaica, reggae is strongly associated with Rastafari, a minor and largely marginalised religion from Jamaica. In many ways, Bob Marley was both a global music star and a prophet in his dissemination of Rastafari (Bilby 1977; Chevannes 1995). The popularity and reputation of Bob Marley is, however, more contentious in Jamaica than it is elsewhere in the world. While Marley is widely acclaimed as a global icon, a rock star, in Jamaica there is resistance to his being named a national hero, due to his religion (Rastafari), his love life (he was promiscuous), and his drug use (he smoked marijuana, a sacrament of Rastafari). Despite Jamaica's strong international association with reggae, Rastafari, and marijuana, there is a decided reluctance and aversion to that image locally. Rastafarians were once considered criminals within Jamaican society, due to their Afrocentric message (which clash with the more Eurocentric Christian values of postcolonial Jamaica) and consumption of marijuana (only decriminalised in 2015 in Jamaica). Bob Marley Day is celebrated with much fanfare in some cities, such as London and Los Angeles. In Jamaica, while observed at the Bob Marley Museum, his former residence, it is not widely celebrated.

Dancehall, a sub-genre of reggae with which it often shares the same stages, speaks to a more local Jamaican message valorising Jamaican ghetto values and lifestyle – the bling, the sex, the violence (Hope 2006; Stolzoff 2000). Despite the difference in their messages, both have a common origin in the Jamaican lower class and are treated similarly by the authorities. In addition, Spence's interviews with people from both dancehall and reggae indicated significant overlap of artists and production talent. We therefore discuss the genres as one, reggae-dancehall.

Dancehall is currently more marginal than reggae within Jamaica. While reggae has become respectable with time, dancehall is now being marginalised on the same grounds that Reggae was previously. This is in part due to dancehall's association with crime through its lyrics. Jamaican journalist Alphea Saunders recently reported on a call by the Jamaican police force to investigate the link between dancehall music and rising criminality in Jamaica to find proof of dancehall's negative influence (Saunders 2016). Interestingly, a similar link had been made earlier between Rastafarians, reggae, and crime (and for hip hop/rap in the US) (Paul 2017).

In the light of the presumed 'indecency' of dancehall, we argue that despised art forms are quite often the only significant way to express dignity for marginalised people. This is what connects styles like dancehall to hip hop: while successful artists may make lots of money, they need 'ghetto' credentials to be taken seriously in subcultural terms.

When 'ghetto people music' becomes economically valuable, cultural credibility becomes cultural capital. But even for those who don't stand to benefit economically, this credibility lends cultural value in the form of dignity. We derive the term 'dignity' from the work of Deirdre McCloskey, who uses it in reference to socio-historical development. In her treatise, *Bourgeois Dignity: Why Economics Can't Explain the Modern World* (McCloskey 2010), she seeks to discover why the Industrial Revolution happened in the UK and not in more technologically advanced China or the Islamic Middle East. The reason, she argues, is that while the Chinese and Middle Eastern bourgeoisie were more advanced than the British bourgeoisie, they lacked support from the wider society. The British bourgeoisie enjoyed high levels of dignity, relative to their counterparts elsewhere in the world. There is however a significant difference between socially acknowledged dignity (as was the case for the British bourgeoisie) and socially disregarded self-worth (as is the case for dancehall artists).

In the Jamaican context, interviewee after interviewee noted the disregard of the reggae and dancehall industry by the government and the wider society. Gregory Alcock, Jamaica Music Society (JAMMS) employee, one of the collection management agencies in Jamaica (see Chapter five), noted in an interview with Kim-Marie Spence that government officials had a negative view of the music industry and that 'they don't even view it as a contributor to the economy. It is just entertainment. Just some guys who smoke weed and grow [dread] locks'. Discussions on the 'cultural industries' and policy assume that minorities and other groups with less 'dignity' will be accepted as long as the economic value of their cultural product is good. But while the earnings of Bob Marley, Sean Paul, and Shaggy are an indication of the economic value of their music, it does not translate into greater 'dignity' for the music within Jamaica. Moreover, one senior entertainment government official explained in an interview with Spence:

> Once the public does not perceive entertainment as an industry, it is difficult for government to spend. Government spending is directed by public acceptance. So, when you put a waiver for the motor vehicle industry or the tourism industry, it is accepted by the public. You put a waiver for entertainment, it is resisted by the public.

Since 1996, Jamaica has identified entertainment and particularly the music industry as an area for potential economic gain in its *National Industrial Policy* (NIP). Despite this formal recognition and economic potential, it remains difficult to justify support for parts of the cultural economy that lack of socially accepted dignity. Policy support instead accrues to cultural sectors that have social 'dignity'. The marginalisation of the reggae and dancehall communities have acted as two-way barrier to inclusion, investment, and local development (of the music industry).

First, poor public perception acts as a hindrance for artists being included in the wider society, as per the case with National Hero recognition for Bob Marley in Jamaica. The music industry in Jamaica is largely seen as a way for lower class people to be 'somebody' and a way of social recognition. Stolzoff (2000) notes in a study of Kingston's dancehall scene that the choices open to lower class men, due to their poor education and lack of social capital, were crime, selling goods, minimum wage employment, or entertainment.

Second, it acts as a hindrance for talent, whether artistic, managerial, or even financial, from entering the industry. In order to attain success, musicians need to be marginal as a way to legitimise their rightful and dignified place within the subculture. Instead of the reggae and dancehall industry being a place of elites, it is a place for the marginal.

Sean Paul, an acclaimed international dancehall artist, has discussed his journey as a middle class, 'uptown' man in Jamaica's dancehall community. In a recent *Fader* interview, he noted that he started his career with 'conscious songs' (the Jamaican term for songs dealing with social justice) characteristic of reggae-dancehall, but noted that they were not accepted by the public as 'people would look at me like, "What the f...k you know about this s...t? You don't know nothing about it 'cause you're from uptown"' (Mistry 2016). This association with the marginal has ensured access to the music industry for the Jamaican lower class. It has also had an effect of keeping the music industry in Jamaica marginal with a lack of social capital, lack of financial capital, and poor public and private investment (Power and Hallencreutz 2002). This is a dilemma and one little addressed in current work around 'cultural industries' policy.

The Jamaican music industry forms an interesting example of the concept of Bourdieu's cultural capital, but in reverse. Pierre Bourdieu and Jean Claude Passeron (1990) argue that the knowledge of the upper class is considered capital valuable in a hierarchical society. Those without such knowledge can always go to school to learn this knowledge or this social capital. This forms the essence of the reproductive system of class. The music industry is one where people actively do emulate the ways of Jamaican mainstream society. This social distance acts against investment in the music industry, as those in the music industry cannot relate to those they need investment from. Moreover, as a reggae-dancehall artist, marginality, the opposite of cultural capital, is essential to street credibility. Similarly Sarah Thornton's (1996) work on British clubbers examines how different groups are identified by their 'disdain' of mainstream society in the construction of subcultural capital. Subcultural capital has had both an investment and policy effect.

This lack of dignity has translated into policy, turning socio-cultural exclusion into systemic and institutionalised exclusion. The Jamaican government, for example, has not passed laws recognising the economic rights of performers (Spence 2018). Moreover, until recently, there were few incentive programs for the Jamaican music industry (Tom Fleming Consultancy 2016). The example of reggae and dancehall demonstrates that cultural sectors don't always exclude in favour of the elite but can also exclude their members from the rest of the society. Reggae is 'ghetto people music' and is associated with marginalised groups in Jamaica, irrespective of the financial wealth they may accrue.

CONCLUSIONS

The cultural economy is a passionate pursuit. But that should not mean the artistic, emotional, social, or intellectual fulfilment should negate the need and ability to earn a living. And yet, that seems to be the case. In her book, *Do What You Love, and Other Lies About Success and Happiness*, art historian Miya Tokumitsu (2015) argues that the pursuit of passion ('do what you love') has become a convenient way to lure people into accepting free labour and low pay as the flip side of having a compelling job in the cultural economy. The fact that many people are willing to make these economic sacrifices speaks to the despair for the future among cultural labour aspirants.

Brooke Duffy, a media scholar, argues that the DWYL ('Do What You Love') maxim is appealing because it alludes to the existence of 'new employment spaces where pleasure, autonomy and income seemingly coexist' (Duffy 2016, 442). George Morgan and Pariece Nelligan further note the disjuncture of working class culture and the new economy, particularly for working-class men. They call the labour needed for the new economy 'labile labour', which they define as 'mobile, spontaneous, malleable, and capable of being aroused by new vocational possibilities. They must also present as eager and ambitious, but, paradoxically, this ambition must be diffuse' (Morgan and Nelligan 2015, 68). Though they argue that working class men are particularly vulnerable for having been socialised into a masculinity defined by stability, humility, and group-loyalty. What connects these three perspectives is that they critique the promise of the cultural economy as empowering and open.

In the global cultural economy, the 'rags to riches' story is prized and there is a discourse of diversity and inclusion. However, the examples in this chapter intimate that inclusion within the cultural economy seems more the exception, more conceptual than in practice. The common thread is that cultural economies reinforce, rather than transform, social structures, unless policies are put in place or a discourse to thwart that tendency. The casual nature of the 'cultural industries' seems to lend itself to mimicking the structures of the host society, as it does not include active advocacy for those who might be excluded.

There are of course exceptions, but artists and cultural economy workers in general may find it difficult to market their work from a 'marginal' position in the cultural economy. Marginality even extends to geographic location. When an artist, producer, manager, or director does not live in or have access to key cities such as London, Paris, Tokyo, or New York, where activity and power clusters, their 'local' inclusion and power may not count for much in the global cultural economy. For example, despite Bollywood being one of the largest film industries, there is little awareness of Bollywood stars elsewhere. Elizabeth Currid-Halkett and Gilad Ravid note in their analysis of US-based stock photo agency *Getty Images* note that Bollywood is nearly absent. They note that despite 'photographs taken in 187 locations, it is missing important parts of the world, namely parts of Africa, India (including Mumbai, Bollywood's film capital), and China' (Currid-Halkett and Ravid 2012, 2660). Making it in these global hubs requires further access to key networks with certain geographic hubs.

This raises two key issues that we address in the following chapters. First, in Chapter three, we discuss attempts to regulate market access in an unequal but globalised world. Second, in Chapter five, we discuss the difficulty to assert intellectual property rights over 'traditional' cultural expressions and the expressions of marginalised groups, which are all prone to cultural appropriation.

NOTES

1   Kangana Ranaut is one of the most popular actresses in Bollywood and is known for her forthrightness. She is not from a film family, hailing from a conservative family in Himachal Pradesh. She moved to Mumbai, despite family disapproval and enrolled for film course. She describes surviving on bread and pickles before her debut.
2   Sahat Chahaun is an alias for an upcoming director. He is not from Mumbai, but from northern India. He has directed one film and worked on a number of others. His film was a success and he is gradually making his name in Bollywood.
3   Reggae and dancehall are two distinct but inter-related forms of Jamaican music. While the sound of each is distinct, the two genres share artists, producers, album charts and even political reaction, Both emanate from the Jamaican lower class and are critiques of mainstream Jamaica. We have decided to recognise both and utilise the term reggae-dancehall.

REFERENCES

Banks, Mark. 2017. *Creative Justice: Cultural Industries, Work and Inequality*. London; New York, NY: Rowman & Littlefield International.

Bastien, Angelica Jade. 2016. "'Insecure' Season 1 Finale: Great Expectations". *New York Times*, November 27, 2016, sec. Television. www.nytimes.com/2016/11/27/arts/television/insecure-season-1-finale-recap.html?rref=collection%2Fcolumn%2Finsecure-tv-recaps&action=click&contentCollection=television®ion=stream&module=stream_unit&version=latest&contentPlacement=1&pgtype=collection.

Bilby, Kenneth. 1977. "The Impact of Reggae in the United States". *Popular Music and Society* 5 (5): 17–22.

Bourdieu, Pierre, and Jean Claude Passeron. 1990. *Reproduction in Education, Society, and Culture*. 1990 ed. Theory, Culture & Society. London; Newbury Park, CA: Sage in association with Theory, Culture & Society, Dept. of Administrative and Social Studies, Teesside Polytechnic.

Butler, Bethonie. 2016. "'Insecure': Everything You Need to Know about Issa Rae's HBO Comedy". *Washington Post*, October 9, 2016, sec. Blogs.

Carbado, Devon W., Kimberlé Williams Crenshaw, Vickie M. Mays, and Barbara Tomlinson. 2014. "Intersectionality: Mapping the Movements of a Theory". *Du Bois Review: Social Science Research on Race* 10 (2): 303–12.

Caves, Richard. 2000. *Creative Industries: Contracts between Art and Commerce*. Cambridge, MA: Harvard University Press.

Chevannes, Barry. 1995. *Rastafari: Roots and Ideology*. Syracuse, NY: Syracuse University Press.

Crenshaw, Kimberle. 1989. "Demarginalizing the Intersection of Race and Sex: A Black Feminist Critique of Antidiscrimination Doctrine, Feminist Theory and Antiracist Politics". *University of Chicago Legal Forum* 1: 139–67.

Currid, Elizabeth. 2009. "Bohemia as Subculture; 'Bohemia' as Industry: Art, Culture, and Economic Development". *Journal of Planning Literature* 23 (4): 368–82.

Currid-Halkett, Elizabeth, and Gilad Ravid. 2012. "'Stars' and the Connectivity of Cultural Industry World Cities: An Empirical Social Network Analysis of Human Capital Mobility and Its Implications for Economic Development". *Environment and Planning A: Economy and Space* 44 (11): 2646–63.

Duffy, Brooke Erin. 2016. "The Romance of Work: Gender and Aspirational Labour in the Digital Culture Industries". *International Journal of Cultural Studies* 19 (4): 441–57.

Ghosh, Samrudhi. 2017. "Karan Johar Regrets Chanting 'nepotism Rocks' at IIFA 2017: I Have Been Ungraceful to Kangana Ranaut". *India Today*, July 19, 2017. www.indiatoday.in/movies/celebrities/story/karan-johar-nepotism-rocks-iifa-2017-kangana-ranaut-1025085-2017-07-19.

Havens, Timothy. 2013. *Black Television Travels: African American Media Around the Globe*. Critical Cultural Communication. New York, NY; London: New York University Press.

Hesmondhalgh, David, and Sarah Baker. 2010. *Creative Labour: Media Work in Three Cultural Industries*. London; New York, NY: Routledge.

Hope, Donna. 2006. *Inna Di Dancehall: Popular Culture and the Politics of Identity in Jamaica*. Kingston: University of the West Indies Press.

Hunt, Darnell, Ana-Christina Ramón, Michael Tran, Amberia Sargent, and Debanjan Roychoudhury. 2018. *Hollywood Diversity Report*. Los Angeles, CA: UCLA College of Social Sciences.

Lorenzen, Mark, and Florian Arun Täube. 2008. "Breakout from Bollywood? The Roles of Social Networks and Regulation in the Evolution of Indian Film Industry". *Journal of International Management* 14 (3): 286–99.

McCloskey, Deirdre. 2010. *Bourgeois Dignity: Why Economics Can't Explain the Modern World*. Chicago, IL: University of Chicago Press.

McRobbie, Angela. 2016. *Be Creative Making a Living in the New Culture Industries*. Chichester: Wiley. www.public.eblib.com/choice/PublicFullRecord.aspx?p=4353616.

Mistry, Anupa. 2016. "Sean Paul Explains Why Dancehall Has Always Been Big". *Fader*. www.thefader.com/2016/07/15/sean-paul-interview.

Morgan, George, and Pariece Nelligan. 2015. "Labile Labour – Gender, Flexibility and Creative Work". *The Sociological Review* 63 (1_suppl): 66–83.

NDTV. 2017. "Varun Dhawan On Nepotism in Bollywood". Video. NDTV. www.ndtv.com/video/entertainment/news/varun-dhawan-on-nepotism-in-bollywood-451096.

Oakley, Kate, Daniel Laurison, Dave O'Brien, and Sam Friedman. 2017. "Cultural Capital: Arts Graduates, Spatial Inequality, and London's Impact on Cultural Labor Markets". *American Behavioral Scientist*, 1–22.

Park, Jane Chi Hyun. 2014. "The Failure of Asian American Representation in All-American Girl and The Cho Show". *Gender, Place & Culture*, 21 (5): 637–49.

Pathak, Ankur. 2017. "It's Dismaying How Blind Bollywood's Star Kids Are about Their Privilege: You Work Hard Doesn't Mean Your Privilege Isn't Real". *Huffington Post India* (blog). 2017. www.huffingtonpost.in/2017/03/22/its-dismaying-how-blind-bollywoods-star-kids-are-about-their-p_a_21905465/.

Paul, Annie. 2017. "Evening Sun Can't Dry Clothes". *Jamaica Gleaner*, April 12, 2017, sec. Commentary. www.jamaica-gleaner.com/article/commentary/20170412/annie-paul-evening-sun-cant-dry-clothes.

Power, Dominic, and Daniel Hallencreutz. 2002. "Profiting from Creativity? The Music Industry in Stockholm, Sweden and Kingston, Jamaica". *Environment and Planning A* 34 (10): 1833–54.

Rosling, Hans. 2018. *Factfulness: Ten Reasons We're Wrong about the World-and Why Things Are Better than You Think*. 1st ed. New York, NY: Flatiron Books.

Ross, Karen. 1995. *Black Minority Viewers and Television: Neglected Audiences Speak Up and Out*. Leicester: Centre for Mass Communication Research, University of Leicester.

Saha, Anamik. 2017. "Diversity Initiatives Don't Work, They Just Make Things Worse: The Ideological Function of Diversity in the Cultural Industries". *Media Diversified* (blog). www.mediadiversified.org/2017/02/16/diversity-initiatives-dont-work-they-just-make-things-worse-the-ideological-function-of-diversity-in-the-cultural-industries/.

Saha, Anamik. 2018. *Race and the Cultural Industries*. Malden, MA: Polity Press.

Saunders, Alphea. 2016. "Police Want Study on Effects of Dancehall Music on Crime: Commissioner Convinced Lyrics Influence Unruly Behaviour". *Jamaica Observer*. www.jamaicaobserver.com/news/Police-want-study-on-effects-of-dancehall-music-on-crime_58703.

Spence, Kim-Marie. 2018. "When Money Is Not Enough – Reggae, Dancehall and Policy in Jamaica". *Journal of Arts Management, Law & Society*, in press.

Statista. 2018. "Leading Film Markets Worldwide from 2007 to 2016, by Number of Films Produced". *Statista*. www.statista.com/statistics/252727/leading-film-markets-worldwide-by-number-of-films-produced/.

Stolzoff, Norman. 2000. *Wake the Town and Tell the People: Dancehall Culture in Jamaica*. London; Durham, NC: Duke University Press.

Sur, Prateek. 2018. "This Actor Feels Nepotism Is an Industry Norm & It's Pointless to Cry About It". Mumbai: 9X Media Pvt Limited.

Thakur, Shreya. 2017. "After Kangana Ranaut, Mahesh Bhatt's Daughter Alia Bhatt Talks about Nepotism". *The Times of India*, February 27, 2017. www.timesofindia.indiatimes.com/entertainment/hindi/bollywood/news/after-kangana-ranaut-mahesh-bhatts-daughter-alia-bhatt-talks-about-nepotism/articleshow/57372415.cms.

Thornton, Sarah. 1996. *Club Cultures: Music, Media, and Subcultural Capital*. 1st U.S. ed. Music/Culture. Lebanon, NH: University Press of New England.

Throsby, David, and Anita Zednik. 2010. *Do You Really Expect to Get Paid?* Strawberry Hills: Australia Council for the Arts.

Tokumitsu, Miya. 2015. *Do What You Love: And Other Lies about Success and Happiness.* First Regan Arts hardcover edition. New York, NY: Regan Arts.

Tom Fleming Creative Consultancy. 2016. "A Business Plan for the Jamaican Cultural and Creative Industries", edited by Ministry of Finance and Planning Institute of Jamaica. Kingston, Jamaica: Government of Jamaica.

UNCTAD, and UNDP. 2008. *Creative Economy Report 2008: The Challenge of Assessing the Creative Economy: Towards Informed Policy-Making.* UNCTAD/DITC/2008/2. Geneva: United Nations.

Wittel, Andreas. 2001. "Toward a Network Sociality". *Theory, Culture & Society* 18 (6): 51–76.

Wortham, Jenna. 2015. "The Misadventures of Issa Rae". *New York Times*, August 4, 2015, sec. Magazine.

Young, Michael Dunlop. 1958. *The Rise of the Meritocracy.* New Brunswick, NJ: Transaction Publishers.

3

DIVERSITY

The German trade journal for librarians *BuB – Forum Bibliothek und Information* published an article that claimed the *Transatlantic Trade and Investment Partnership* (TTIP) could impact German libraries and book publishers (Barbian 2014).[1] Jan-Pieter Barbian, who wrote the article, is a cultural historian and the director of the city library of Duisburg, and forewarns of the impact TTIP may have on trade in culture, and thereby on cultural diversity (see also Loisen and Pauwels 2015; Richieri Hanania 2016; Vlassis 2016). Barbian focuses particularly on the possible impact of the TTIP on existing policies and regulations pertaining to libraries and book publishers in Germany. When Barbian wrote his comments, they were entirely speculative, as no information about the secretive (and fundamentally undemocratic) TTIP negotiations was public.

Barbian's concerns are valid and reflect a long-standing tension between 'culture' and 'economy' (which we try to move beyond by focusing on the 'cultural economy'). This raises the question of whether individual governments (at national, local, or regional levels) can help maintain and promote cultural diversity. Moreover, it is argued that Barbian's refusenik perspective (see Introduction) fails to acknowledge the inherent complexities of the cultural economy. Rather than providing a grounded argument, he outlines three worst-case scenarios based largely on rumours and fears.

First, the fixed book price could cease to exist. This mechanism allows book publishers to set a fixed retail price for their books, thereby making it impossible for retailers to engage in price competition (Ringstad 2004). As price competition between book retailers would create an incentive for them to pressure publishers to lower their prices, this system has primarily benefited book publishers as they claim it allows them to publish a greater variety of works. The fear is that eliminating the fixed book price will lead to a retail monopoly.

Second, existing subsidies to culture and education could be seen as a barrier to trade (*Handelshemmnis*) for foreign players, as market orthodoxy considers subsidies to result in unfair competition. The fear is that commercial firms in education and retail of books (and other cultural expressions) would be able to sue states for their support for culture – through free education and fixed book prices, for example. The underlying threat is that this would undermine cultural diversity. Citing Olaf Zimmermann, the director of the German *Kulturrat* (Cultural Council), Barbian argues that it is easier to make money with more simplistic and smaller cultural offerings.

Third, Barbian is concerned that the strong protection of individuals' copyrights in Germany may come under pressure in an attempt to create a more homogeneous copyright regime as part of the TTIP negotiations. This could undermine the stronger moral and inalienable copyrights of individual creators in Germany, which are protected differently (and perhaps better) than those of creators in the US.

Several months before the publication of Barbian's opinion piece, the European Commission released a document (*TTIP and Culture*) that challenged the fears on which Barbian builds his claims about the diversity of the cultural economy. The European Commission debunks the three major arguments that Barbian makes. First, the Commission argues that US companies would not be able to 'use investor-to-state dispute mechanisms to challenge laws on book pricing' (European Commission 2014, 4). Second, they assert that 'claims that TTIP will limit subsidies to cultural activities are simply wrong' (European Commission 2014, 6). Third, the Commission clarifies that TTIP 'will not cover the kind of intellectual property enforcement issues that were included in the Anti-Counterfeiting Trade Agreement (ACTA)' and further stresses that 'any claims that it will are merely "urban myths"' (European Commission 2014, 6). The strong language of the European Commission doesn't mean much: The TTIP negotiations took place in great secrecy – until Greenpeace leaked a range of documents in May 2016[2] that neither confirmed nor denied these suspicions – so the Commission simply asks us to believe them.

A simple binary opposition between free trade in culture on the one hand and the protection of and support for culture by (and within) the state is however a false dichotomy. Neither of these positions actually exists in practice; they are mere ideological ideal-types that frame complex practices. The free market is a political construct that relies on the political and bureaucratic institutions to create regulatory frameworks (and often also markets themselves by selling off public assets to private investors). The protection of and support for culture by and within the state is equally illusory, as there is both limited congruence between people's cultural worlds and the territorial sovereign boundaries of the state.

Even so, the tension between the German book and library lobby and the TTIP free trade agreement reflects an old debate in political economy of culture: 'culture' versus 'economy' (more about this below). The threat these companies pose has arguably increased through globalisation. But what does cultural diversity mean in the context of a global cultural economy?

The remainder of this chapter explores the tension between the commitment to cultural diversity in the global cultural economy and the difficulty in governing it. First, we address what the *exception culturelle* means in international trade agreements and why it matters in debates around cultural diversity. Second, we explain how UNESCO tries to 'protect and promote' cultural diversity through a legally binding Convention. And third, we explain how the *African Writers Series*, and 'African' literature more generally, shows that the global cultural economy is not neatly organised country by country. In conclusion, we make the case that this creates tensions between intergovernmental regulations and individual countries that have to implement and enforce them.

THE *EXCEPTION CULTURELLE*: GOVERNING CULTURAL DIVERSITY BETWEEN WTO AND UNESCO

Diversity is key to the cultural economy. But because there are incompatible perspectives on how to support diversity (see Chapter four), some countries have argued for an *exception culturelle,* or cultural exception. France coined the term in 1993 as a way to keep culture (audio-visual productions, to be precise) out of GATTS (General Agreement on Trade in Services). The French argued that, in line with their cultural and foreign policies, culture should be exempt from free trade negotiations because of its particular status as something with symbolic status that cannot be separated from its value in trade – hence *exception culturelle* (Vlassis 2015).

In the cultural economy, 'difference' is currency in a market for creative, artistic, and innovative expressions where rapid changes dictate the game. Audiences are always looking for new stories, ideas, images, and sounds, so producing new *texts* while tapping into existing taste patterns is a constant challenge in the cultural economy. When looking at diversity at a global level, there are two major ways of increasing such diversity for audiences.

First, trading cultural expressions *among* countries gives people in all countries involved greater access to a variety of cultural expressions, often in other languages, set in different cultural contexts, and building on a different aesthetic. Increasing diversity through international trade builds both on similarity and difference in order to build and maintain new audiences.

Second, increasing diversity also takes places *within* countries when new genres, styles, and stories are developed; or when local issues give rise to artistic reflections – such as the films Fatih Akin's *Head On* (*Gegen Die Wand*) or Asghar Farhadi's *A Separation (Jodaí-e Nadér az Simín*) that negotiate conflicting cultural norms *within* countries. While most people herald diversity of cultural products (as opposed to diversity within societies) as inherently desirable, governments and academics continue to debate on how to best ensure that the cultural economy continues to produce a variety and diversity of cultural expressions.

Here, we sketch two opposing approaches: free trade and protectionism. On the one hand, in a 'classical' approach to cultural economics, scholars like Tyler Cowan argue that the 'gains from trade' in culture makes 'individuals who engage in cross-cultural exchange expect those transactions to make them better off, to enrich their cultural lives, and to increase their *menu of choice*' (Cowen 2002, 12, emphasis added).[3] In practice, a varied 'menu of choice' allows for a small number of cultural expressions to circulate around the world, which contribute to stereotyping complex and rich cultures. Depending on the strength of local producers, distributors, and audience preferences, such an influx may co-exist with local cultural expressions, but the global cultural economy may also overpower niche and minority 'cultural industries'. Cowen acknowledges this, stating, 'the diversity of modern commercial society nonetheless presents a paradox: a growing menu of choice in a particular society may limit the menu of choice for the world as a whole' (2002, 71). He substantiates his claim by arguing that the most open societies are also the most diverse, but we take a global perspective and argue that the 'menu of choice for the world as a whole' is more important that what is available within any given country. The argument he presents is thus little more than an ideological reflection on the consumer end of diversity.

The World Trade Organisation (WTO) and its predecessor, the General Agreement on Tariffs and Trade (GATT), have staunchly defended the free market argument, since 1994 and 1948 respectively – even if some cultural expressions (i.e. audio-visual or cinematographic industries) have remained a contentious category in GATT negotiation rounds (Vlassis 2015; Voon 2007). The aim of the multilateral WTO negotiations and regional free trade agreements is generally to reduce trade barriers (tariffs, subsidies, tax incentives, etc.) that may hamper international trade. Theories of trade presume that trade is generally beneficial to all parties involved and that these parties trade on equal footing. While mainstream economic thinking may recognise that there are inequalities in trading relations, it argues that these inequalities would be resolved through more free trade, not that they are its result.

On the other hand, those who take a more statist approach argue that the state has an active role to play in maintaining cultural diversity *within* its borders. This argument is based on the premise that the state is the guardian and patron of cultural expressions that reflect the national identity of a country – even if the underlying identity politics have become increasingly complex and layered. France is a prime example of this approach for two main reasons. First, the French state has a long history of active political involvement in the realm of culture that became official policy with the foundation of France's first Ministry of Cultural Affairs (*Ministère des Affaires Culturelles*) under President Charles De Gaulle and minister André Malraux in 1959. Second, France has an active cinema culture that thrives on government subsidies.

While generating a significant number of feature films every year, the state intervenes in order to 'promote and protect' (to use the words of the 2005 UNESCO Convention) the viability and reach of these films. Their 'protectionist' approach includes measures such as government subsidies, market access restrictions, tax measures, licensing restrictions, limitations of foreign investment and ownership, domestic content requirements, and measures relating to intellectual property rights (Van den Bossche 2007, 20–24). But who is protecting what? And what is the cultural economy being protected from?

The production, distribution, and consumption of audio-visual expressions (mainly film and television) illustrate the tension between 'national' expressions in a 'global' cultural economy. While the tension between free trade and protectionism plays out politically between nation-states through 'inter-national', or rather 'inter-governmental' organisations such as the WTO and UNESCO, culturally, these tensions are far more complex. This has much to do with the high fixed costs and the low marginal costs of audio-visual productions. The initial fixed cost (the production of the film) is high, while the marginal cost of the distribution in cinemas, on DVD, on television, and through on-demand platforms is relatively low (even if the success of blockbusters relies on significant marketing budgets). The former is called a fixed cost because it is the amount necessary to produce the film or television series in the first place; once the product is finished it becomes a non-rival good, which means that the very same film can be watched by millions of others without incurring additional (or marginal) cost. As a result, there is a relatively small number of films produced every year (in particular when compared with music albums or books), which circulate quite extensively for a relatively long time.

The debate sketched above places the tension between free trade and protectionism in a new context but adds little to the long-standing ideological opposition between both. As the history of the fixed book price can be traced back to the early 19th century (Ringstad 2004).[4] In the simplest (and perhaps most simplistic) manner, the argument holds that culture needs protecting from commercial interest, particularly the commercial interests of global corporations, as they tend to care about diversity in function of sales, but less about diversity that does not sell. This raises the question of how we can best 'protect and promote the diversity of cultural expressions' (UNESCO 2005).

UNESCO'S 'GLOBAL' SOLUTION TO A 'LOCAL' CHALLENGE?

The high fixed costs and low marginal costs make it appealing to export audio-visual productions: Once they have been finalised, the cost of releasing them elsewhere is limited. But the ease with which one country is able to export their films depends on the extent to which the importing country makes that easy. This is where countries with strong internal audio-visual markets and productions with significant international appeal (traditionally, the US has been the key example of this) clash with countries with weaker internal markets or with audio-visual productions that are not commercially viable abroad (France puts itself in that category). International tensions about trade in culture have been around since well before Louis Le Prince filmed his first moving picture in Leeds in 1888, and before Auguste and Louis Lumière organised their first moving picture screening in Lyon, seven years later in 1895.

Long before the global circulation of audio-visual productions became an issue of economic importance in the context of the international and regional economic integration, the trade in books had already been a matter of concern and conflict. Since the early days of book printing, conflicts about cross-border trade in (what would later be called) intellectual property rights have been rife. At the time, two major differences make a comparison with today's trade issues difficult. First, legal jurisdictions did not map onto nation-states for the simple reason that the latter did not exist in the way we know them today. Second, given the lack of an international legal framework to settle disputes between jurisdictions did not exist; even if the term inter-national is an anachronism here: nation-states did not commonly exist as sovereign entities until the 19th century, even if the 17th century Treaty of Westphalia marks the birth of the nation-state.

In the Introduction to this book, we showed that cultural production does not easily map onto the imagined unity and territoriality of the nation-state. The flows of culture connect many places around the world without necessarily being truly global – many networks are regional (Appadurai 1996; Scott 2008). Yet the marketplace for cultural expressions is now a global arena, where international organisations develop legal frameworks in order to regulate and govern anxieties and conflicting interests (Singh 2011).[5]

The ideological tension between the WTO and UNESCO has resulted in a formal global norm-setting and regulatory document: the UNESCO (2005) *Convention on the Protection and Promotion of the Diversity of Cultural Expressions* (henceforth the Convention). It is the only legally binding international agreement that regulates the *diversity of cultural expressions*.[6] The UNESCO General Conference adopted the Convention on October 20, 2005, during the 33rd Session of its General Conference. The Convention came into action on March 18, 2007, after the Convention came into force upon the ratification by the 30th party to the convention as outlined in Article 29.

The premise at the core of the Convention is that the current rules of the global cultural economy are unequal, unbalanced, and unfair. The underlying contention of the document is that state intervention through support for cultural production is needed to rectify these issues that would be exacerbated by unfettered free trade. This resonates throughout the Convention but is at its strongest when addressing global imbalances between 'developed' and 'developing' countries – even if that division is misleading, misguided, and out-of-date (De Beukelaer 2014).

Article 1 stipulates the objectives of the Convention; section (h) of the article clarifies UNESCO's stance on global trade in cultural expressions:

> The objectives of the Convention are:
>
> [. . .]
>
> (h) to reaffirm the sovereign rights of States to maintain, adopt and implement policies and measures that they deem appropriate for the protection and promotion of the diversity of cultural expressions on their territory.
>
> (UNESCO 2005)

With this section, the Convention cements the rights of parties to the Convention to provide support for 'cultural industries' *within* their territories. Many countries with a weaker cultural economy do indeed need support for (and investment in) the high fixed cost of setting up production, distribution, and exhibition companies. In making this point in the name of cultural diversity, UNESCO legally became a stakeholder in debates around free trade and protectionism regarding cultural expressions, aiming to put in question the authority of WTO.

First, the convention originates in the *exception culturelle* (Loisen and Pauwels 2015; Neuwirth 2013, 2015; Vlassis 2015). Unlike wheat or petrol, which are traded in bulk, cultural products and services are unique, which makes it difficult to claim that films from the US or France can be traded as equivalent goods – that is, it is difficult to argue that any single film is as good as any other, much like any litre of diesel whether it comes from Indonesia or Nigeria is equivalent at the petrol station.

Second, the *exception culturelle* has shaped the legal provisions enshrined in the *Convention on the Protection and Promotion of the Diversity of Cultural Expressions* (UNESCO 2005). This convention explicitly limits its scope to providing a framework for the governance of cultural expressions, and not to culture more broadly (De Beukelaer and Pyykkönen 2015; Pyykkönen 2011, 2012). The path dependency of the normative and legal stances in this debate illustrate how the process of international and regional economic integration pushed for a more explicit and clear articulation of countries' interests, which often did not exist in such an explicit manner (Singh 2008, 147).

Third, tensions between free trade agreements and UNESCO's Convention remain pressing. JP Singh (2011, 82–83) points out that Article 20.2 of the Convention means that the WTO can in fact supersede UNESCO's document: "Nothing in this Convention shall be interpreted as modifying rights and obligations of parties under any other treaties to which they are parties" (UNESCO 2005). Antonios Vlassis takes a different view, in arguing that the Convention is a 'hard instrument' in that it is legally binding but has 'soft content' in that its aims remain ambivalent, making its inclusion in national law and its enforcement an area of contestation (Vlassis 2011). In sum, neither UNESCO nor WTO have managed to gain the upper hand (Loisen and Pauwels 2015).

The institutional battles continue. But as the complexity of the paradox between trade and culture increases, it has become increasingly difficult to frame any analysis in a strict UNESCO or WTO approach. This is mainly because the global flows of culture have become more difficult to track and monitor, in spite of 'big data'. The difficulty results from illicit digital distribution, VPN-connections and proxy servers (Nolin 2015), migration and diaspora communities, and – perhaps most importantly – a healthy curiosity about the expressions of 'others'. This renders national borders and laws inefficient and insufficient to address the challenge of protecting and promoting cultural diversity.

In spite of its genesis in the cultural exception, the 2005 Convention is not simply a legal instrument to guarantee the right of nation-states to take protectionist measures in the realm of culture. The Convention recognises the benign and widely embraced positive traits of global trade in cultural expressions. In response to this, the convention proposes a range of measures that would allow countries to support their 'cultural industries', so they can become competitive in the global marketplace. While the film industries of Nigeria are an often-quoted example of how this can work (Witt 2017), and despite the optimism about the rise of digital distribution platforms as a way to create a level-playing field, the challenges remain rife.

DIVERSITIES IN THE GLOBAL CULTURAL ECONOMY

Cultural diversity does not exist as an abstract independent entity, separate from the cultural economy. The diversity of culture is rather deeply entwined with its economy. Trade in culture relies on diversity, but diversity can only exist to the extent that it is traded or exchanged – even if 'trade' in this context is in no way limited to monetary exchange or domestic frontiers. Earlier in this chapter, we have seen that neoclassical economist Tyler Cowen argues increased trade *between* countries may increase diversity *within* countries but decrease diversity *between* countries and in the world as a whole. Legal scholar Rostam Neuwirth posits that this forms a paradox in the trade of culture, because 'as a consequence of increased volumes of trade, the very foundation of trade appears to become threatened by tendencies towards a homogenisation of the conditions originally providing the incentive for trade' (2015, 97). In practice, the complexity of such a paradox makes it difficult to consider how to govern cultural diversity in the global cultural economy.

The global networks and networks that drive book publishing form an apt example of the complexities of diversity on the cultural economy. The case of Chinua Achebe is telling in this regard. Achebe, an

Igbo author from Ogidi in Nigeria, signed his works to *Heinemann Educational Books*, which shows that cultural diversity in the global cultural economy transcends many boundaries, while others remains firmly intact. Achebe, who lived from 1930 until 2013, is one of the main figures in 'African' literature of the 20th century. To a great extent, this is because of the magnificent books he has written (who hasn't read *Things Fall Apart*?). Through his writings, Achebe has enriched many lives through prose, symbolic messages, and political reflections. But alongside his work as an author, he has made a mark on the literary world in another way too.

Beyond his literary contributions, Achebe also made a significant mark on the genesis of 'African' literature through his work as the editor of the *African Writers Series* (AWS). Alan Hill, who worked for Heinemann Educational Books, started this series in 1962. He saw the opportunity to fill an emerging gap in the 'African' book market by responding to the need for educational and fiction works that reflected the 'African' experience. The demand for this sprung from the nationalist and pan-Africanist sentiments that developed in tandem with the push for independence and the ensuing decolonisation of many countries across the continent since Ghana declared its independence on March 6, 1957. Hill's motives were more shrewd than noble, as he 'recast the imperial adventurer as a global entrepreneur [who] wrote quite unabashedly of backward countries providing the perfect opportunity to augment sales of its locally produced textbooks, but also of specially commissioned books for the overseas market' (Low 2002, 32). The AWS proved successful in both economic and cultural terms. Commercially, the success of the series relied significantly on the adoption of its titles in the school curricula across Anglophone East and West Africa. The East and West African Examinations Councils were keen on prescribing texts from 'Africans' as they captured the political spirit of early independence – without having a long tradition of selecting established, and long dead, writers as their UK counterparts did (Currey 2003, 579). As a result, the series sold well, with around 80% of sales occurring across Africa (Currey 2003, 581; Low 2002, 34).

The cultural significance of the series is crucial as well. The AWS provided a 'forum where African writers could and continue to argue about their history, culture, and identity' (Mpe 1999, 108). There was however a growing number of local publishers that provided opportunities for writers to get their works out as well. Though the AWS provided 'African' writers with better circulation in the West *and* across Africa (Mpe 1999, 109). At the same time, being a London-based publishing house (albeit with editorial offices in Ibadan and Nairobi), Heinemann Educational Books could circumvent some government censorship and developed a rather progressive and open-minded editorial ethic. As a result, the AWS now consists of 273 novels, poetry collections, and plays that were published between 1962 and 2000. This has contributed to the emergence of the notion of 'African' literature.

The emergence of 'African' literature shows that trade in cultural goods is the norm, in all its complexity. But it also shows the remnants (or rather, the enduring legacy) of colonial connections. This is why we keep on referring to 'Africa' and 'African' authors or publications in quotes. The African-ness of these works remains contested. One of the most vocal critics is perhaps Ngũgĩ wa Thiong'o, a Kikuyu (*Gĩkũyũ*) writer from Kamirithu, Kenya. He argues that literature written by writers from the African continent cannot be 'African' if is written in colonial languages (notably English, French, and Portuguese), as they are actually more a part of the bodies of British, American, French, or Portuguese literatures (Ngũgĩ and Cantalupo 2016).[7] Moreover, while 'African' may be a marker of difference in Western literary markets, it is in fact a deeply flawed homogenising label that creates an imaginary 'type' of literature of the continent, even if the vast variety of writers across the continent produce many different styles and genres.

While the *African Writers Series* has facilitated access to large audiences across the continent and beyond, the emergence of 'African' literature in colonial languages has come at a cost for the diversity of publications across the continent. The AWS created a niche market for 'African' literature beyond the continent, but at the same time contributed to the ghettoisation of African literatures. Saha (2015) argues that the relegation of 'minority' texts to racialised niche markets through the production and marketing logics of the 'cultural industries' is both common and surprising. It is common because cultural markets are segmented into stereotypical consumers, niche markets, and divisions based on age, gender, race, and class. Though it is surprising because marketing these cultural expressions solely or predominantly to the likes of those who have produced these texts undermines the commercial appeal of 'niche' cultural expressions. Saha suggests that this builds on a contradiction within the 'cultural industries':

> If capitalism was only concerned with profit, hence it would be in the best interests of the cultural industries to stress the universal qualities of the minority-produced cultural commodity, rather than foregrounding its ethnic particularity. Yet through niche strategies, USPs, market research, audience segmentation and subsequent aestheticization techniques, the cultural commodity is racialized in a deeply problematic manner, framed as it is through the Orientalist gaze of the status quo.
>
> (Saha 2015, 520)

This raises the question of whether stereotyping is merely one of the markers of difference on which value creation in the cultural economy rests, or whether it reflects deeper tensions and inequalities in society. More practically, it calls into question whether cultural diversity, exclusion, and discrimination can be adequately addressed within the logics of the cultural economy (see Chapter two for a detailed discussion). In the case of the AWS, this manifests as an 'anthropological short circuit', where African texts are paradoxically celebrated for their exotic difference but also assimilated into Western models on interpretation and understanding.

The *African Writers Series* is also exemplary of the concentration of financial interests in the cultural economy in Western capital cities such as Paris, London, and New York. This means that not only symbolic, but also economic power shifts away from (in this case) African countries to former colonial metropolises (see also Singh 2011). With its focus on strengthening the 'cultural industries' across 'developing' countries, the UNESCO 2005 Convention explicitly aims to rectify that imbalance. The Convention is a tool to rethink cultural policies for artistic creation in a global era characterised by complex competition between territories, but also between public and private organisations operating in this field.

The Convention provides a framework to protect countries' ability to supply public funds to support creation. But the Convention also sets out a framework to support emerging 'cultural industries', to rectify power imbalances in global cultural trade, and to strengthen capacities around the world – particularly in so-called 'developing' countries and strengthening cultural cooperation by calling to integrate culture in sustainable development strategies (Article 13), by creating a framework for cooperation (Article 14), by fostering collaboration between countries (Article 15), and by encouraging countries to develop preferential treatment mechanisms for artists and cultural workers from 'developing' countries (Article 16). Moreover, the creation of the *International Fund for Cultural Diversity* (Article 18) creates a practical (that is, financial) tool to facilitate the development of 'cultural industries' in 'developing' countries.

The insight needed to strengthen and develop 'cultural industries' requires insight in the broader cultural economy in which they operate (De Beukelaer 2015; Stupples 2014). Developing such 'cultural industries' in order to increase their ability to compete in the global marketplace is a complex issue that requires attention at the level of education, skills development, policy, finance, and infrastructure. Often, these developments are driven by people who do not only want to see their books published, music recorded, or films produced, but who also care about the context in which they materialise and who benefits from this. Nigerian writer Sarah Ladipo Manyika, for example, realised the unequal relationship between publishers in different parts of the world after signing away the global rights to her debut *In Dependence* to London-based *Legend Press*. However, Manyika sold the global rights to her second book, *Like A Mule Bringing Ice Cream To The Sun*, to Cassava Republic, a Nigerian publisher based in Abuja. This could potentially signal a shift in global publishing, where authors, in Nigeria and elsewhere, increasingly publish with local houses and use them to connect to global distributors. This shift relocates both the editorial and economic epicentre of their creative activity to commercial hubs outside of the capitals of former colonial powers. There is however little evidence that cultural production is becoming less anchored in the regional hubs Arjun Appadurai mentioned in his seminal work on the cultural economy over 20 years ago (Appadurai 1996).

CONCLUSIONS

There is little, if any, disagreement on the need to maintain and stimulate the diversity of cultural practices and expressions. Though there is ample disagreement on the ways in which we can do this in normative terms.

This then results in disagreements about how to address diversity through policy.

The question of what German book publishers should do is merely one of many questions about how governments can (and often cannot) 'protect and promote' cultural diversity. While Barbian and German book publishers in general may claim to speak in the name of cultural diversity, they also speak in their own economic interest. They have every right to lobby for their interests, while claiming to protect and foster cultural diversity. Though no one should necessarily believe the arrangement they have is the only one that could maintain diversity in their sector. And yet, the formal lack of transparency – or at times the opacity of information overload – makes it difficult to gauge what trade agreements may actually change, if approved.

We opened this chapter with criticism on TTIP. This issue, to which different groups voiced strong criticism against its possible implications in 2014 and 2015, all but disappeared from public debate. This probably has a lot to do with the fact that in August 2016, Sigmar Gabriel – then German Federal Vice-Chancellor and Minister of Economic Affairs and Energy – publicly declared the trade agreement a failure (Deutsche Welle 2016). This happened before the election of Trump and the Brexit referendum that crystallised strong anti-globalisation sentiments and indicates that such agreements are difficult to attain. However, negotiations resumed in mid-2017, but again remain out of public sight and scrutiny.

At face value, UNESCO's *Convention on the Protection and Promotion of the Diversity of Cultural Expressions* serves as a legally binding tool to guarantee the exclusion of culture from free trade negotiations. Article 20 restricts the power of the Convention, as it cannot supersede any other agreement, making it very difficult to enforce its principles, particularly given the lack of a strong arbitrage mechanism. This article does however not preclude any party from invoking the 'cultural exception' in free trade talks, as the European Union has done in relation to TTIP. This 'cultural exception' is however not a neutral basis on which the Convention is built; it is historically a particular issue between France and the US, in which most UNESCO member states have now taken sides. As a result, both its limitations and history make it difficult to see how the document can be a neutral instrument that does not favour any industry or sector over any other, or any sector over any other.

This raises the question of whether inter*governmental* organisations (as opposed to *global* ones) can be the level at which we can devise solutions. They may perhaps help find a narrative that transcends countries, but they will rely on their member states, that is, nation states, to transform these ideas into practice.

Ultimately, there are ample examples of commercial initiatives that have greatly contributed to cultural diversity. But they have done so in ways that are never without contestation, for they will simultaneously perpetuate and challenge stereotypes – through not necessarily the same ones. This raises the question of whose diversity we aim to uphold. Anecdotal accounts of successes do not constitute evidence for ideological stances; they merely illustrate how difficult it is to reduce messy practice to any such approach.

Cultural diversity is not simply a matter of finding a balance between free trade and protectionism. It is a matter of making the cultural economy function despite a lack of such a balance. That is why the next chapter on public/private raises the question of how to balance public support and governmental regulation with private initiatives and companies *within* countries, rather the trade *between* countries.

NOTES

1 The TTIP is a regional free trade agreement that would liberalise trade between the US and member states of the European Union. The European Commission claims that this agreement will boost economic growth and employment on both sides of the Atlantic, but critics challenge this strongly (De Ville and Siles-Brügge 2016).

2 www.ttip-leaks.org/.

3 Interestingly, Tyler Cowen was one of the 15 independent experts who prepared the draft of the *Convention on Protection and Promotion of the Diversity of Cultural Expressions* (UNESCO 2005), see *Gouvernance Mondiale et Culture: de l'Exception à la Diversité* (Vlassis 2015) for background on these negotiations.

4 The *Börsenverein des Deutschen Buchhandels* (the Association of German Book Trade) established these rules to protect local publishers and bookstores – while price-setting by producers is generally not legal (Bittlingmayer 1988). The same era saw a major transatlantic trade dispute between the US and the UK, because the US allowed the wholesale pirating of British books – until 1891, the US treated the works of foreign authors as being in the public domain. We will discuss the tensions around ownership and piracy in Chapter four, of importance here is that the debates about what countries protect, why they wish to do so, and how they go about it predate the current debate about regional trade agreements (Balasz 2011).

5 Our chapter in this book does not provide a comprehensive history and politics of the global governance of culture and cultural diversity, simply because this would take a book of its own: see Vlassis (2015) or Van den Bossche (2007) for such book-length approaches.

6 For an extensive engagement with the history of the negotiations of the UNESCO's 2005 Convention, see the edited volume by Sabine von Schorlemer and Peter-Tobias Stoll (2012), in which every single article of the document is discussed in great detail and the initial critical assessment of the Convention edited by Nina Obuljen and Joost Smiers (2006). For an initial assessment of the operation and use of the Convention see the edited volume by De Beukelaer et al. (2015) and UNESCO's own reports on the Convention (UNESCO 2015, 2017).

7 Even if Ngũgĩ wa Thiong'o has written both *in* Kikuyu and *on* the de-Anglicisation of his and other Africans' writings (1994), Phaswane Mpe argues that he has continued to publish predominantly in English (Mpe 1999, 118).

REFERENCES

Appadurai, Arjun. 1996. *Modernity at Large: Cultural Dimensions of Globalization.* Minneapolis, MN: University of Minnesota Press.

Balasz, Bodó. 2011. "Coda: A Short History of Book Piracy". In *Media Piracy in Emerging Economies*, edited by Joe Karaganis, 399–413. New York, NY: Social Science Research Council.

Barbian, Jan-Pieter. 2014. "Das Freihandelsabkommen TTIP Betrifft Auch Die Biblio-theken". *BuB: Forum Bibliothek Und Information.* December 11, 2014. www.b-u-b.de/freihandelsabkommen-ttip-betrifft-auch-bibliotheken/.

Bittlingmayer, George. 1988. "Resale Price Maintenance in the Book Trade with an Application to Germany". *Journal of Institutional and Theoretical Economics (JITE)/Zeitschrift Für Die Gesamte Staatswissenschaft* 144 (5): 789–812.

Cowen, Tyler. 2002. *Creative Destruction.* Princeton, NJ: Princeton University Press.

Currey, James. 2003. "Chinua Achebe, the African Writers Series and the Establishment of African Literature". *African Affairs* 102 (409): 575–85.

De Beukelaer, Christiaan. 2014. "Creative Industries in 'Developing' Countries: Ques-tioning Country Classifications in the UNCTAD Creative Economy Reports". *Cultural Trends* 23 (4): 232–51.

De Beukelaer, Christiaan. 2015. *Developing Cultural Industries: Learning from the Palimpsest of Practice.* Amsterdam: European Cultural Foundation.

De Beukelaer, Christiaan, and Miikka Pyykkönen. 2015. "Introduction: UNESCO's 'Diver-sity Convention' – Ten Years On". In *Globalization, Culture and Development: The UNESCO Convention on Cultural Diversity*, edited by Christiaan De Beukelaer, Miikka Pyykkönen, and J. P. Singh, 1–10. Basingstoke: Palgrave Macmillan.

De Beukelaer, Christiaan, Miikka Pyykkönen, and J. P. Singh, eds. 2015. *Globalization, Cul-ture and Development: The UNESCO Convention on Cultural Diversity.* Basingstoke: Palgrave Macmillan.

De Ville, Ferdi, and Gabriel Siles-Brügge. 2016. *T.T.I.P.: The Truth about the Transatlantic Trade and Investment Partnership.* Cambridge; Malden, MA: Polity Press.

Deutsche Welle. 2016. "Germany's Vice Chancellor Gabriel: US-EU Trade Talks 'Have Failed'". *Deutsche Welle,* August 28, 2016. www.dw.com/en/germanys-vice-chancellor-gabriel-us-eu-trade-talks-have-failed/a-19509401.

European Commission. 2014. "TTIP and Culture". Brussels: European Commission. www.trade.ec.europa.eu/doclib/docs/2014/july/tradoc_152670.pdf.

Loisen, Jan, and Caroline Pauwels. 2015. "Competing Perspectives? WTO and UNESCO on Cultural Diversity in Global Trade". In *Globalization, Culture and Development: The UNESCO Convention on Cultural Diversity,* edited by Christiaan De Beukelaer, Miikka Pyykkönen, and J. P. Singh, 43–58. Basingstoke: Palgrave Macmillan.

Low, Gail. 2002. "In Pursuit of Publishing: Heinemann's African Writers Series". *Wasafiri* 17 (37): 31–35.

Mpe, Phaswane. 1999. "The Role of the Heinemann African Writers Series in the Development and Promotion of African Literature". *African Studies* 58 (1): 105–22.

Neuwirth, Rostam Josef. 2013. "L'exception Culturelle: Retour Permanent Ou Abandon Final(Ement)?" *Culture, Commerce et Numérique* 8 (5): 7–9.

Neuwirth, Rostam Josef. 2015. "The 'Culture and Trade' Paradox Reloaded". In *Globalization, Culture and Development: The UNESCO Convention on Cultural Diversity,* edited by Christiaan De Beukelaer, Miikka Pyykkönen, and J. P. Singh, 91–101. Basingstoke: Palgrave Macmillan.

Ngũgĩ, wa Thiong'o. 1994. *Decolonising the Mind: The Politics of Language in African Literature.* Nairobi; London; Portsmouth, NH; Harare: East African Educational Publishers; J. Currey; Heinemann; Zimbabwe Pub. House.

Ngũgĩ, wa Thiong'o, and Charles Cantalupo. 2016. "African Literature . . . Says Who?" *Transition,* 120: 4.

Nolin, Jan. 2015. "Cultural Policy by Proxy: Internet-Based Cultural Consumption as a Copygray Zone". *International Journal of Cultural Policy* 21 (3): 273–90.

Obuljen, Nina, and Joost Smiers, eds. 2006. *UNESCO's Convention on the Protection and Promotion of the Diversity of Cultural Expressions: Making It Work.* Zagreb: Culturelink Joint Publications Series 9.

Pyykkönen, Miikka. 2011. "All in the Name of Diversity? Dialectics of the Naming and Framing in Cultural Heterogeneity". *Nordisk Kulturpolitisk Tidskrift* 14 (1–2): 120–25.

Pyykkönen, Miikka. 2012. "UNESCO and Cultural Diversity: Democratisation, Commodification or Governmentalisation of Culture?" *International Journal of Cultural Policy* 18 (5): 545–62.

Richieri Hanania, Lilian. 2016. "The UNESCO Convention on the Diversity of Cultural Expressions as a Coordination Framework to Promote Regulatory Coherence in the Creative Economy". *International Journal of Cultural Policy* 22 (4): 574–93.

Ringstad, Vidar. 2004. "On the Cultural Blessings of Fixed Book Prices: Facts or Fiction?" *International Journal of Cultural Policy* 10 (3): 351–65.

Saha, Anamik. 2015. "The Marketing of Race in Cultural Production". In *The Routledge Companion to the Cultural Industries,* edited by Kate Oakley and Justin O'Connor, 512–21. London: Routledge.

Schorlemer, Sabine von, and Peter-Tobias Stoll, eds. 2012. *The UNESCO Convention on the Protection and Promotion of the Diversity of Cultural.* New York, NY: Springer.

Scott, Allan J. 2008. "Cultural Economy: Restrospect and Prospect". In *The Cultural Economy*, edited by Helmut Anheier and Yudhishthir Raj Isar, 307–23. Los Angeles, CA; London: Sage.

Singh, J. P. 2008. "Agents of Policy Learning and Change: US and EU Perspectives on Cultural Trade Policy". *The Journal of Arts Management, Law, and Society* 38 (2): 141–60.

Singh, J. P. 2011. *Globalized Arts: The Entertainment Economy and Cultural Identity.* New York, NY: Columbia University.

Stupples, Polly. 2014. "Creative Contributions: The Role of the Arts and the Cultural Sector in Development". *Progress in Development Studies* 14 (2): 115–30.

UNESCO. 2005. *Convention on the Protection and Promotion of the Diversity of Cultural Expressions.* Paris: UNESCO.

UNESCO., ed. 2015. *Re|shaping Cultural Policies: A Decade Promoting the Diversity of Cultural Expressions for Development.* Paris: UNESCO.

UNESCO., ed. 2017. *Re|shaping Cultural Policies: Advancing Creativity for Development.* Paris: UNESCO.

Van den Bossche, Peter. 2007. *Free Trade and Culture: A Study of Relevant WTO Rules and Constraints on National Cultural Policy Measures.* Amsterdam: Boekmanstichting.

Vlassis, Antonios. 2011. "La mise en oeuvre de la Convention sur la diversité des expressions culturelles: Portée et enjeux de l'interface entre le commerce et la culture". *Études internationales* 42 (4): 493.

Vlassis, Antonios. 2015. *Gouvernance mondiale et culture: de l'exception à la diversité.* Sciences politiques et sociales. Liège: Presses Universitaires de Liège.

Vlassis, Antonios. 2016. "European Commission, Trade Agreements and Diversity of Cultural Expressions: Between Autonomy and Influence". *European Journal of Communication* 31 (4): 446–61.

Voon, Tania. 2007. *Cultural Products and the World Trade Organization.* Cambridge Studies in International and Comparative Law. Cambridge; New York, NY: Cambridge University Press.

Witt, Emily. 2017. *Nollywood: The Making of a Film Empire.* New York, NY: Columbia Global Reports.

4

PUBLIC/PRIVATE

In 1993, Universal Pictures released the Steven Spielberg movie *Jurassic Park* (the first one), which grossed just over US$1 billion in box office revenues. The popular belief in South Korea is that these revenues exceeded the revenues of the Hyundai chaebol in the same year. This mythical moment in South Korean cultural policy history, popularly known as the, 'Hyundai Argument' or the 'Jurassic Park Syndrome', led to a turning point in thinking about the economic value of culture in Korea (Kang 2004).

In 1994, in response to this realisation, the Korean government set up a Cultural Industries Division within the Ministry of Culture. Through this body, it started *investing* in the cultural economy, eventually allocating over 1% of public spending to culture by 2002 (Hong 2014; Shim 2006). The main beneficiary within the Korean cultural economy was the *Korean Wave*, known in Korean as *Hallyu*, an umbrella term for Korean popular culture. Korean public investment in the cultural economy continued as a strategy to drive export diversification, which continued throughout and after the Asian Financial Crisis of 1997. This crisis taught the Korean government that it could not rely on chaebols alone to drive the Korean export economy (see Introduction).

The marked increase in public funding for culture and the changed rationale raises several important questions. The most important one is probably whether *Jurassic Park* really generated greater revenues than Hyundai. (The answer to this question is, unfortunately no, as we explain below.) But beyond this anecdote, there was a significant shift in the way governments have allocated public funding to the cultural economy since the 1990s in many countries around the world, not just in Korea.

In this chapter, we discuss the variety of motives behind the public funding for the cultural economy with the popularity of the 'creative industries' discourse. For much of the 20th century, governments provided public funding for the arts and culture because of their status as a public good that is valued highly in cultural terms, but subject to market failure. We explore the influence of the discourse of the cultural, and more significantly, the 'creative industries' on this rationale. We do so by discussing the Korean case in greater detail, exploring the cultural and economic contradictions of Bollywood, the instrumentalisation of the Trinidadian Carnival, and China's attempts to establish itself as a cultural powerhouse in order to garner influence and reputation.

Before we explore these cases, we highlight how our approach to understanding the role of public funding and government intervention differs from models that were common in cultural policy studies before the cultural economy garnered the celebratory appeal it has had over the past two decades.

FUNDING CULTURE

The US American cultural policy author Schuster notes that 'each country has its own conception of the arts and of culture and its own view as to what implies about the role of the government in providing support to activities that fall within the definition' (1989, 18). Bearing in mind the specificity of countries, Harry Chartrand and Claire McCaughey (1989) proposed a taxonomy of approaches. While their approach is now some 30 years old, it still serves as an important tool to understand government intervention in arts and culture (Bell and Oakley 2015). They distinguish the *patron* model; the *architect* model; the *engineer* model; and the *facilitator* model (see Table 4.1). These models focus on the structure of the funding within the government, whether through deferred taxes, through arts councils, through a culture ministry, or under the state's express approval.

Table 4.1 Models for allocating public funding to the arts

Role of state	Exemplar	Policy objective	Funding mechanism
Facilitator	USA	Diversity and independence	Tax incentives for donors and tax-free status for select cultural organisations
Patron	UK	Excellence and access	Public funding through arts councils ('at arm's length' of ministry)
Architect	France	Democratisation of culture	Direct funding by ministry of culture
Engineer	USSR	Political education	Ownership control of means of artistic production

Source: Adapted from Chartrand and McCaughey (1989).

The underlying assumption is that the arts and culture are examples of 'market failure' and that reliance on the market would result in an under-production of some forms of culture (Keat 2000). We argue that while policy rationales for funding the cultural economy have changed since the 1990s. This shift is from *subsidising* activities prone to market failure on the basis that the cultural economy produces public goods that have cultural value that is not economically viable, to *investing* in parts of the cultural economy that will likely contribute to economic growth. Despite this shift, market failure persists in many parts of the cultural economy.

The *patron* model best characterises the way the UK and Australia engage with arts and culture. The primary objective of the policy is to foster excellence, ensuring that local organisations and companies can compete with other institutions at international standards. In order to do this, arts funding is administered 'at arm's length' (see below) of politicians and funding is allotted by peer evaluation. This system provides strong support for artistic excellence and the limited political intervention in the particular organisations and projects that are funded. But it often favours more traditional art forms and elite organisations.

The *architect* model best characterises the French approach. In this context, the ministry of culture of the central government plays a pivotal role in defining priorities and administering institutions. The idea behind this is that direct support and a blanket approach to activities and institutions benefits the country as a whole. Significant support for key institutions makes them less reliant on their own income (through box office and sponsorship), which should allow them to take greater creative risk. Yet this paternalistic form of (social welfare) policy implies that the state (thinks it) knows what is best.

The *engineer* model best characterises the approaches in post-Soviet states and countries like Cuba. The primary objective of cultural policy in these countries is the promotion of a national culture in tandem with political education. The strategy to attain this builds on government ownership of artistic production. The school of *Socialist Realism* articulates the emblematic result of such policies: the elevation of socialist political structures, institutions, and principles through art. Yet, while this approach has the potential to create a unified political sphere through culture on the surface, these cultural policies underestimate the subversive potential of artists.

The *facilitator* model best characterises the approach of the US. While the absence of a formal policy text at the federal level in the US might lead some to think that the country has no cultural policy at all, this is not true. The primary role the state plays in the facilitation of diversity of culture throughout the country is through tax incentives. Some private cultural organisations are recognised as non-profit organisations under Internal Revenue Code §501(c)(3), which allows donors to get tax breaks. The exemption is a measure without which many organisations would not be able to survive (Burch 2010). Yet it also allows wealthy benefactors to steer cultural policy in a direction of their choosing, without direct government interference in the beneficiaries of their gifts. Though the tax breaks mean that there is a de facto public contribution, as donors do not pay taxes on the amounts donated. This means that some flagship organisations may benefit disproportionately from donor funds and public support (by means of foregone tax revenues). So, while the public supports the arts indirectly, there is no direct government policy to steer this, nor any accountability to the public. While the National Endowment for the Arts is a small body with very limited funds and stifled power (Miller and Yúdice 2002, 46–50), they are not the key 'institution' in US cultural policies.

The four approaches above are ideal-types of government intervention. And in our approach to the cultural economy, we note some significant changes since Chartrand and McCaughey proposed this model. The world itself has changed; the Soviet Union does not exist anymore, the UK and France now have cultural policies that are far more similar, and many countries (including Korea) have pursued their own trajectories.

But while these changes mainly affect *how* countries fund culture, there have also been significant changes in the reasons *why* countries fund culture. In the introduction to this book, we proposed five perspectives on the cultural economy: Celebratory, Aspirational, Refusenik, Agnostic, and Reflexive. By using these perspectives, we argue for an approach to the relation between public and private institutions that moves beyond Chartrand and McCaughey's model. We do so by considering *why* governments invest in the arts, rather than explaining *how* they do so.

The emergence of the celebratory 'creative industries' discourse in the 1990s builds on the agnostic perspective that was common in the 1980s (Hesmondhalgh 2013). This celebratory perspective highlights the positive contributions the cultural economy makes to societies, primarily in economic terms, which is what George Yúdice calls the 'expediency of culture' (Yúdice 2003). While this approach has helped secure public support for the cultural economy, it has also further undermined the 'public good' argument in favour of market failure correction. That is why we focus on the emergence of the 'cultural' and, more strongly, 'creative industries' as a policy discourse that changed cultural policy priorities away from 'subsidy' in the arts to 'investment' in culture. Table 4.2 is an illustrative exploration (and not an exhaustive treatment) of how different countries have dealt with the shifting priorities in cultural policy and even the definition of 'cultural industries'.

Economist Jason Potts and media scholar Stuart Cunningham propose four possible relationships between the 'cultural industries' and the economy: that of welfare (market failure), standard industry, growth, and innovation driver (Potts and Cunningham 2008). While they argue for a teleological perspective on these different models, leading to one where market failure is no longer the norm, we have argued earlier in this book that these models continue to exist in parallel (see Chapter one).

We therefore maintain that the public funding decision is a political, cultural, and economic one. Our empirical knowledge of cultural policy spheres beyond the US and Europe allows for a more nuanced

Table 4.2 Rationales for funding culture in Korea, Trinidad and Tobago, China, and India

Country	Significant supported activity	Term used	Funding objective	How they support
Korea	Commercial popular culture (particularly the Korean Wave)	'Cultural industries', content industries, 'creative industries', creative economy	Economic growth	Research institutes, funds, grants, public-private partnership
Trinidad and Tobago	Carnival	'Creative industries'	Economic diversification, global cultural significance	Marketing, overseas collaborations
China	Film	'Cultural-creative industries'	Soft power	Confucius institutes, quotas, requiring local partners, co-production agreements
India	Crafts	Village industries	Rural economic development	Central Cottage Industries Emporium (national network)

Source: The authors.

understanding of localised interactions with the global cultural economy discourse, informs these five approaches. We argue that the cultural economy is more complicated including both the monetary and non-monetary aspects of the way culture is produced, disseminated, and exchanged. The examples in this chapter demonstrate the varying interactions between those two aspects and how that has impacted what is defined as culture and what is supported, important aspects of the political economy of culture.

1 *JURASSIC PARK* = 2 HYUNDAI

Many people working in the Korean cultural economy locate the genesis of its government's commercial, export-driven cultural economy strategies in the realisation that *Jurassic Park* realised higher revenues than Hyundai in 1993. Whether or not this is true makes little difference in terms of Korea's shifted policy priorities. But we will tackle that question before turning to a discussion of the political shifts that surround the success of the Korean Wave. The shifts directed policy attention from nation-building (and strict state censorship) to support for commercial success, which while ostensibly depoliticising, in fact concealed strong oppression of political art.

One popular theory in Korea regarding the movement from cultural censorship to the embrace of the cultural economy discourse refers to *Jurassic Park* and a particular line of Hyundai cars, the Sonata. The story goes that in 1994, the South Korean (hereafter Korean) *Presidential Advisory Council on Science and Technology* in a briefing entitled *Strategic Plan for the Growth of the High-Tech Visual Arts Industry* presented that the movie *Jurassic Park* had generated US$1,029.7 million globally (including the US).[1] The story goes that the revenues of that one movie were twice the revenues generated Hyundai's export of 700,000 Sonatas in 1993. Hyundai would need to have sold 1.5 million cars to attain the same revenues (Kang 2015; Ryoo 2005; Shim 2006). While many argue that this represents the start of the adoption of the cultural economy discourse in Korea, the story does not hold up: Hyundai's cars would have to be sold at a bit under US$700 each in order to make this comparison work. However, the popularity of this story demonstrates the willingness of the Korean government to change policy discourse based on the proof of economic benefit.

Since the Korean War of 1945 to 1953 that led to the separation of North and South Korea, the South Korean government has regulated and supported the cultural economy in different ways.[2] Cultural policy scholar Kiwon Hong cites the 1972 *Act of Promoting Culture and the Arts* in which the Korean government defines culture (for funding purposes) as 'literature, fine arts, music, dance, drama, cinema, artistic entertainment, traditional music, photography, architecture, language and publishing' (Article 1, cited in Hong 2012, 3). Popular culture was not on the Korean government's agenda for funding.

President Park Chung-hee (Park Geun-hye's father) referred to culture as the 'second economy' in 1968 (Yim 2002, 43), a means to motivate people to work harder in the name of Korean economic growth and patriotism in the aftermath of the Korean War (Kim 2017; Yim 2002). The role of culture was to inculcate good values of thrift, hard work, and 'optimism', which resulted in heavy censorship (Kim 2017; Shin and Lee 2017; Yim 2002). In 1975, for example, Presidential Emergency Decree #9 was promulgated, banning 222 South Korean songs and 261 foreign songs. The reasons for banning these songs ranged from negative influence on national security and foreign (often Japanese) content to pessimistic content (Shin and Lee 2017).

The Hyundai Argument changed that perspective. The government started funding the cultural economy through the Division of the Cultural Industries within the Ministry of Culture in 1994. At the same time, it also permitted the entry of chaebols and multinationals into the previously heavily censored cultural sectors (Kang 2015; Kwon and Kim 2014). In 1998, the cultural market was also opened to Japanese products, marking a definitive turn away from previous Korean cultural policies of cultural nationalism. Economic value and benefit overwrote postcolonial sentiment.

What is funded has also changed. The creation of a 'cultural industries' division within the Ministry of Culture shifted attention and funding to popular culture for its economic potential. This has happened in Western countries as well since the late 1980s and early 1990s. The significant difference between the West and Korea (and many other countries in the majority world) is that in Korea, the rationale for public funding of culture shifted from a concern with postcolonial nation-building to a concern about economic benefit and export diversification.

The combination of the 1994 Hyundai Argument and the 1997 Asian Financial Crisis has created a degree of path dependence in relation to 'cultural industries' policy in the Korean government. President Kim Dae-Jung (1998–2003) declaring himself 'President of Culture', demonstrated the focus on the cultural economy at the highest levels of the Korean government (Spence 2018). He oversaw the creation of a cultural promotion fund of approximately US$150 million and a new cultural policy in 1998 (Kim 2017; Hong 2012).

The Korean decision to fund the cultural economy seems a simple one that relies on its economic potential. In the Korean case, the government's response to the demonstration of the film industry's economic value was to invest in these industries, as was done previously with manufacturing and the economic sectors associated with the chaebols. The Korean political discourse values economic strength, even above nationalistic, anti-Japanese sentiment. The Korean government adheres to a developmental state model in relation to its perspective on the economic sector. Under these circumstances, public funding of the now-economically viable 'cultural industries' aligned with general public spending objectives.

In the Korean case, the institution around the cultural economy has changed from one of censorship to one of economic gain. But President Park Geun-hye (2013–2017) reminded the citizens of Korea that a long history of censorship and culture being politically correct does not just disappear. Under her presidency, the Ministry of Culture kept an unofficial black-list of artists who were not allowed to get any public funding, most commonly based on their political views or criticism of Park's conservative government (Kim 2018). The ostensibly pragmatic shift from censoring culture to supporting it for economic growth thus went hand in hand with a secretive suppression of dissonant voices in the arts. This tension between economic potential and moral threat is one that also influences India's approach to the cultural economy.

BOLLYWOOD AS A MORAL THREAT, CRAFT AS AN ECONOMIC OPPORTUNITY?

India's film industry produces far more titles than Hollywood, with respectively 1,903 and 789 in 2016 (Kanzler and Talavera 2017).[3] One significant difference is that Bollywood generates lower revenues on average than Hollywood films. In 2016, the Indian box office receipts accounted for US$1.9 billion, only 5% of the global box office (Motion Picture Association of America 2018). In contrast, the North American (US and Canada) box office accounted for US$11.4 billion. But this is not the only difference. In the US, the film industry benefits from tax breaks and supportive regimes that have helped the sector develop into the most lucrative in the world (see Table 4.3).

In India, however, the opposite is true. Despite high taxes, Bollywood has managed to become one of the world's key film industries. The Indian approach to its lucrative industry is thus very different from the tax breaks and political support Hollywood receives and the significant public funding Korea spends on the cultural economy, including its film industries. This raises the question of what explains the government's vastly different approaches: Why would India actively hamper investment in one of its most iconic 'creative industries' with immense economic potential?

The Indian film industry faces a double tax regime with both entertainment and service taxes, the only industry in India to be doubly taxed. Moreover, the service tax burden varies according to the state. Maharashtra's (home of Bollywood) service tax is 45% (Kumar 2015). Asian entertainment consultant Rob Cain (2015) notes that the various state governments also regulate ticket prices to be as low as US$1.20, hence the low box office receipts. Despite the film industry being granted official status by the Government of India, allowing the industry permission to receive private investment in the 1990s by the Indian government, the film industry's tax and piracy issues have made the film industry an unattractive investment option. This investment difficulty resulted in black market money being utilised to finance Bollywood films (Athique 2008; Lorenzen and Täube 2008). Official support for the industry is virtually non-existent. None of the tax revenue is invested in the film industry. In short, the Indian government sees the film industry as a revenue-raising sector.

Historian Robin Jeffrey argues that India's political history in relation to the broadcast industries offers some answers. He argues the government of newly independent India had inherited both restrictive colonial broadcast policies and the puritanism (also anti-media) of the Gandhi independence movement. Both of these were coupled with a

Table 4.3 Film production, revenues, and support in 2016

	Number of films	Global box office revenues (US$ billions)	Global box office share	Support mechanism	Taxation
India	1,903	1.9	5%	None	Entertainment tax; service tax
China	944	8.7	23%	Co-production treaties, film funds	Foreigners pay 20% on revenue earned in China***
Nigeria	1,000*	0.59* 0.1**	1.5%* 0.2%***	Film funds, state government funding, cinema construction	Income taxes
USA	789	10.31	27%	Incentives via taxes and location incentives (film commissions)	Motion picture incentive (MPI) programmes (some states)****

Sources: The authors, based on data from Kanzler and Talavera (2017) and Motion Picture Association of America (2018) for India, China, and the US. Bauer (2015), PricewaterhouseCoopers (2017), Kemp's database (2018).

*Estimates for Nollywood include both cinema and DVD.

**This figure only includes ticketed box office.

***Sourced from Kemp's Film and Television (KFTV) yearbook (www.kftv.com/country/china/guide/incentives).

****MPI often includes consumption tax waivers, tax credits for hiring, and infrastructure spending (Thom and An 2017).

fear of inciting sectarian violence, a hangover of the 1947 India-Pakistan partition.[4] Both radio and television were 'starved of funds' and heavily controlled in newly independent India, with even live broadcasts considered 'dangerous', a hangover from a colonial legacy where radio was seen as 'an additional problem for a colonial state preoccupied . . . with a national movement transformed by Gandhi' (Jeffrey 2006, 208).

The censorial attitude of the Indian government towards film and broadcast also stemmed from the devout Gandhian sympathies of the earliest ministers in the first 15 years of the post-independence era in India. Gandhi saw 'radio and recording [ranked] as distractions and temptation, capable of diverting people from the national quest for freedom and reformation' and heartily declared that 'I am the only person who has never seen a film' except for one 'depressing experience' (cited in Jeffrey 2006, 211).

The 1966 Chanda Report, written by the Ashok Chanda-led committee investigating Indian broadcasting, criticised the Indian government's intervention in radio and television. It argued that, 'television [is] an expensive luxury intended for the entertainment of the affluent society and [. . .] should be left alone until our plans for of economic development have been completed' (cited in Jeffrey 2006, 212). More recently, film studies scholar Nandana Bose notes the continuation and even exacerbation of the pre- and post-independence fear of the movies with the political rise of the Hindu Right in India in the 1990s, which espoused a more conservative vision of India (Bose 2010).

While the reluctance to support the film industry is consistent with the Indian government's history of media censorship, it is inconsistent with its attitude towards other 'cultural industries'. The Indian government has tried to pursue 'cultural policy [that is] centrally tied to India's development vision' (Rajadhyaksha et al. 2013, 7). In this context, 'culture' meant heritage but also economic resource.

The traditions of the village, particularly handicrafts, were seen as an economic resource and key to the development of India's masses. These handicrafts were distributed through a national network of emporia run by the Khadi and Villages Industries Commission under the Ministry of Micro, Small and Medium Enterprises (now the Ministry of Small Scale Industries and Agro and Rural Industries). One of the assumptions was that such cultural resources could not be found in the cities and so support of such industries served both heritage revival and economic purposes (Rajadhyaksha et al. 2013). Even in later discussions within what was described as the Indian government's definitive turn to a culture industries strategy, the focus continued to be on the rural.

In 2005, UNESCO organised a meeting in Jodhpur (India) to advance its *Creativity and Cultural Industries Programme* in Asia and the Pacific aimed at the utilisation of the 'creative industries' for local economic development. In response to the resulting *Jodhpur Consensus*, India's Planning Commission established a Task Force on Culture and Creative Industries in 2005 with the aim to facilitate 'the transition of cultural industries (defined as *traditional art and craft*) into creative industries with the help of design and media industry' (Rajadhyaksha et al. 2013, 75–76, emphasis added).

The economic value and potential of Bollywood and the other film industries of India was not enough to surmount the previous customs and views of the film industry by Indian policymakers. Symbolic value outweighed other considerations. While Korea, at least officially, moved beyond censorship in its support for commercially viable activities in the cultural economy, India continues to support heritage activities with commercial potential and raises additional taxes on Bollywood, rather than subsidising production or export.

THE MANY FACES OF CARNIVAL

The Trinidad Carnival (hereafter Carnival) takes place on Shrove Monday and the Tuesday before Ash Wednesday, when one receives absolution for one's sins before the beginning of the Lent period according to Catholic traditions. In Trinidad, these days are the pinnacle of Carnival time – the annual festivities, characterised by floats, parades, costumes, and mas bands. Carnival originates from a mix of various European traditions, Afro-Trinbagonian[5] protest, and festivities. In Trinidad, within Carnival's hybrid provenance (which is a mix of European Christianity, rebellion, and festivities) lie the seeds of its contradiction as a national cultural product.

The Trinidad Carnival in Port of Spain, the country's capital, is the largest in the Caribbean region. In 2017, Carnival visitor spending alone was approximately US$50 million (353 million T&T dollars) (Central

Statistical Office 2017) and generates US$156 million per annum (Burke 2014). It is through the realisation that the annual celebration generated high revenues that the Trinbagonian government started focusing on the 'cultural industries', including Carnival, in the 1990s as part of economic diversification from the oil and gas industry.[6] The linking of commerce and Carnival in Trinidad [re]emerged in May 1993 with the announcement in London of T&T 10 million dollars (approximately US$2 million) events tourism program by the then Trinbagonian Prime Minister Patrick Manning (Garth 2002).

The contestation around Carnival did not, however, end with government commitment to public funding and support for Carnival. Caribbean popular culture scholars Rohlehr (1990) and Cowley (2002) both highlight a longstanding class (and at times racialised) ambivalence towards Carnival in Trinidad and Tobago. In the post-slavery period,[7] middle-class merchants were content to benefit economically from the sale of costumes and material, but still criticised what they characterised as the vulgarity and obscenity of the festivities. Local educational programmes designed by the intellectual and cultural elite tends to emphasise 'old time' Carnival with its tableau of folkloric characters. However, the idea that Carnival needed to be 'cleaned up' persisted (Burke 2014; Green 2007).

Carnival played a significant part in Trinidad and Tobago's national identity-making exercise. In a multiethnic and multicultural state such as Trinidad and Tobago,[8] the politically ascendant black and brown creole class sought to privilege their cultural forms and Carnival was principal amongst these forms. Green characterises Carnival as part of a 'folkloric cultural resistance model' where 'Carnival is primarily an African-inspired performance event in which the marginalized strive for liberation, express their identity, and mock the hypocrisy of the ruling classes' (Green 2007, 208).

This Afro-Trinbagonian identity conflicts with economic access required of a national cultural product. Garth Green tells us the story of Robert Amar,[9] an Indo-Trinbagonian, who started Kiskidee Karavan, which produced a show including calypso, soca, brass band, and even Jamaican dancehall performers in a different location each week, culminating in a big show during Carnival week. Due to his lack of roots within the Carnival community, he was unsuccessful and was characterised (by some) as another 'Indo- Trinbagonian businessman who was trying to take advantage of Afro-Trinbagonian culture' (Garth 2002, 291). This is despite essentially having, from a business perspective, done everything right as other bands had done – hiring the most talented people and conducting an extensive marketing campaign both locally and regionally.

International marketing of Carnival has focused on 'bikini, beads, and feather' (BBF) (Copeland and Hodges 2014, 186) almost to the exclusion of the other aspects of Carnival (Green 2007). The BBF version of Carnival clashes with the Afro-Trinidadian protest model of carnival. This version focuses on the stress release, partying, and, as the Trinbagonians say, bacchanal aspect of Carnival. Here, the costuming is more akin to the skimpy attire of Las Vegas showgirls than the traditional folkloric characters. This is the Carnival enjoyed by many Trinbagonians and tourists.

The National Carnival Commission (NCC), a centralised government body established in 1991, increasingly manages Carnival as a cultural product rather than a dynamic cultural event. The NCC seeks to be a central point for external interests by managing the media rights to the Carnival, local and international marketing, and revenue generating mechanisms, in collaboration with private interests, such as Pan Trinbago and the Trinbago Unified Calypsonians Association.

Commoditisation resulted in the fragmentation of cultural policy. The NCC emphasises one aspect of Carnival, the Afro-Trinbagonian, and the tourism ministry highlights another, the riotous party aspect. This raises the question of who Carnival makes money for. Carnival is big business but makes little money for participants. Trade policy specialist Keith Nurse (1999) argues that most of the earnings come from tourist spend in restaurants, bars, and costume payments. Those who organise festivals make little, as demonstrated by the regional carnivals. He further highlights that 'Caribbean carnivals exhibit something of a contradiction: the carnivals generate large sums of money but the organizing units retain very little of the profits' (Nurse 1999, 679).

The Trinbagonian government has turned to a more aspirational engagement with the cultural economy by positioning itself as a global carnival leader. Nurse (1999) notes that Carnival has now become part of the national branding of Trinidad, with attempts to form mutually beneficial relationships with overseas (versions of) carnivals, including Notting Hill in London, the Labor Day parade in New York City, and Caribana in Toronto. But this raises questions about how Trinidad and Tobago can benefit from this global emergence of these 'successor' events (which resembles Jamaica's struggle to reap the benefits of reggae's global popularity, as we discuss in the Chapter five).

Public investment (rather than subsidy) in Carnival celebrations has helped strengthen the economic importance of the annual celebrations. But the focus on projecting identity and preserving heritage through Carnival has not grown with the focus on economic impact. This raises questions about what public funds should be invested in, and to whose benefit, and is characteristic of the Celebratory approach, ignoring contestation.

CHINA'S SOFT POWER AMBITIONS

Variety reported that the Wanda Group, a big Chinese business conglomerate, bought AMC, the largest American cinema chain, and became the world's largest cinema owners (Stewart 2012). Given the high growth in Chinese film production, of 700% between 2000 and 2015 (Yang 2016), Chinese interest in an American theatre chain is hardly surprising. This growth in feature film production in China materialised in large part thanks to government supports and intervention according to Chinese media scholar Yanling Yang (2016). China's accession to the WTO and the popularity of the 'cultural industries' discourse resulted in acknowledgement of the importance of film industries in 'cultural industries' and soft power strategies (Keane 2009; Yang 2016). Film production, distribution, and exhibition were decentralised. State Administration of Radio, Film and Television (SARFT) issued a document 'Interim Provisions on Operation Qualification Access for Movie Enterprises', which allowed international investors to invest in Chinese films up to 49% (Yang 2016). One result was the aforementioned increase in feature film production.

Film production in China had previously been seen as a tool of cultural exchange with other socialist countries from 1950 to 1976. Later, until approximately 2000, film was considered a tool of propaganda for promoting correct values and education among the masses. Film production and distribution remained centralised during these periods (Yang 2016). This situation had raised questions about the implementation of the 'cultural industries' discourse in China. Jing Wang asks, 'how do we begin to envision a parallel discussion in a country where creative imagination is subjugated to active state surveillance?' (Wang 2004, 13). What explains this funding and policy shift?

The response lies in the way China combined an interest in the conservative and heritage factor of China's cultural prominence and the innovation of the creative. Stuart Cunningham notes the 'prestige 'factor in China's cultural 'creative industries' initiatives, stating that the leadership of the country is 'as much concerned with reasserting its historic claims to cultural/spiritual eminence as it is about inscribing itself into technological modernity and contemporary innovative thinking' (Cunningham 2009, 380). After initial caution in adopting the cultural economy discourse, China scholar Michael Keane further notes the acceptance was based on a wish to 'construct an alternative vision of an emerging China' (Keane 2009, 433). International relations scholar Antonios Vlassis highlights the decision of the 17th Central Committee of the Chinese Communist Party in October 2011 to promote the 'international influence of Chinese culture' (Vlassis 2016, 481). All three scholars comment on an increasingly outward focus and concern about China's place in international public perception by Chinese policymakers. Cultural economy scholars Justin O'Connor and Xin Gu (2014) concur, describing an aspirational balancing act within Chinese cultural policy, noting that:

[China's] concerns for the educative/normative function of culture have increasingly spilled over from 'high' into commercial culture. Any attempt to uncouple creative industries from cultural policy concerns would always be suspect. At the same time, its search for 'soft power' suggests an investment in cultural industries that might go beyond their purely economic function.

(O'Connor and Gu 2014, 3)

China's conception of its prominent place in the global economy necessitates a similarly prominent place within the global cultural economy. The cultural economy turn was as much about business as about the international and explains the nature of the public investment in cultural economy. The Chinese government issued the *Plan for Promotion of the Cultural Industries* (2009) and the *Guidelines on Facilitating the Development of the Film Industry* (2010). Both advocated for active overseas promotion of film as part of China's soft power policy.

China's execution of film promotion reflects a focus on the exterior and global prominence, rather than just economic goals. China has one of the largest domestic markets, accounting for 22% of global box office revenue and therefore its domestic market is profitable. However, China has also emerged as a major global film-funding source (Keane 2006). China has signed ten co-production agreements since 2000 with Australia, Spain, and so on.[10] In a recent TIME magazine article, noted Asian film industry analyst Rob Cain cited China's financial clout as the reason Hollywood villains were still Russian. China is bringing the films to its market and exerting its influence in the international film market through funding.

The aspiration to global cultural prominence is shared by Chinese business. Vlassis (2016) shares the example of Wang Jialin, CEO of the Wanda Group, now the world's largest cinema owners (after the AMC acquisition), noting that 'in ten years, the Chinese economy will be on [its] way to dethrone US as dominant economic power. But in terms of cultural power, China is still far behind . . . this project is an opportunity to implement a national policy in order to promote cultural power' (Vlassis 2016, 484).

Despite China's efforts, Chinese films themselves have not become as popular within the global market place as they have domestically. According to Table 4.3, China was the third largest film market in the world, ahead of Hollywood. While 682 Chinese films were distributed in 34 nations and regions in 1981, 121 Chinese films were distributed in 16 nations in 1993 (Yang 2016). This relative lack of success is in large part due to heavy censorship, embedded propaganda, and Hollywood dominance (Sun 2015; Vlassis 2016; Yang 2016). Vlassis cites the Hollywood global distribution infrastructure as one reason for the lack of success. Paradoxically, China has focused its international efforts less on addressing the Hollywood issue and more on joining organisations such as UNESCO and other international organisations to increase its political influence rather than its economic influence (Vlassis 2016).

Both Vlassis (2016) and Yang (2016) locate China's film strategy in a bid for soft power. While we have issues with soft power given confusion about how it is used, created, or measured, we do acknowledge the impact of the soft power concept on Chinese strategy. The focus on soft power allows for a focus on the international and external, reducing the focus on domestic change and revolution. Yang argues that China continues its censorship of film, but more discreetly. The cultural economy is associated with progress as symbolised by the slogan, 'Made in China to Created in China' (Keane 2006).

The focus on the exterior and appearance of being a cultural power could explain the over-funding at even local levels. In a detailed analysis, Gu (2014) highlights that the first project of the Shanghai Creative Industries Centre (SCIC) was a creative cluster building called 1933. It cost 10 million RMB (approximately 1.5 million USD) and took two years to construct. The expense was justified by the rents that could be charged. The same high rent meant that 60% of businesses were catering and services, in short, cultural consumption business rather than to those involved in production. Gu (2014) notes that the most creative aspect was the architecture. The aim to have a grand exterior surpassed the desire to support creative businesses: '1933 was a grand exercise in exterior spectacle and the integration of high-end leisure consumption' (Gu 2014, 129). The result was that Shanghai's cultural economy, albeit defined more by cultural consumption than production, continued to grow. This model is, in some ways, similar to an older cultural development model where the focus was on real estate in the form of the establishment of local branches of world-class institutions such as the Guggenheim Bilboa (Plaza and Haarich 2015). However, the difference was that the Chinese government built their own world-class real estate and branding, rather than utilise an already-established name.

Despite moderate successes, such as an expansion in feature film production for the domestic market, but not the international, and an increase in businesses, but non-creative businesses, the funding and support continues. As in our other examples, the interaction between the global economy discourse and the local political discourse is specific to the Chinese context, but here success is judged by size, appearance, and numbers (of films and CICS). China aspires to be a cultural power and is willing to invest to achieve soft power in much the same way it has invested in its economic power. The scale of the investment and the type of investment betrays a focus on outward perception rather than the economics of the cultural economy, one reliant on innovation, clustering, and interaction. We argue that the concern with the external appearances and international reputation dominates much of the strategy regarding the 'cultural industries' as with the 1933 buildings and the cultural organisation membership. The Chinese government has turned to the cultural economy both as a solution for the engendering of international goodwill and to support the transition from a manufacturing to an innovative economy. Prominence in the global cultural economy has become a new aspiration, a new space program. Both at home, through creative clusters, and abroad, through film.

CONCLUSIONS

The rise of the 'creative industries' in the 1990s has led to a shift in thinking about the relationship between public and private institutions in the cultural economy. Prior to this shift, in 1989, Chartrand and McCaughey assumed that funding for arts and culture operated in a context where correcting for market failure is the norm. In the examples we address in this chapter, the concerns are rather different. All countries we look at 'invest' in the cultural economy with clear economic returns in mind.

The cases of Korea, India, Trinidad and Tobago, and China illustrate the extent to which the economic expediency of culture dominates the engagement with the cultural economy, even while very local, distinct and cultural interpretations of this policy discourse abound. However, what has not changed is that many parts of the cultural economy, such as classical music, and the visual arts, are subject to market failure. This means they need continuous support (*subsidy*) and not start-up funding (*investment*) to survive. Even those activities that are commercially viable remain subject to the inherent uncertainties of the cultural economy: it is very difficult (if not impossible) to predict success and when successes emerge, they disproportionally benefit a few winners (Caves 2003; Hesmondhalgh 2013). Moreover, the government's balancing act between the 'arts that cost' and the 'arts that pay' (Hughson and Inglis 2001, 466) continues to be an inexact art as the Trinbagonian and Jamaican cases demonstrate.

This creates the challenge of how to balance what kind of expressions can be created and supported or funded in particular socioeconomic and cultural contexts and who should own and benefit from these creations and in which ways. That is why the next chapter on ownership tackles the political economy of culture at the level of ownership of specific 'symbolic texts' in the global cultural economy.

NOTES

1 Jurassic Park made US$15.8 million in South Korea and US$1,029 million overall (www.boxofficemojo.com/movies/?page=intl&country=KR&id=jurassicpark.htm).

2 Japan colonised Korea between 1910 and 1945. It was at the end of this period that the capture of the Korean peninsula by Soviet and American forces resulted in the creation of North and South Korea.

3 This figure is for the entire Indian film industry and likewise the Hollywood figure is for the entire US film industry

4 British India had consisted of a landmass including present-day India, Pakistan, and Bangladesh. The agreement for Indian independence included the creation of a Muslim state of Pakistan, which consisted of both East and West Pakistan. East Pakistan became independent as Bangladesh in 1971.

5 We use the term 'Trinbagonian' instead of Trinidadian to reflect the fact of the two-island nature of the Republic of Trinidad and Tobago. However, regarding Carnival, we are referring to the Carnival in Port of Spain (not the Carnival in Tobago), therefore use the term Trinidad/Trinidadian Carnival.

6 Trinidad and Tobago is the largest gas and oil producer in the Caribbean region, totalling over 3 billion barrels so far (http://caribbean.cepal.org/content/overview-oil-and-gas-industry-trinidad-and-tobago).

7 Slavery ended in the Anglophone Caribbean on August 1, 1838.

8 Trinidad and Tobago has two major ethnic groups, those of Indian descent and those of African descent. They account for approximately 35% of the population. The rest of the population consists of mixed, white, Chinese, Amerindian, and Middle Eastern.

9 Robert Amar is the owner of many 'cultural industries' enterprises including Kiskadee Caravan and Caribbean Sound Basin. He was also chairman of the Small Business Development Corporation among other entities in Trinidad and Tobago.

10 www.mpa-i.org/wp-content/uploads/2014/12/Co-Production_Handbook_English.pdf.

REFERENCES

Athique, Adrian M. 2008. "The 'Crossover' Audience: Mediated Multiculturalism and the Indian Film". *Continuum* 22 (3): 299–311.

Bauer, Roxanne. 2015. "Media (R)Evolutions: The Epic Nollywood Machine". *The World Bank*. www.blogs.worldbank.org/publicsphere/media-revolutions-epic-nollywood-machine.

Bell, David, and Kate Oakley. 2015. *Cultural Policy*. Key Ideas in Media and Cultural Studies. London: Routledge.

Bose, Nandana. 2010. "The Central Board of Film Certification Correspondence Files (1992–2002): A Discursive Rhetoric of Moral Panic, 'Public' Protest, and Political Pressure". *Cinema Journal: The Journal of the Society for Cinema and Media Studies* 49 (3): 67–87.

Burch, Micah. 2010. "National Funding for the Arts and Internal Revenue Code § 501(c)(3)". *Florida State University Law Review* 37: 1–34.

Burke, Suzanne. 2014. "Creative Clustering in Small Island States: The Case of Trinidad and Tobago's Carnival Industry". *Caribbean Quarterly* 60 (1): 74–95.

Cain, Rob. 2015. "India's Film Industry – a $10 Billion Business Trapped In a $2 Billion Body". *Forbes*, October 23, 2015. www.forbes.com/sites/robcain/2015/10/23/indias-film-industry-a-10-billion-business-trapped-in-a-2-billion-body/#7534999870d2.

Caves, Richard E. 2003. "Contracts between Art and Commerce". *Journal of Economic Perspectives*, 17(2): 73–84.

Central Statistical Office (Trinidad and Tobago). 2017. Central Statistical Office (Trinidad and Tobago) Survey. edited by Trinidad and Tobago Central Statistical Office. Port of Spain: Ministry of Planning and Development, Government of Trinidad and Tobago.

Chartrand, Harry Hillmann, and Claire McCaughey. 1989. "The Arm's Length Principle and the Arts: An International Perspective – Past, Present and Future". In *Who's to Pay for the Arts: The International Search for Models of Support*, edited by M. C. Cummings and J. Mark Davidson Schuster. New York, NY: ACA Books. www.compilerpress.ca/Cultural%20Economics/Works/Arm%201%201989.htm.

Copeland, Raedene, and Nancy Hodges. 2014. "Exploring Masquerade Dress at Trinidad Carnival: Bikinis, Beads, and Feathers and the Emergence of the Popular Pretty Mas". *Clothing and Textiles Research Journal* 32 (3): 186–201.

Cowley, John. 2002. *Carnival, Canboulay and Calypso: Traditions in the Making*. Cambridge: Cambridge University Press.

Cunningham, Stuart. 2009. "Trojan Horse or Rorschach Blot? Creative Industries Discourse around the World". *International Journal of Cultural Policy* 15 (4): 375–86.

Garth, L. Green. 2002. "Marketing the Nation: Carnival and Tourism in Trinidad and Tobago". *Critique of Anthropology* 22 (3): 283–304.

Green, Garth L. 2007. "'Come to Life': Authenticity, Value and the Carnival as Cultural Commodity in Trinidad and Tobago". *Identities: Global Studies in Culture and Power* 14 (1–2): 203–24.

Gu, Xin. 2014. "Cultural Industries and Creative Clusters in Shanghai". *City, Culture and Society* 5 (3): 123–30.

Hesmondhalgh, David. 2013. *The Cultural Industries*. 3rd ed. London: Sage.

Hong, Euny. 2014. *The Birth of Korean Cool*. London: Picador.

Hong, Kiwon. 2012. *Country Profile: South Korea*. International Database of Cultural Policies. Sydney: International Federation of Arts Councils and Cultural Agencies.

Hughson, John, and David Inglis. 2001. "Creative Industries and the Arts in Britain: Towards a 'Third Way' in Cultural Policy?" *International Journal of Cultural Policy* 7 (3): 457–78.

Jeffrey, Robin. 2006. "The Mahatma Didn't like the Movies and Why It Matters: Indian Broadcasting Policy, 1920s–1990s". *Global Media and Communication* 2: 204–24.

Kang, Inkyu. 2015. "The Political Economy of Idols: South Korea's Neoliberal Restructuring and Its Impact on the Entertainment Labour Force". In *K-Pop – The International Rise of the Korean Music Industry*, edited by Roald Maliangkay and JungBong Choi, 51–65. Media, Culture and Social Change in Asia 40. New York, NY; London: Taylor & Francis.

Kang, Myungkoo. 2004. "There Is No South Korea in South Korean Cultural Studies: Beyond the Colonial Condition of Knowledge Production". *Journal of Communication Inquiry* 28(3): 253–68.

Kanzler, Martin, and Julio Talavera. 2017. *Focus 2017: World Film Market Trends*. edited by European Audiovisual Observatory Paris: Marche du Film, Cannes Film Festival.

Keane, Michael. 2006. "From Made in China to Created in China". *International Journal of Cultural Studies* 9 (3): 285–96.

Keane, Michael. 2009. "Creative Industries in China: Four Perspectives on Social Transformation". *International Journal of Cultural Policy* 15 (4): 431–43.

Keat, Russell. 2000. *Cultural Goods and the Limits of the Market: Beyond Commercial Modelling*. Basingstoke: Macmillan.

Kim, Ju Oak. 2018. "Korea's Blacklist Scandal: Governmentality, Culture, and Creativity". *Culture, Theory and Critique* 59(2): 81–93.

Kim, Soojin. 2017. "Controlling or Supporting? A History of Cultural Policies on Popular Music". In *Made in Korea: Studies in Popular Music*, edited by Hyunjoon Shin, Seung-Ah Lee, and Goffredo Plastino, 181–90. Routledge Global Popular Music Series. New York, NY: Routledge.

Kumar, Bala Senthil. 2015. "How India's Government Surprisingly Cripples Its Own Film Industry". *Forbes*, August 19, 2015. www.forbes.com/sites/robcain/2015/08/19/how-indias-government-surprisingly-cripples-its-own-film-industry/.

Kwon, Seung-Ho, and Joseph Kim. 2014. "The Cultural Industry Policies of the Korean Government and the Korean Wave". *International Journal of Cultural Policy* 20 (4): 422–39.

Lorenzen, Mark, and Florian Arun Täube. 2008. "Breakout from Bollywood? The Roles of Social Networks and Regulation in the Evolution of Indian Film Industry". *Journal of International Management* 14 (3): 286–99.

Miller, Toby, and George Yúdice. 2002. *Cultural Policy*. London; Thousand Oaks, CA: Sage Publications. www.catalog.hathitrust.org/api/volumes/oclc/49871805.html.

Motion Picture Association of America. 2018. "2017 Theme Report: A Comprehensive Analysis and Survey of the Theatrical and Home Entertainment Market Environment (Theme) for 2017." In *THEME Report*. Washington, DC: Motion Picture Association of America.

Nurse, Keith. 1999. "Globalization and Trinidad Carnival: Diaspora, Hybridity and Identity in Global Culture". *Cultural Studies* 13 (4): 661–90.

O'Connor, Justin, and Xin Gu. 2014. "Creative Industry Clusters in Shanghai: A Success Story?" *International Journal of Cultural Policy* 20 (1): 1–20.

Plaza, Beatriz, and Silke N. Haarich. 2015. "The Guggenheim Museum Bilbao: Between Regional Embeddedness and Global Networking". *European Planning Studies* 23 (8): 1456–75.

Potts, Jason, and Stuart Cunningham. 2008. "Four Models of the Creative Industries". *International Journal of Cultural Policy* 14 (3): 233–47.

PricewaterhouseCoopers. 2017. "Entertainment and Media Outlook: 2017–2021 An African Perspective". Johannesburg: PricewaterhouseCoopers. www.pwc.co.za/en/assets/pdf/entertainment-and-media-outlook-2017.pdf.

Rajadhyaksha, Ashish, P. Radhika, and Raghavendra Tenkayala. 2013. *Country Profile: India*. International Database of Cultural Policies. Sydney: International Federation of Arts Councils and Culture Agencies.

Rohlehr, Gordon. 1990. *Calypso & Society in Pre-Independence Trinidad*. Tunapuna: Gordon Rohlehr.

Ryoo, Woongjae. 2005. "The Role of the State in the National Mediascape: The Case of South Korea". *Gloabl Media Journal* 4 (6): 1–32.

Shim, Doobo. 2006. "Hybridity and the Rise of Korean Popular Culture in Asia". *Media, Culture & Society* 28 (1): 25–44.

Shin, Hyunjoon, and Seung-Ah Lee. 2017. *Made in Korea: Studies in Popular Music*. Routledge Global Popular Music Series. New York, NY; London: Routledge.

Spence, Kim-Marie. 2018. "When Money Is Not Enough – Reggae, Dancehall and Policy in Jamaica". *Journal of Arts Management, Law & Society*, in press.

Stewart, Andrew. 2012. "Wanda Group Acquires AMC Entertainment". *Variety*. www.variety.com/2012/film/news/wanda-group-acquires-amc-entertainment-1118058647/.

Sun, Wanning. 2015. "Slow Boat from China: Public Discourses behind the 'Going Global' Media Policy". *International Journal of Cultural Policy* 21 (4): 400–418.

Thom, Michael, and Brian An. 2017. "Fade to Black? Exploring Policy Enactment and Termination Through the Rise and Fall of State Tax Incentives for the Motion Picture Industry". *American Politics Research* 45 (1): 85–108.

Vlassis, Antonios. 2016. "Soft Power, Global Governance of Cultural Industries and Rising Powers: The Case of China". *International Journal of Cultural Policy* 22 (4): 481–96.

Wang, Jing. 2004. "The Global Reach of a New Discourse: How Far Can 'Creative Industries' Travel?" *International Journal of Cultural Studies* 7 (1): 9–19.

Yang, Yanling. 2016. "Film Policy, the Chinese Government and Soft Power". *New Cinemas: Journal of Contemporary Film* 14 (1): 71–91.

Yim, Haksoon. 2002. "Cultural Identity and Cultural Policy in South Korea". *International Journal of Cultural Policy* 8 (1): 37–48.

Yúdice, George. 2003. *The Expediency of Culture: Uses of Culture in the Global Era*. Durham, NC: Duke University Press.

5

OWNERSHIP

Jamaica is known worldwide for Bob Marley and reggae. But do Jamaicans 'own' reggae, or does Jamaica 'own' it as a county? In recent years, there has been much discussion about the extent to which Jamaica and Jamaicans have benefitted from reggae economically. This ties in with practical issues around payment of royalties, but also more abstract questions around what ownership constitutes in the cultural economy. Three issues illustrate the pertinence of this question.

In August 2012, *Jamaica Observer* entertainment reporter, Cecelia Campbell-Livingston wrote about 'millions of dollars' in digital performance royalties owed to Jamaican artistes (without specifying an exact sum). Some of these royalties are administered by US-based collection agency *SoundExchange* (Campbell-Livingston 2012). One reason was the then-recent nature of a reciprocal agreement by *Sound Exchange* with Jamaica Music Society (JAMMS), a Jamaican Collective Management Organisation (CMO).[1]

JAMMS has also been involved in longstanding cases with major Jamaican music users, such as broadcasting companies and hotels. Musicians asked JAMMS to enforce copyright compliance and royalties payments (Jamaica Observer 2010). In an interview with Kim-Marie Spence, JAMMS employee, Gregory Alcock, noted the struggle JAMMS had for Jamaicans to recognise the importance of copyright, particularly the major users such as hotels and broadcast companies refusing to pay for years.

Jamaica is where music styles such as mento, ska, rocksteady, dub, nyahbinghi, reggae, and dancehall originate. But despite the success of these genres, it is often non-Jamaican reggae artists who reap high cultural and economic successes. This is why some Jamaicans have raised the question of whether Jamaica is still the capital of reggae (Campbell 2012). In response to this, the Minister of Culture, Gender, Entertainment, and Sports (MCGES) has sought to inscribe reggae on UNESCO's Representative List of Oral and Intangible Heritage since 2016. Naila Morgan, a Jamaican Culture Ministry official, told Spence that UNESCO inscription could reclaim reggae for future generations of Jamaicans. The ministry chose UNESCO, and not WIPO, nor WTO, as the organisation with which to register such a claim, as neither organisation acknowledges or could acknowledge this kind of cultural ownership.

These three Jamaican examples present three different levels of issues regarding the concept of ownership within the wider global cultural economy. Though a key underlying question remains: Why do some people argue copyright legislation and enforcement is a non-negotiable precondition for the cultural economy to function, while the success of reggae shows that Jamaican music has managed to thrive for decades, despite the absence of an effective copyright regime? Surely, many musicians could have earned more money, but Jamaicans still developed a highly influential music genre, much like Nigerians developed a leading film industry (Larkin 2008; Lobato 2010; Witt 2017), despite very similar issues in copyright legislation and enforcement.

In this chapter, we explore ownership of intellectual property rights (IPR) in the cultural economy. At a micro level, it raises the question of how present-day reggae musicians make a living. At a macro level, it urges us to probe who benefits from the international success of reggae. It further opens up the question of how a small country like Jamaica can defend its cultural and material interests from reggae in the light of cultural appropriation. And finally, it makes us ponder what kind of influence these struggles have on the dignity of reggae musicians and other creators in the global cultural economy.

COPYRIGHT, A PRECONDITION?

Copyright is one of the mechanisms to regulate and enforce intellectual property rights over immaterial goods such as music. In *A Handbook of Cultural Economics*, a key textbook, William Landes makes the case that in the absence of copyright, 'the incentive for authors to write new books will diminish, as will the supply of new books' (Landes 2011, 100). Historically, there is little evidence to support this claim and the global cultural economy continues to illustrate that this mainstream copyright 'orthodoxy' (literally, the right or correct opinion) does not chime with the development of cultural creation, distribution, and consumption (see e.g. Kernfeld 2011).

Many things created in the cultural economy, including music, are intangible and non-rivalrous goods. This means that what the intellectual property is not in the thing, whether it is a CD or even an audio file, it is the music itself. But because music is non-rivalrous, meaning that *my* listening to the music does not diminish *your* ability to listen to the very same music, this creates problems for commercialisation. Because if we can copy the music very easily and cheaply and sharing it does not diminish its value for anyone – if anything, sharing music increases its social meaning – how can we make money from selling it?

We make money from music, films, literature, and so on through artificial scarcity. Intellectual property represents the legal right to exploit an idea or concept. Copyright essentially grants the (recognised) author a monopoly from which they can charge for the right to use (Sell 2010; Towse 2011). This approach is now virtually universal, and many economists, lawyers, musicians, and writers will argue that copyright is absolutely essential for the cultural economy to function. But is this the case? Before evaluating that question in detail through the case of Jamaica, we will make the case that copyright as a legal framework emerged in very particular contexts in response to very particular needs.

The *Statute of Anne*, enacted in England in 1709, is considered the first copyright act for *publishers* (and not *creators*). Media and communications scholars Bethany Klein, Giles Moss, and Lee Edwards (2015) highlight three main tenets of modern copyright: first, the right to the fruit of one's labour; second, incentivising production; and third, the author as creative genius (the individual creator). However, some argue that these underlying ideas are not universal, unlike the reach of the principles of copyright:

> This standard . . . has a distinct local history; it basically evolved from British utilitarian legal models and German idealist notions of personal authorship, but travelled quickly across the Atlantic and beyond.
> (Eckstein and Schwarz 2014a, 2)

These principles have worked well enough *within* countries but posed difficulties when trying to enforce copyright beyond the national boundaries of the country the rights owner was based. In response to this, a large number of countries agreed to the Berne Convention, which created reciprocity between countries. Once the Berne Convention was in place, the international trade in copyrighted cultural goods became primarily a matter of trade, rather than of legal concern. By gradually moving to a broad agreement on legal frameworks through the Berne Convention, and later the World Intellectual Property Organization, the legal interests of copyright owners have been ensured. The emergence of a global copyright regime has shifted legal concerns (that were in fact the economic concerns of individual rights owners) to country-level economic tensions around trade in culture in a globalising world.

There are however two major issues. First, at the time the Convention was drawn up and signed, there were far fewer countries in the world than there are today: most countries that exist today were 'colonies' of European countries. While colonialism has ended, former colonies had to join this (and other conventions) in order to gain access to global markets, without the possibility of renegotiating their terms (De Beukelaer and Fredriksson 2018; Peukert 2016). Second, the notion of the artist as an individual creative genius reflects the Western cultural context in which copyright as a legal regime emerged. While this idea continues to influence copyright legislation, it does not adequately account for collective creation and ownership (Boateng 2011).

The Western origins and principles of copyright mean that, despite the early spread and agreement on the concept of IPRs and of copyright, only the citizens of certain countries could benefit. Under the Berne Convention, colonies and overseas territories were subject to the same judicial frameworks of their colonisers. Alexander Peukert notes that while there was no explicit citizenship requirement to benefit from copyright protection, particular requirements limited the effective protection of creators in the colonies, because 'until the UK International Copyright Act of 1886, a work had to be published first in the United Kingdom in order to acquire copyright throughout the British Empire' (Peukert 2016, 41).

The US used similar methods to its own advantage, even if the country is a (settler) colony, which declared its independence in 1776 (merely 28 years before Haiti). From 1790 to 1891, the US granted territorial copyright protection to US citizens only. Which meant that US publishers could freely publish works by foreigners (mostly British writers), who felt their rights were violated. This was possible, because the 1790 US Federal Copyright Statute only recognised copyright claims of US citizens and the 1891 Chace Act included limited copyright protections for foreigners (Balasz 2011, 408). Most importantly, this remained possible because the US did not sign the 1886 Berne Convention until 1989 – barely a few decades ago. A year before signing this convention, the US established Section 301 of the US Trade Act, which mandates the president to address any infringement of international trade agreements. A 1988 amendment of Section 301 allowed the US to compile a list of countries infringing on US property rights every year, thereby creating a blacklist of countries failing their international obligations. This mechanism remains in place to this day.

The irony is that, because strict IPR regulation and enforcement benefits them greatly, the US is now the most vocal and powerful enforcer of international IPR agreements. They heavily police and enforce their own IPRs across the world and insist on compliance to the WIPO and Trade-Related Aspects of Intellectual Property Rights (TRIPS) regulations as well as bilateral and multilateral agreements through the Office of the US Trade Representative (USTR) when negotiating trade deals. In this context, the legacy of the German publishing industry lobby – as we discuss at the start of Chapter three – acts as the guardian of the sector's interest. Their arguments make most sense when interpreting them in relation to the history of book publishing, as such industry bodies were the sole organisations that offered reliable protection in a sector with limited protective regulation (Balasz 2011).

The colonial legacy tells us one half of the story. The other half of the story is increasing recognition of the perpetuation of a copyright regime that does not adequately benefit the majority of the world. Consequently, the 'development agenda' emerged in the early 2000s in the WTO and the WIPO, with 'calls for a moratorium on new treaty-making and instead demands that WIPO give greater attention to public access to knowledge and to non-proprietary systems of creativity and innovation' (Helfer 2007, 974). The rise of the global cultural economy in a neoliberal political economy has made copyright increasingly important.

The US's transformation from worst offender to global enforcer raises questions about whose interests these agreements serve at a global level. Sell (2010) argues that internal political changes within the US have resulted in the international lobbying for IPRs, which has reaped success. In the post-Nixon political fallout, responsibility for trade policymaking moved from that of the president to the international trade commission as part of reforms for greater transparency. Gradually, responsibility for international action on American intellectual property rights moved to the specific portfolio of the US Trade Representative (USTR), facilitating bilateral promotion of intellectual property rights that would be to the advantage of Americans.

The US's first international IPR achievement was the inclusion of IPR provision in the Caribbean Basin Economic Recovery Act of 1983, which stated that 'countries pirating US copyrighted products would lose non-reciprocal tariff waivers on their imports under the Generalized System of Preferences (GSP)' (Sell 2010, 772). Through a sequence of events, IPR was also incorporated into GATT in 1985. Susan Sell further identifies the ability of rich countries to utilise forum-shifting to achieve their agendas. They have the power to argue in whichever organisation or bilateral or regional level that suits their needs, thereby influencing the 'synchronisation' of ideas and policies (Alasuutari 2016).

Due to a deficit of power and resources, less wealthy or less powerful countries have fewer options. This is quite evident in the sphere of copyright and IPR. We have noted Jamaica moving to UNESCO to secure the acknowledgement of its ownership of reggae. However, the US has utilised regional (CBERA), multilateral (GATT), and other bilateral fora to achieve its IPR enforcement goals. Music scholar Dennis Howard notes in a recent newspaper interview that Jamaica being on the USTR trade watch list has prevented Jamaican artists from [direct] access to iTunes, Apple Music, Spotify, or other such music 'e-tailers' (Campbell 2016).

Practically, copyright is not just a technical issue; it is an issue that revolves around economic, political, and cultural power. But if copyright has colonial roots and its enforcement perpetuates power imbalances (De Beukelaer and Fredriksson 2018; Peukert 2016), and if piracy is not a mere lack of enforcement but also a form of postcolonial resistance (Eckstein and Schwarz 2014b),[2] the question is how can copyright be postcolonial and move beyond its colonial foundations?

POSTCOLONIAL COPYRIGHT?

In a recent *Fader* interview, veteran reggae artist Sister Nancy mentioned she had no idea her song *Bam Bam* was a huge success before she moved to the US in 1996: 'I never had a clue because the producer never wanted me to know' (Kochhar 2017). Sister Nancy's producer used her lack of knowledge about the international market as a lower-class Jamaican to her disadvantage, despite her having filled out her copyright registration: 'I did copyright the album, but I think he went behind my back and took *Bam Bam* . . . from the album, the copyright, changed it totally' (Kochhar 2017). In the end, Sister Nancy negotiated with the producer's family for the copyright.

This case illustrates that copyright legislation alone is not enough to protect artists, who may be unaware of its economic logic and legal intricacies. On top of this, the net flow of royalty payments between Jamaica and the rest of the world has always been from the former to the latter (Howard 2009; JACAP 2017; Taylor 2013;). The Jamaica Association for Composers, Authors and Publishers (JACAP) is one of two CMOs for the music industry. Figure 5.1 demonstrates a net outflow of royalties in the last ten years from 2007 to 2016. An average of 25.6% of collections is paid out to local artistes (or locally registered artistes). It questions the predominant approach of a copyright-centric music development model.

Despite the global popularity of reggae, many musicians in Jamaica have not been able to make a living from their work. Few musicians in the global cultural economy earn enough to live off music alone. Roger Wallis and Krister Malm moreover documented that

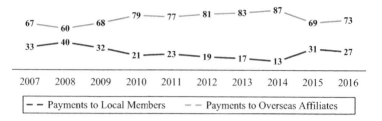

Figure 5.1 JACAP royalties payment shares to local and overseas members 2007–2016

Source: The authors, based on JACAP (2017).

the challenges to do so are particularly salient in 'small countries' (Wallis and Malm 1984). But what are the particular issues about making a fair share from music in a former colony that has an internationally significant music scene?

Jamaica's first Copyright Act dates back to 1911 and was enacted to secure the rights of British citizens in the colonies, but not those of Jamaicans, as was considered standard within colonial governmentality. Jamaica's Copyright Act of 1993 was its first after its independence in 1962, despite reggae being an international musical force since the 1970s. Sharma Taylor, an IPR scholar, argues that the Jamaican Parliament passed the 1993 copyright act in an attempt to protect the rights and earning power of the Jamaican music industry for Jamaica's economic development (Taylor 2013).

The 1990s and early 2000s saw the establishment of the Jamaica Association of Composers and Publishers (JACAP), the first local collection management organisation (for music) in 1998, the Jamaica Intellectual Property Office (JIPO) in 2002, followed by the Jamaica Music Society (JAMMS), a collection management organisation of record producers, in 2006.

Jamaican musicians either don't know or don't care about the copyright act. This is in large part because given its colonial legacy, public knowledge about the benefits and rights embedded in copyright has been limited (Howard 2009; Taylor 2013; Toynbee 2010). Its mere existence therefore has thus failed to resolve copyright and royalty payments issues experienced by Jamaican artists, particularly in the 1970s when reggae was popular. In this context, cultural economy specialists Nurse (2006), James (2001), and Taylor (2013) indicate that the copyright-centric development model is intrinsically flawed, as securing benefits from copyright is difficult, as Figure 5.1 illustrates.

A related issue is that due to is colonial history, some Jamaican artists have registered their works with foreign CMOs as opposed to local ones, which means that royalties do not necessarily flow back to Jamaica. Some performers, particularly the top-selling ones, had a belief that maybe the overseas CMOs were more effective, alongside a general deficit in public knowledge about copyright (James 2001; Nurse 2006; Taylor 2013).

Institutionally, there are negotiation issues within and without Jamaica. The main registered music users in Jamaica are reluctant to pay. The notion that broadcasters and hoteliers among others should pay for the use of music in their establishment is not controversial. Yet the CMOs had to take Jamaican broadcasters to court to be paid. The fact that it took a court case in Jamaica is demonstrative of the local power imbalances in copyright negotiation, despite the recognition of the Jamaican government of the importance of copyright in the exploitation and investment in the music industry, despite the law (Schultz and van Gelder 2008; Taylor 2013).

At the heart of these conflicts is the implicit assumption that copyright is wholly beneficial for everyone and for all activities in the cultural economy. However, the case of Jamaica argues for caution according to ethnomusicologists. Toynbee (2010) notes that 'reggae music would never have emerged had copyright been implemented [as] local forms of creativity . . . were inimical to intellectual property' (Toynbee 2010, 357). Likewise Dennis Howard describes the environment during the period of reggae's evolution as 'open domain', and as 'an environment devoid of copyright enforcement [that] was characterized by the exploitation of creators who were not aware of copyright protection nor was concerned with its implications with regard to its economic benefits' (Howard 2009, 512).

In this context, the absence of copyright enforcement was key to the development of reggae as it encouraged the use of elements of the Anglo-American pop music (learnt through doing cover versions for the local Jamaican market) and then the intermingling with local styles from African retentions such as Kumina. Here, access to the material and innovation by singers was facilitated by less copyright. The open domain also facilitated cheap access to the music by Jamaicans at dances and through sound and audio-visual recordings of dances. While access to music facilitated experimentation and increased its popularity, it made commercial exploitation of music a major challenge. Given the colonial and postcolonial history of Jamaica and many other countries, there is a difficulty in building institutions that reflect both cultural and commercial interests that can help copyright legislation to move beyond its colonial foundations and the inequalities it helps uphold to this day.

CULTURAL RIGHTS VERSUS INTELLECTUAL PROPERTY RIGHTS

Laurence Helfer argues that there is a tension between the protection of cultural rights and copyright (Helfer 2007). A key example of this tension is the traditional knowledge of indigenous communities, which is often exploited by third parties, particularly in the area of medicine, with little benefit for the originators. Along the same lines, Peter Drahos and John Braithwaite argue that IPRs protect 'the knowledge and skills of the leaders of the pack' (Drahos and Brathwaite 2003, 12).

De Beukelaer and Fredriksson (2018) explicitly highlight tension between cultural rights and copyright by discussing the issue with reference to the 1948 Universal Declaration of Human Rights. Article 27 of this declaration pertains to cultural rights and contains two clauses. One guarantees every human being the freedom to participate in the cultural life and to benefit from the effects of scientific advancement. The other stipulates the guarantees creators the right to benefit from the moral and material interests of their cultural expressions and scientific discoveries. While both these rights are *cultural* rights, only the latter pertains to copyright. Copyright as a guarantee of a temporary monopoly to the creator is incompatible with a notion of a right to one's cultural expression as a member of a community and to the notion of a right to a global culture. This raises the question of which right takes precedence: cultural rights or copyright? This tension raises two questions. First, does copyright recognise this tension? Second, how can this tension be resolved?

First, copyright, as a legal construct, refers to private economic rights in the Paris, Berne, and Rome Conventions as well as TRIPS. The Paris Convention was adopted in 1883 and applies to industrial property including patents, trademarks, geographical indications, and unfair competition. This international agreement was the first major step taken to help creators ensure that their intellectual works were protected outside of their home country. The Berne Convention was adopted in 1886 and addresses the protection of works and the rights of their authors. It provides creators such as authors, musicians, and so on, with the means to control how their works are used, by whom, and on what terms. It has three foundational principles – national treatment, automatic protections, and independence of protection. It also determines the minimum protection to be granted, as well as special provisions for developing countries. The Rome Convention secures protection in performances for performers, in phonograms for producers of phonograms, and in broadcasts for broadcasting organisations.

None of these approaches explicitly recognise the simultaneous and conflicting existence of copyright and cultural rights. Copyright does not address this tension as it still promotes the model of the singular creator and pays little attention to the cultural rights of access to the heritage of humanity or moral rights of access by creator communities. In this context, Helfer argues that 'trade and intellectual property negotiators should embrace rather than resist opening up these organizations to human rights influence' (Helfer 2003, 61). This brings us to the question of how this debate can be opened up and the significant economic implications this may have.

Second, in her capacity as Special Rapporteur on Cultural Rights for the UN Office of the High Commissioner for Human Rights (OHCHR), Farida Shaheed, acknowledges the tension between copyright and the cultural right of access. This tension has become more pronounced because of the increased commercial importance of the cultural economy that resulted in the simultaneous expansion of copyright and the increasingly vocal contestation of the dominant intellectual property regime (Eckstein and Schwarz 2014b; Röschenthaler and Diawara 2016). Shaheed notes both the right of authors to benefit from their work and public access to it were recognised in both the Universal Declaration of Human Rights and the International Covenant on Economic, Social and Cultural Rights.

However, in 2000, the OHCHR Sub-Commission on the Promotion and Protection of Human Rights adopted a resolution on intellectual property and human rights calling for the primacy of human rights over trade law. But there is little on how the negotiation of the current breadth of copyright would occur. Given inequity embedded within the current copyright system, and the reality of such a negotiation by those who require it, without a supportive institution and mechanism (easily accessible, resource extensive), such a disputes tribunal is unlikely.

Shaheed, in her role as special rapporteur also reports on the right to freedom of artistic expression and creativity raising more. She argues that 'removing artistic and creative expressions from public access is a way to restrict artistic freedom' (Shaheed 2013, 3). This claim does, however, prompt the need to define public access. She cites the 2005 *Convention on the Protection and Promotion of the Diversity of Cultural Expressions* (UNESCO 2005, see also Chapter three), shows commitment to the idea of a global culture, as 'a common heritage of humanity' (UNESCO 2005, 1). Shaheed notes that

> under article 7 [of UNESCO's 2005 Convention], states endeavour to create an environment which encourages individuals and social groups to create, produce, disseminate, distribute and have access to their own cultural expressions as well as to diverse cultural expressions from within their territory as well as from other countries of the world.
>
> (Shaheed 2013, 6)

However, to secure material rights, public access might need to be abrogated.

Farida Shaheed is not the only person to make this argument. Legal scholar Helfer (2003, 2007) also acknowledges the tension between intellectual property rights and cultural and human rights. He cites the UN Committee on Economic, Social and Cultural Rights' first General Comment on intellectual property in 2005, and arguing for national protection of moral and material rights of creators with other copyright protections being supplementary, providing access to the creations.

His argument then is for a greater appreciation of cultural and social rights of access by members of the public, while protecting the moral and material right of the creators. If appealing, his proposal raises the question of how public access contends with group cultural rights. As of yet, a mechanism to balance and administer these conflicting interests is lacking. We are however aware that, as conflicts in supranational bodies have demonstrated, a mechanism for dispute resolution is one step but rendering this accessible to all countries and peoples is another. The tension between cultural appropriation and national ownership illustrates this difficulty.

CULTURAL APPROPRIATION AND NATIONAL OWNERSHIP

When Norwegian jazz saxophonist Jan Garbarek released his album, *Visible World*, in 1996, he adapted *Sweet Lullaby* by the French world music band Deep Forest. He attributed it both to Deep Forest and as 'a traditional African melody' (Feld 2000, 204). When Deep Forest released their album *Deep Forest* in 1992, anthropologist Hugo Zemp, who had recorded the lullaby contested their use of the melody without due permission. Zemp had initially recorded the song *Rorogwela*, sung by Afunakwa, as part of ethnographic fieldwork among the Baegu community of the Solomon Islands. The song is thus neither Deep Forest's nor African.

An ethnographic recording by a Swedish anthropologist was licensed by an international organisation to a French duo. The French duo then attributed it to a Central African tribe. The song was then heard by a Norwegian saxophonist who then adapted the song, therefore only earning Norwegian royalties for the performer and a Norwegian folk music fund. How would a small Solomon Islands community have the resources to challenge this, especially as both Deep Forest and Jan Garbarek have paid their licence fees?

Steven Feld explains that when Garbarek was alerted to the contested origins of the song, he promised to correct the attribution (to the Solomon Islands) during a concert, thereby following the letter of the law. Indeed, in Norway, the payment for songs from 'oral tradition' is 'split between the performer and a fund (administered by TONO, the Norwegian CMO) to promote folk music' (Feld 2000, 208). There is thus no legal obligation to compensate Afunakwa or other members of the Baegu community.

This is but one of many cases where Western musicians use 'traditional' music without due credit or compensation to its creators. Legally, performers do not have to pay if the music is 'traditional' because it supposedly does not have an individual as its creator and owner. On top of this, Afunakwa could not have easily monetised the song Hugo Zemp recorded in the Solomon Islands, though it was a highly marketable product for Deep Forest and Jan Garbarek, thanks to their access to a paying audience and an international distribution system, demonstrating the uneven ability to exploit the global heritage of humanity. But while they operated legally under French and Norwegian law, Afunakwa's moral and material rights as the 'author' of the song were not honoured.

This kind of intercultural exploitation highlights the importance of location and social networks in asserting one's moral and material interests in the global cultural economy. Kim-Marie Spence argues that the case of Popcaan and Lucas DiPasquale is demonstrative (Spence 2018). Lucas DiPasquale was discovered due to a recording of different acoustic covers of songs by Popcaan, a talented but 'unsigned' Jamaican dancehall artist, and an ability to speak patois (Kameir 2015). DiPasquale, the cover artist, is now signed to Universal Canada, while Popcaan is signed to Brooklyn-based independent label Mixpak (home to a number of Caribbean artistes). As a signed musician, Lucas DiPasquale has 6,040 followers on Instagram and 2,235 on Twitter as of April 8, 2018. Whereas Popcaan has 1 million followers on Instagram and 219,000 on Twitter. What might explain this situation is that Lucas DiPasquale is a white Canadian man who gets credit for his use of Afro-Jamaican music and culture.

These two examples are forms of cultural appropriation in which the moral rights of a particular cultural expression (a song) or a culture at large are not attributed. Often this also means that no compensation is made for the use of the material. Richard Rogers, a communications scholar, identifies four types of cultural appropriation: exchange, dominance, exploitation, and transculturation (Rogers 2006). He further argues that the cultural appropriation rests on the essentialisation of cultures. This does not happen on a level playing field but is rooted in unequal power dynamics with a colonial legacy. While we agree with the caution against cultural essentialism as well, we argue that cultural appropriation happens and power dynamics are important defining it.

Exchange, for example, occurs between equals. Along the same lines, philosopher Erich Matthes argues the importance of power differentials but not cultural essentialism. Matthes, like us, accepts the hybridity of culture that makes it difficult to identify insiders or outsiders. But Matthes notes 'oppressive systems and practices do not necessarily require the identification of an oppressor' (Matthes 2016, 356).

In cases of cultural appropriation between individuals, litigation is a possible way out. But it becomes far more difficult when the creator is not a single person (which, as we have discussed, is essential in copyright legislation) but a group of people. Boatema Boateng's discussion of the copyright issues around Ghanaian fabrics, kente and adinkra, demonstrates the inconsistencies between the individual authorship and notions of communal creation (Boateng 2011). Kente and adinkra cloth and the patterns and symbols that respectively characterise them do not have sole creators in the Western sense of the term. Even so, individual do make distinguishable modifications and innovations, which make the cloths the result of both individual and communal authorship.

We argue that these cases illustrate forms of cultural appropriation in conjunction with national or communal claims to ownership. The use of Afunakwa's performance of the song *Rorogwela* by Deep Forest and Jan Garbarek is a form of cultural appropriation because the original creators of the music are in a legally and economically weaker position than Deep Forest and Jan Garbarek. They do not have the same recourse to copyright protection, due to a lack of resources, national copyright laws, as well as limited infrastructure and distribution platforms. Lucas DiPasquale's use of music inspired by Popcaan in specific and Jamaican dancehall in particular raises questions about how both individual artists and countries with particular music traditions can assert their ownership rights. In the Ghanaian case, while individuals assert the rights to the contributions they make to traditional cloth weaving and printing, these claims are regulated through indigenous social relations, but not by Western copyright. This makes the contestation of its use by Chinese industrial wax printing facilities and African-American college graduates very difficult. Because who will make that claim and on what basis?

We argue that rather than resolving these issues solely through stronger enforcement of Western copyright, they need political attention ('how to protect creators in weak legal positions?'). Copyright alone will not resolve issues around 'traditional' expressions or communal creation, because it lacks the framework to deal with ownership claims where the originator is not a unique and sole individual.

CONCLUSIONS

Reggae is both a private endeavour of individual musicians and a matter of Jamaican national pride. However, as a globally popular music form, it is not only performed by Jamaicans. There are national reggae scenes and even reggae styles. For example, *Billboard* reggae writer, Pat Meschino, wrote of the distinct Hawaiian or Jawaiian reggae (Meschino 2018). The global popularity of reggae is what has made it a focus of government policy. Because what matters is both dignity *and* money.

Geographers Dominic Power and Daniel Hallencreutz conducted a comparative study of Stockholm and Kingston as cases of small cities that were innovation centres within the international music industry. They conclude that 'although Kingston's products have a far higher global commercial value than those from Stockholm, it is Stockholm's local production system and urban economy that make the bigger profit in real terms' (Power and Hallencreutz 2002, 1834). We argue that McCloskeyian dignity is a significant factor in this distinction between Kingston and Stockholm. Power and Hallencreutz focus on the differences IPR structure but fail to account for the high regard that Swedes and the Swedish government have for music as a part of the arts, facilitating significant public investment in the Swedish music industry.

In a 2017 survey on public music funding, Marc Hogan (2017) reported for *Pitchfork* Magazine that at least US$7.8 million went towards music in Sweden in 2016. In addition, there is considerable private sector funding of the industry with industry bodies reinvesting in their sector. One such is Export Sweden that coordinates Swedish participation in international trade fairs, festivals, seminars, and the like. Export Sweden is funded by major bodies within the Swedish music industry. Culture was funded and supported publicly by the Swedish government prior to the introduction of the cultural economy discourse. The Swedish Arts Council was founded in 1974 and the goal of Swedish cultural policy is to 'increase access for all who live in Sweden to culture, both via contact with culture of high quality and through creative activity of their own. Financial support for artists and cultural institutions is a key element of this policy'.[3]

The identity-oriented cultural policies of early independent Jamaica favoured building both the national project to legitimise the state and foster dignity in response to colonial oppression. In this context, the independence movement led to official acknowledgement of popular African and Afro-Jamaican cultural forms, but strictly within the cultural space. There was no discussion of the economic nationalism advocated by some elements within the black nationalist movement (Thomas 2004). Jamaican music became the soundtrack of resistance to this definition of nationhood (Chevannes 1995; Hope 2006; Stolzoff 2000). But while critics of the celebratory perspective of the cultural economy stress the need not to overplay the economic impact, it is helpful for cities, countries, and regions to balance a healthy concern for dignity with an equally healthy concern for money. The cultural economy is after all predicated on the economic benefit to both the individual creator and to the place of creation.

This chapter has highlighted the fraught nature of copyright in the global cultural economy. The systems to guarantee individual copyright are not enough to ensure that individuals are compensated if the power and knowledge is not in their favour. We spoke of songs being stolen by producers or copyright unacknowledged by broadcast companies. We see issues regarding the relative power of large corporations or citizens of certain countries whose copyright system is crafted for their own benefit, paralleling the colonial sensibilities of the earliest days of copyright. Lack of knowledge and economic resources can mean non-access to copyright's economic benefits that are collected, as in the case of Afunakwa and a number of reggae artistes.

We therefore argue that creativity is not only an individual endeavour, but one where we often stand on the shoulders of our ancestors, to paraphrase Bernard of Chartres and Isaac Newton. Early reggae artists were inspired by earlier artists. Kente and adinkra presented centuries of tradition and innovation in their designs. How do we ensure the moral and material rights of creators and creative communities are being protected? The discussion on the place of cultural and social rights with regard to IPRs is a long overdue discussion. However, we argue that discussion about accessible dispute mechanisms, particularly at the UN level, is overdue.

We therefore conclude that copyright, as presently implemented, is not an intrinsic guarantor of economic benefit, especially for the powerless in the global cultural economy. We do believe they are developmental outcomes that the global cultural economy can deliver, such as cultural and social rights, economic benefits, and identity. We also argue for a more expansive view of ownership and translating that into copyright, beyond a methodologically individualist legal regime that fails to equitably share both the moral and material interests of the global cultural economy, as the Universal Declaration of Human Rights argues it should.

NOTES

1 JAMMS is one of Jamaica's two music CMOs, which administers broadcasting and performance rights. It was incorporated in 2006, under the Copyright Act of Jamaica, and is a member of the International Federation of the Phonographic Industry (IFPI).
2 We are not arguing for wholesale copyright infringement. But we do question the vilification of piracy, as there are ample situations where weak copyright legislation and enforcement turns piracy into the only effective distribution mechanism.
3 www.kulturradet.se/en/In-English/Cultural-policy/.

REFERENCES

Alasuutari, Pertti. 2016. *The Synchronization of National Policies: Ethnography of the Global Tribe of Moderns*. 1st ed. London; New York, NY: Routledge.

Balasz, Bodó. 2011. "Coda: A Short History of Book Piracy". In *Media Piracy in Emerging Economies*, edited by Joe Karaganis, 399–413. New York, NY: Social Science Research Council.

Boateng, Boatema. 2011. *The Copyright Thing Doesn't Work Here: Adinkra and Kente Cloth and Intellectual Property in Ghana*. Minneapolis, MN: University of Minnesota Press.

Campbell, Curtis. 2012. "Is Jamaica Still the Reggae Capital of the World?" *Jamaica Gleaner*, sec. Entertainment. www.jamaica-gleaner.com/gleaner/20120715/ent/ent8.html.

Campbell, Curtis. 2016. "U.S. Watch List Limits Online Record Sales for Jamaicans". *The Sunday Gleaner*, July 17, 2016.

Campbell-Livingston, Cecilia. 2012. "Millions Owed". *Jamaica Observer*, August 26, 2012. www.jamaicaobserver.com/entertainment/MILLIONS-OWED_11092311.

Chevannes, Barry. 1995. *Rastafari: Roots and Ideology*. Syracuse, NY: Syracuse University Press.

De Beukelaer, Christiaan, and Martin Fredriksson. 2018. "The Political Economy of Piracy: The Paradox of Article 27 in Practice". *Review of African Political Economy*.

Drahos, Peter, and John Brathwaite. 2003. *Information Feudalism: Who Owns the Knowledge Economy?* Oxford: Oxford University Press.

Eckstein, Lars, and Anja Schwarz. 2014a. "Introduction: Towards a Postcolonial Critique of Modern Piracy". In *Postcolonial Piracy: Media Distribution and Cultural Production in the Global South*, edited by Lars Eckstein and Anja Schwarz, 1–25. Theory for Global Age. London; New York, NY: Bloomsbury.

Eckstein, Lars, and Anja Schwarz., eds. 2014b. *Postcolonial Piracy: Media Distribution and Cultural Production in the Global South*. London; New York, NY: Bloomsbury.

Feld, Steven. 2000. "A Sweet Lullaby for World Music". *Public Culture* 12 (1): 145–71.

Helfer, Laurence R. 2003. "Human Rights and Intellectual Property: Conflict or Coexistence". *Minnesota Intellectual Property Review* 5 (1): 47–61.

Helfer, Laurence R. 2007. "Toward a Human Rights Framework for Intellectual Property". *U.C. Davis Law Review* 40: 971–1020.

Hogan, Marc. 2017. "How Countries around the World Fund Music – and Why It Matters". *Pitchfork*, June 26, 2017.

Hope, Donna. 2006. *Inna Di Dancehall: Popular Culture and the Politics of Identity in Jamaica*. Kingston: University of the West Indies Press.

Howard, Denis. 2009. "Copyright and the Music Business in Jamaica – Protection for Whom?" *Revista Brasileira Do Caribe* 9 (18): 503–27.

JACAP. 2017. "JACAP Report to Ministry of Culture, Gender, Entertainment & Sport 2016". Kingston: Jamaica Association of Composers, Authors and Publishers (JACAP).

Jamaica Observer. 2010. "JAMMS Goes after Non-Compliant Music Users". *Jamaica Observer*, October 17, 2010, sec. Entertainment. www.jamaicaobserver.com/entertainment/JAMMS-goes-after-non-compliant-music-users_8062956.

James, Vanus. 2001. "The Caribbean Music Industry Database (CMID), 2000". Fort Lauderdale, FL: UNCTAD WIPO.

Kameir, Rawiya. 2015. "Is Dancehall Going to Be Mainstream Again?" *Fader*, June 12, 2015. www.thefader.com/2015/06/12/is-dancehall-going-to-be-mainstream-again.

Kernfeld, Barry Dean. 2011. *Pop Song Piracy: Disobedient Music Distribution since 1929*. Chicago, IL: University of Chicago Press.

Klein, Bethany, Giles Moss, and Lee Edwards. 2015. *Understanding Copyright: How the Digital Age Has Changed Intellectual Property*. Thousand Oaks, CA: Sage Publications.

Kochhar, Nazuk. 2017. "Ain't No Stopping Sister Nancy Now". *Fader*. www.thefader.com/2017/06/14/sister-nancy-interview-bam-bam.

Landes, William M. 2011. "Copyright". In *A Handbook of Cultural Economics, Second Edition*, edited by Ruth Towse, 2nd ed., 100–12. Cheltenham; Northampton, MA: Edward Elgar.

Larkin, Brian. 2008. *Signal and Noise: Media, Infrastructure, and Urban Culture in Nigeria*. Durham, NC: Duke University Press.

Lobato, Ramon. 2010. "Creative Industries and Informal Economies: Lessons from Nollywood". *International Journal of Cultural Studies* 13 (4): 337–54.

Matthes, Erich Hatala. 2016. "Cultural Appropriation Without Cultural Essentialism?" *Social Theory and Practice* 42 (2): 343–66.

Meschino, Patricia. 2018. "The Green on New Album 'Marching Orders' & Hawaii's Unique Reggae Scene". *Billboard*, February 21, 2018. www.billboard.com/articles/news/8098971/hawaiian-reggae-the-green-marching-orders.

Nurse, Keith. 2006. "The Cultural Industries in CARICOM: Trade and Development Challenges". Port of Spain: Caribbean Regional Negotiating Machinery. www.acpcultures.eu/pdf/The%20Cultural%20Industries%20in%20CARICOM.pdf.

Peukert, Alexander. 2016. "The Colonial Legacy of the International Copyright System". In *Copyright Africa: How Intellectual Property, Media and Markets Transform Immaterial Cultural Goods*, edited by Ute Röschenthaler and Mamadou Diawara, 37–68. Canon Pyon: Sean Kingston Publishing.

Power, Dominic, and Daniel Hallencreutz. 2002. "Profiting from Creativity? The Music Industry in Stockholm, Sweden and Kingston, Jamaica". *Environment and Planning A* 34 (10): 1833–54.

Rogers, Richard A. 2006. "From Cultural Exchange to Transculturation: A Review and Reconceptualization of Cultural Appropriation". *Communication Theory* 16 (4): 474–503.

Röschenthaler, Ute, and Mamadou Diawara, eds. 2016. *Copyright Africa: How Intellectual Property, Media and Markets Transform Immaterial Cultural Goods*. Canon Pyon: Sean Kingston Publishing.

Schultz, Mark, and Alec van Gelder. 2008. "Creative Development: Helping Poor Countries by Building Creative Industries". *Kentucky Law Journal* 97: 79–147.

Sell, Susan K. 2010. "The Rise and Rule of a Trade-Based Strategy: Historical Institutionalism and the International Regulation of Intellectual Property". *Review of International Political Economy* 17 (4): 762–90.

Shaheed, Farida. 2013. *Report of the Special Rapporteur in the Field of Cultural Rights, The Right to Freedom of Artistic Expression and Creativity*. A/HRC/23/34. Geneva: UNHCR.

Spence, Kim-Marie. 2018. "When Money Is Not Enough – Reggae, Dancehall and Policy in Jamaica". *Journal of Arts Management, Law and Society*, in press.

Stolzoff, Norman. 2000. *Wake the Town and Tell the People: Dancehall Culture in Jamaica*. London; Durham, NC: Duke University Press.

Taylor, Sharma. 2013. *Reggaenomics: The Relationship between Copyright Law and Development in the Jamaican Music Industry*. Wellington: Victoria University of Wellington.

Thomas, Deborah. 2004. *Modern Blackness: Nationalism, Globalization, and the Politics of Culture in Jamaica*. Durham, NC: Duke University Press.

Towse, Ruth. 2011. "What We Know, What We Don't Know and What Policy-Makers Would like Us to Know about the Economics of Copyright". *Review of Economic Research on Copyright Issues*, 8 (2): 101–20.

Toynbee, Jason. 2010. "Reggae Open Source: How the Absence of Copyright Enabled the Emergence of Popular Music in Jamaica". In *Copyright and Piracy: An Interdisciplinary Critique (Cambridge Intellectual Property and Information Law)*, edited by Lionel Bently, Jennifer Davis, and Jane Ginsburg, 357–73. Cambridge: Cambridge University Publishers.

UNESCO. 2005. *Convention on the Protection and Promotion of the Diversity of Cultural Expressions*. Paris: UNESCO.

Wallis, Roger, and Krister Malm. 1984. *Big Sounds from Small Peoples: The Music Industry in Small Countries*. London: Constable.

Witt, Emily. 2017. *Nollywood: The Making of a Film Empire*. New York, NY: Columbia Global Reports.

6

HUMAN DEVELOPMENT

In his address at Arterial Network's inaugural *African Creative Economy Conference* in Nairobi, Mike van Graan, Secretary General of the network at the time, gave a paper titled *The Creative Economy, Development, Culture, Human Rights and Democracy in Africa: Joining the Dots* (2011). This talk teased out some of the tensions between the cultural economy and human development. There are a few apparent paradoxes when it comes to the relationship.

While many African countries are renowned for their cultural diversity, vibrancy, and creativity, the spending power of most of their populations is too low to generate a healthy cultural economy (De Beukelaer 2015). Moreover, at the same time, UNCTAD reported that the combined share of 'creative goods' exports from African countries was less than 1% of global exports:

> In Africa, for instance, despite the abundance of creative talents, the creative potential remains highly underutilized. The continent's share in global trade of creative products remains marginal at less than 1 per cent of world exports despite sharp increases.
>
> (UNCTAD and UNDP 2008, iv)

The combined share of African countries in the global trade of 'creative goods' has however been more modest than this, as Figure 6.1

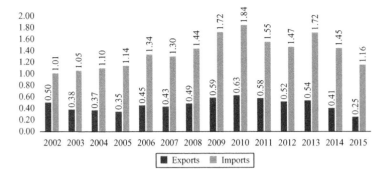

Figure 6.1 Combined share of African countries in global creative goods exports (2002–2015).

Source: UNCTAD www.unctadstat.unctad.org.

highlights. Exports averaged 0.46% throughout the period between 2002 and 2015, well below 1%. While there was some increase, there were decreases too, with the share dropping off to a mere 0.25% by 2015. Imports, on the contrary, are more significant at an average of 1.42%. At no point during this period do exports exceed imports, resulting in a constant negative balance of trade.

Mike van Graan does however stress that economic activity comes in different forms. In Nigeria for example, Nollywood – its film industry – employs more people than the oil industry, even if the latter generates more income (van Graan 2011, 2).[1] This raises questions about what to prioritise in policy: sectors that have high turnover, but employ relatively few people (such as the oil industry), or sectors that employ far more people, but have a more modest turnover (like the film industry)?

Development is far more than 'export earnings' or 'employment' alone. This is why the United Nations Development Programme (UNDP) has stressed the need to focus on 'human development'. This way of defining and measuring development includes non-economic indicators such as health and education. While the UNDP's Human Development Index paints a more nuanced and complex picture of the lives people are able to lead than gross domestic product (GDP) per capita, it remains limited in its ability to reflect the underlying capabilities they allude to (more about these capabilities below).

Arterial Network, a pan-African umbrella organisation for arts and culture, operates in a political context in which it cannot simply focus on arts and culture. Members of the network have to frame their work in relation to the development goals they seek to attain in order to get the recognition and credibility they need to find partners and funds. But rather than aligning with the development definition or focus of such partners, they have taken a more independent stance by defining development as:

> the ongoing generation and application of resources (financial, human, infrastructural and other) to create the optimal conditions (political, cultural, social, economic and other) in which human beings may enjoy the full range of human rights and freedoms enshrined in the Universal Declaration of Human Rights.
>
> (Cited in Graan 2011, 4)

The focus on the 'conditions' in which people live chimes with the 'capabilities' that underlie human development. These 'capabilities' are the concept at the core of the liberal normative theory that underpins the idea of human development. Amartya Sen, its chief architect, argues that development does not lie in the mere utility of development (for which the disposable income someone may have is a useful, but incomplete, proxy), but in the ability of people to have the social, political, and economic freedom (Sen 1999) to choose the life 'they have reason to value' (Sen 1992, 5), which implies the significance of human rights as we discuss later in this chapter – but also dignity, as we argue throughout this book.

In the next section, we will explore in greater detail what 'human development' ought to entail in our view. What matters here is that Arterial Network's definition of 'development' is far more rights-based than 'human development'. And having high levels of human development does not mean human rights are adequately protected:

> Libya and Tunisia were at the top of the 2010 African HDI list, before the recent revolutions. What the overthrows of the Libyan and Tunisian dictatorships show is that human development is not sufficient and do not compensate for the absence of other human rights and

freedoms . . . The lessons from North Africa for tl
you can have levels of economic growth, high
development in terms of life expectancy, educatio
you can serve the geo-political, security and econor
powerful north, but ordinary people will demand tl
and fundamental freedoms.

(Graan 2011, 3–4)

In response to these challenges, Arterial Network has rightly set an ambitious goal for both the development of the continent and for the role the cultural economy can play in this. The underlying message is clear: for the cultural economy to work there is a need for economic development, human development, and human rights. But cultural expressions are also a part of the struggle to get there. This raises a key question: how does the cultural economy contribute to human development (as we will discuss in the next section), while also relying on other dimensions of human development to function properly? And how do we ensure human rights are respected in when talking about the cultural or creative economy, which has in many ways depoliticised the discourse about the arts by favouring economic performance over cultural value? (Da Costa 2016; see also Chapter one).

To that end, we break down the link between the cultural economy and human development. First, we explore what kind of claims cultural economy reports and documents make about human development. Second, we explore what human development stands for in the literature. Third, we explore the difference between *capacity building* and advancing *capabilities*. Fourth, we explore how cultural rights relate to human development.

CULTURAL ECONOMY AND HUMAN DEVELOPMENT?

The cultural economy elicits claims about the economic impact of culture in societies around the world. But it also inspires a broad range of other claims concerning the role culture can, could, and does play in those societies. One of the claims that features prominently in United Nations *Creative Economy Reports* and discourses is the role culture and creativity can play in terms of 'human development'.

e United Nations Conference on Trade and Development (UNCTAD)[2] made such a claim explicit in their *Creative Economy Reports:*[3]

> [The creative economy] can foster income generation, job creation and export earnings while promoting social inclusion, cultural diversity and *human development.*
>
> (UNCTAD and UNDP 2010, 10, emphasis added)

The United Nations Educational, Scientific and Cultural Organisation (UNESCO)[4] made a similar claim.

> This special edition of the Creative Economy Report argues that creativity and culture are processes or attributes that are intimately bound up in the imagining and generation of new ideas, products or ways of interpreting the world. All these have monetary and non-monetary benefits that can be recognized as instrumental to *human development.* Transformational change is thus understood within a broader framework of *human development* and is recognized as a process that enhances the effective freedom of the people to pursue *whatever they have reason to value.*
>
> (UNESCO and UNDP 2013, 16, emphasis added)

Yudhishthir Raj Isar also contextualises this narrative as follows:

> For the 2013 report, UNESCO made the reasoned choice of a perspective that would analyse the potential of the cultural economy at the local level in developing countries and locate it squarely within a less economistic paradigm, that of human development.
>
> (Isar 2015, 480)

The United Nations *Creative Economy Reports* are not the only ones to make such claims. When Danielle Cliche (UNESCO's Chief of Section on the Diversity of Cultural Expressions) argues that 'public support for new emerging, experimental art forms and expressions should therefore not be considered mere subsidy to consumption but an investment in *human development*' (Cliche 2015, 18).[5]

Across the board, the claim is clear: the cultural economy is instrumental to human development. But a clear articulation of what human development means in this context, how culture contributes to it, and how we can substantiate such claims is lacking. Yet UNESCO's 'special edition' of the Report (2013) does not systematically demonstrate how the 'panoply of practice' contributes to human development. While the evidence that is provided may be sufficient for readers who work in the cultural economy and will draw such conclusions by following implicit assumptions, the examples and arguments lack the precision and systematic treatment needed to convince others. We therefore think there are good reasons to ask for clear evidence-based reasoning to flesh out such claims, which are rooted in a rigorous empirical but also theoretical understanding of human development.

These Reports do not seek to define with clarity and precision what 'human development' means. Human development is a complex concept that is central to a normative theory developed by political philosophers Sen (1999) and Martha Nussbaum (2011). It has a very specific meaning that relates to the way individuals may attain the capabilities that allow them to live the lives 'they have reason to value', as Sen (1992, 5) puts it. There is much in the cultural economy that may help towards attaining greater capabilities. But these contributions are not self-evident. Or more specifically, do the products and processes of the cultural economy help us lead the lives 'we have reason to value'? In any case, insufficient research has been done to provide such evidence.

In recent years, there has been some engagement with the links between capabilities and the cultural economy (Dave 2015; De Beukelaer 2015; Hesmondhalgh 2016; Moss 2018), but the tone and message of this literature is far more cautious than that of the *Creative Economy Reports*. Before we engage with these questions in detail, let us reiterate how the claims made in the *Creative Economy Reports* go largely unsubstantiated in two significant ways – despite the different framing of UNCTAD's (2008, 2010) and UNESCO's (2013) reports.

First, there is no systematic basis on which these reports and the work of other advocates of the cultural economy establish the processes and outcomes through which it contributes to human development. The causal link is assumed and not explained or evidenced. This does not mean the claims are necessarily false, but that there is no conceptual framework against which these claims can be measured. There is thus no explicit theoretical connection between the cultural economy and human development in these policy-oriented documents. As these writings do not clearly define or conceptualise human development, the evidence they provide of the contributions the cultural economy makes to *development* are difficult to evaluate against contributions of the cultural economy to *human development* – which are two different things.

However, international trade flows serve as a proxy for development in UNCTAD's *Creative Economy Reports*. This goes against the core principle of human development that stresses that the economy is *not* a sufficient indicator of development. Moreover, these reports (and their associated datasets) retain a simple dichotomy between developed and developing countries, without using the more nuanced degrees of human development as used by UNDP. There is no explicit evidence of how the cultural economy contributes to education or health (the two other key indicators UNDP uses), nor a discussion of how it relates to the underlying principles of human development and the capabilities approach.

Second, the academic and policy literature on human development and capabilities has paid little attention to culture so far. Amartya Sen and Martha Nussbaum both argue that the capabilities approach has emerged from global debates between academics, which would give the approach universal validity beyond cultural specificity (Nussbaum 2011; Sen 1999), even if their theory presupposes a liberal foundation (Fabre and Miller 2003).

The more convincing (although not entirely unproblematic) defence of the global validity of the capabilities approach is that it is a normative tool. In that function, it effectively serves as a global basic framework for justice, much like human rights (e.g. Sen 1999, 227–248), which builds on fundaments from all across the world. Against a more culturally relativist reading, Sen (1999, 242) argues that 'while there is some danger in ignoring the uniqueness of cultures, there is also the possibility of being deceived by the presumption of ubiquitous insularity'.

The explicit engagement with how culture can play a helpful part in articulating and working towards capabilities remains limited. The book *Culture and Public Action* edited by Rao and Walton (2004a) is a rare exception. Following Sen's discourse, they argue that 'culture is part of the set of capabilities that people have – the constraints, technologies, and framing devices that condition how decisions are made and coordinated across different actors' (Rao and Walton 2004b, 4). Overall, this book primarily focuses on the role of culture (as a *way of life*) on development processes and institutions (see e.g. Arizpe 2004). A more innovative approach is articulated by Appadurai (2004), who focuses on the *Capacity to Aspire* as a fundamental tenet of development thinking. He starts from the observation that 'it is in culture that ideas of the future, as much as those about the past, are embedded and nurtured' (2004, 59). He thus reads 'Sen's work as a major invitation to anthropology to widen its conception of how human beings engage their own futures' (2004, 63). But here too, explicit accounts of the cultural economy remain marginal at best.

On the whole, the human development and capabilities approach does not address the way the cultural economy relates to human development in practical terms. Human development theorists have become interested in how culture could help articulate the future, but they pay no attention to how these cultural expressions may operate in a socio-economic context (through 'cultural industries' or otherwise) and make no mention at all about the possible role these industries could play to help attain human development – contrary to UN reports that claim these industries can play such a role.

More importantly, rather than merely going unchecked, claims about human development are constructed as a circular argument: the cultural economy supposedly fosters human development, but it does in fact rely on human development in order to function (De Beukelaer 2015). The claims about human development combine diverse ideas as if they are pretty much the same. We argue they are not. Throughout this chapter we aim to expose this paradox by clarifying how the cultural economy *can* indeed contribute to human development, but it is a sector that also strongly *relies* on high levels of human development in order to function.

While arguing for the role culture can play in development processes, both UNCTAD and UNESCO do however stress the need for a range of interventions, investments, and improvements to make the 'creative industries' work. UNCTAD's 2010 edition of the report indicates that:

> Developing countries face huge obstacles, such as lack of investment and entrepreneurial skills, inadequate infrastructure, absence of appropriate financing mechanisms and weak institutional and legal frameworks to support the growth of the creative industries.
>
> (UNCTAD and UNDP 2010, 224)

UNESCO's 2013 'special edition' of the report addresses a range of structural constraints, such as access to finance, IPR and copyright regulation and enforcement, institution-building, mobility, and access to global markets as structural constraints limiting the working of the 'creative industries' in 'developing' countries. At the same time, the report proposes investing in local capacity-building: 'investing in skills, education, training, and infrastructure so as to allow the 'creative industries' to grow and operate in a wider context' (UNESCO and UNDP 2013, 112).

Before discussing the difference between 'capabilities' (which are central to human development) and 'capacities' (a staple term in development-speak, referring to knowledge and skills), we'll explore the meaning of *human development* in the literature.

HUMAN DEVELOPMENT: DEVELOPING HUMANS?

Development refers to both an intransitive dynamic process (*developing*) and a transitive static objective (*being developed*). Because of this dual meaning, debates around development often talk about objective and process as one and the same. When in the mid-20th century, the term took on its present-day meaning, the 'static objective' of development was the attainment of the 'modernity' that characterised advanced industrialised economies. The 'dynamic process' to get there was the 'development' of economies, institutions, and people to the image of countries that had allegedly been developed already. However, the use and history of the term is contested and it remains subject to ongoing debate about what it is, how it should be executed, and whom it should benefit (see, for example, Nederveen Pieterse 2010). Before we'll look into the precise meaning of 'human development', we will explore what 'development' means.

In his seminal book *Encountering Development: The Making and Unmaking of the Third World*, Arturo Escobar identifies the inaugural speech of US President Harry S. Truman in 1949 as the starting point of the contemporary use of 'development'. In that speech, Truman argued that the solution to the 'misery' of poor countries would be to adopt 'modern scientific and technical knowledge' as a way to ascertain progress (Truman 1949, cited in Escobar 1995, 3). This led to the conflation of 'modernisation' with development and meant that the teleological shift towards a known endpoint ('development') was taken for granted. However, modernisation is no longer the self-evident objective of development, not at least because it is unclear *which* modernity is the objective of this process (Nederveen Pieterse 2010). Some critics in fact question if modernisation ever really was a viable and desirable goal, as it undermines existing knowledge, social structures, and economic arrangements (Rahnema and Bawtree 1997). And yet, since the 1950s, the business of 'development' has been the moral obligation of 'developed' countries towards 'developing' countries; William Easterly paraphrases Rudyard Kipling's poem *The White Man's Burden* in his critical account of the (often failed) attempts to help 'develop' countries (Easterly 2006).[6]

Beyond the discussion of what development *is*, there is much disagreement about how to attain development. Here too, perspectives depend greatly on political ideology. Free-market proponents like Moyo (2010) argue that 'overseas development assistance' (or 'aid') does not work because it distorts markets. Some argue 'good governance' is needed to ensure development, even if that narrative is often a thin cover for structural adjustment (Abrahamsen 2000). While others make the case that 'development' serves to depoliticise attempts to eradicate poverty (Ferguson 1990). Anti- or post-development scholars like Rahnema and Bawtree (1997) argue that the root problem of the ineffectiveness of development interventions is its static objective, rather than the dynamic process meant to attain it.

Some argue the issue runs deeper than whether or not 'development' is effective. The dichotomy between 'developed' and 'developing' countries, that have respectively either reached the static objective of development or are in the dynamic process of development.

This dichotomy is however difficult to maintain. At its extremes of this continuum (for no country is either developed or underdeveloped in absolute terms), one could somehow argue that the distinction holds up; people do generally lead more secure and prosperous lives in Norway than they do in Niger. But how do we know this?

The easiest way to gauge the level of development is by looking at the economic activity that takes places. This activity is measured through the combined turnover of all economic transactions, which is expressed as gross domestic product (GDP). In 2016, World Bank data reveal that there were ten countries with a GDP per capita of less than US$500 per year:[7] The Gambia, Liberia, Somalia, The Democratic Republic of Congo, Madagascar, Central African Republic, Mozambique, Niger, Malawi, and Burundi. This means that the average sum of economic transactions in that year was less than US$1.5 per day per person. In contrast, there are ten countries with a GDP per capita above US$50,000 per year: Switzerland, Macao (SAR), Norway, Ireland, Iceland, Qatar, the US, Denmark, Singapore, and Sweden. Luxembourg tops that list, with a GDP per capita of just over US$100,000.

While GDP is an easy indicator of economic performance as it goes up when economy grows (good) and goes down when the economy contracts (bad), we can ask if it is also a useful indicator. Fioramonti (2013) is one of the many critics who argues it is not. If it is, we should be able to indicate when a country shifts from being 'developing' to being 'developed', when it shifts from being in the dynamic process to having attained the static objective. Take China, for example. The country's GDP stood at US$8,123.18 in 2016, just above the average of the World Bank's category of *Upper Middle Income* countries, which stands at US$7,994.02. Does that mean China is a developed or a developing country? It's hard to tell, because even when we use the developed and developing in opposition to each other, and as categories, there is no agreed-upon threshold.

When does a country stop being 'developing' and start being 'developed'? This distinction is so vague that the United Nations statistical office has no official definition or categorisation, they even state this explicitly: 'There is no established convention for the designation of 'developed' and 'developing' countries or areas in the United Nations system'.[8] The International Monetary Fund similarly argues that 'This classification is not based on strict criteria, economic or otherwise, and it has evolved over time. The objective is to facilitate analysis by providing a reasonably meaningful method of organizing data'.[9]

In 2016, however, the World Bank Group dropped the distinction from their statistical datasets and reporting, because the distinction 'is becoming less relevant' (Fantom et al. 2016). Though it is not clear if the distinction is less relevant because differences are getting smaller *between* countries, because differences are increasing *within* countries, or if the simple opposition simply not a useful one. Either way, while the classification based on GDP data is arbitrary (because there is no rationale), the reliance on the data remains prominent.

The prevailing conception remains that development is a straightforward analytical tool to understand the world. This relies in part on the way development is commonly expressed: through economic measures. In Chapter one, we have explored and explained the complex relation between culture and the economy. What matters here is that development is reduced to the economy, and that the economy is reduced to a single indicator: GDP. Simon Kuznets developed this in the 1930s for the US Department of Commerce. The measure had one simple purpose: 'generate a series of aggregate measures capable of condensing all economic production by individuals, companies, and the government into a single number, which should rise in good times and fall in bad' (Fioramonti 2013, 25–26). While this is a useful – and popular – way of expressing economic performance, it reduces human activity to economic performance. The underlying issue is that GDP does not reflect development; it is a proxy *for* development. This in turn means that there is a political incentive to devise policies to improve the performance of the proxy, which is not necessarily the same as improving people's livelihoods. Human development is a philosophical approach that aims to resolve this issue in a normative, yet pragmatic manner.

Martha C. Nussbaum and Amartya Sen, two of the key thinkers behind this approach, frame human development in terms of 'capabilities', or the extent to which we have the freedom and ability to make choices about our lives that reflect our own (development) objectives that we have 'reason to value' (Sen 2009, 231). Amartya Sen frames these capabilities very loosely in terms of 'political freedoms, economic facilities, social opportunities, transparency guarantees, and protective securities' (Sen 1999, 10), but refrains from providing a clear list of capabilities that we should focus on in terms of practical intervention.

Martha C. Nussbaum does however propose a clear list of capabilities that ought to form the basis of an aspirational articulation of well-being (Nussbaum 2016). She argues that their use of capabilities goes beyond their comparative use in the UNDP reports, as they focus more on the underlying political philosophy (Nussbaum 2011, 17). That underlying political philosophy is liberal one, rooted in methodological individualism. It provides a basis to compare the extent to which people are able to make choices about their lives. The focus is on choices (*capabilities*) rather than their outcomes (*functionings*), as the former allows for pluralism when it comes to people's values: this illustrates the liberal slant of the capability approach:

> The purpose of global development, like the purpose of a good domestic national policy, is to enable people to live full and creative lives, developing their potential and fashioning a meaningful existence commensurate with their equal human dignity.
>
> (Nussbaum 2011, 185)

While 'development' is about humans' contribution to the economy, 'human development' is about advancing people's capabilities in society. So, development is about what people *do*, while human development is about what people are *able to do*.

The human development approach builds rationale because 'development' is more complex and broader than economic growth; GDP is an inadequate measure and pursuing a policy agenda that prioritises economic growth will not be able to address major underlying challenges. Worse, it is in fact counterproductive to only measure economic growth, as this provides political incentives to focus on economic growth as a policy objective instead of incorporating health, wellbeing, cultural vitality, and so on. This is why the United Nations Development Programme (UNDP) economist Mahbub ul Haq developed the Human Development Index (HDI), which is central to UNDP's annual Human Development Reports.

The HDI is a composite index that includes three elements in equal measure: health (life expectancy), education (a composite of mean and expected years of schooling), and income (gross national income per capita, indexed on a scale from US$100 to US$75,000). Including these measures gives politicians a reason to include health and education, alongside economic performance, in order to rise in the UNDP human development rankings. While less imprecise and less skewed than GDP, the HDI remains a crude measure for development.

At its extremes, the Human Development Index is quite sensible, as Norway is somewhere on top and Niger somewhere at the bottom again. But what about the countries in the middle?

Some academics, like Neuwirth (2013), make the case that the dichotomy between 'developed' and 'developing' countries makes little or no sense. In contrast, he argues that 'we all live in developing countries' because being able to ever really attain a static objective (*being developed*), every country is in fact in a constant process of change that is reflected in the dynamic process (*developing*). While this does not absolve us from the need of analytical categories, it does stress the deeply flawed basis of this particular one. And yet, the opposition of developed and developing countries does not only exist as an analytical tool, but as an expression of power. As quite a few countries benefit from this classification, they are unwilling to let go of it, even if it is important when it comes to rethinking how development is approached both in multilateral and bilateral relations (Baumann 2017).

In sum, it should be clear by now that 'human development' is not something the cultural economy intrinsically contributes towards, as the UNCTAD *Creative Economy Reports* suggest. There is so much disagreement about both what the objectives are and how to attain them, that claims about how the cultural economy will somehow drive human development should be met with caution. More specifically, we argue that the claims about culture's contribution to development and the cultural economy's needs conceal an important fact: the cultural economy may contribute to development, but it relies on development too. For example, in order to accrue the societal benefit of well-run cultural institutions, the social, economic, and political context must enable people to set up and maintain such institutions, which is often a major challenge (De Beukelaer 2016). This implies that the cultural economy is at once a driver and the result of development.

In a conventional development framework, this is sensible: investing in infrastructure, access to finance, and enforcing legislation will help a sector grow and make it contribute to development – at least in economic terms. But when it comes to *human* development, one would expect a focus on capabilities as a means to strengthening the cultural economy, not just capacities. And yet, these reports neither clarify if and how the cultural economy would enhance people's *capabilities*, nor how we should strengthen capabilities for the cultural economy to flourish, as they rather focus on capacity-building (De Beukelaer 2015). But what is the difference between 'capacities' and 'capabilities', and why does this matter?

POLICY AND PRACTICE: CAPACITY BUILDING AND CAPABILITIES

The relation between capabilities and the cultural economy is difficult to pinpoint because the former is the basis of an abstract normative theory of justice, while the latter are a concept that helps us look at social and economic processes in the economics of culture in a pragmatic and empirical way.

Martha Nussbaum argues that capabilities are 'fundamental entitlements' (2003) in the sense that they form a more practical and concrete set of rights than the notions (and declarations) of human rights allow. Nomi Dave points out that:

> Nussbaum distinguishes between Western conceptions of rights as 'negative liberties', in which legal protections exist and the state must 'keep its hands off', and the conception of rights as affirmative, which emphasizes states' obligations to act (Nussbaum 2003, 39). The capabilities approach shares this latter 'right to' emphasis. In this regard, Nussbaum has outlined ten central human capabilities that she sees as fundamental entitlements.
>
> (Dave 2015, 13)

In the practical context of linking the cultural economy to human development, our objective is twofold. First, we need to define the 'achieved functionings' that development is meant to foster through *capabilities*. Second, this agenda can then help define what kind of *capacities* are needed to do so.

The first step is to build on the freedoms and capabilities of people (within and beyond) the 'cultural industries' to help think about what the 'achieved functionings' are that they want to attain. The UNESCO *Creative Economy Report* (2013, see chapter six) provides a helpful overview of categories in which planners and policy makers may consider developing indicators. Selecting indicators presupposes a debate about what the objectives are of focusing on 'cultural industries'. Particularly section 6.5 of the report (UNESCO and UNDP 2013, 128–131) focuses explicitly on outcomes: what are the economic, social, cultural, and environmental outcomes to be attained through working with the 'cultural industries'? As there are more options than can realistically be focused on, this is thus a matter of choice. The freedoms and capabilities to choose and deliberate the path towards a life 'we have reason to value' (Sen 1992, 5) is thus crucial.

Sen's approach has been criticised. Pierluigi Sacco, Guido Ferilli, and Giorgio Blessi, for example, claim that Sen's approach is prone to 'cultural parochialism, i.e. a self-indulgent, community-centered approach to cultural expression and participation that need not evolve into developmental social dynamics' (2014, 9) even though, they continue that:

> In principle, this bias is in contrast with a rigorous interpretation of the capability approach, which makes room for virtually unlimited paths of personal and community human development and thus for the gradual construction of a comprehensive, inclusive knowledge society. But in practice, if individuals have little interest in the quality (i.e. in the cognitive richness and articulation) of cultural contents, beyond some basic level they will likely be willing to trade off further improvements of their cultural capabilities for the social reward of more inclusive, easy-going forms of cultural participation, thereby jeopardising cultural innovation, originality and sophistication of contents both on the side of supply (production) and on that of demand (access and participation).
>
> (Sacco et al. 2014, 9)

This critique does however overlook that greater capabilities will allow people to make informed choices about what they deem worthy. That is why capabilities are crucial to defining the *kinds* of cultural expressions and industries that should be pursued and the *kinds* of 'achieved functionings' culture *for* development are meant to foster.

The second step, once policy objectives in terms of *capabilities* have been defined and the current state of things is assessed, is to assess what kinds of *capacities* are needed to attain the set objectives. In this context, Andy Pratt (2013) argues that 'capacity building is about removing a barrier to development through the investment in skills, training, education, and infrastructure such that industries are "scalable"'. While this is a valid argument, it does not address what *kinds* of capacities need building. Pratt argues that 'in most places the creative economy is new, [and] there is no pre-existing tradition of extended production to build on, hence the project is almost to begin from scratch'. But much depends on the definition of 'extended production'.

The cultural economy however preceded the jargon we currently use (e.g. 'creative industries'), even if existing practices might have been makeshift, informal, or even illegal. While this is not true of Pratt's approach, capacity building perspectives that fail to address existing practices, may risk operating in a framework of modernisation that fails to recognise existing socio-economic structures. Moreover, he argues that there is an 'entire range of support skills without which many creative events and processes cannot take place'. This is true, but defining the objectives of the 'cultural industries' (*what should they help attain?*) precedes the definition of activities (*what kind of activities are needed to attain the said goals?*) and those, in turn, precede the assessment of skills needed to develop such events and processes. This is why the identification and articulation of the 'achieved functionings' should precede the articulation of the capacity building needs.

There is however a resulting need to articulate the capacity building needs and the ways in which these skills can be learned. So, while both capabilities and capacities are essential, the former is the primary concern of human development, whereas the latter is central to practical interventions. And we argue that if policy documents and reports are making claims about the contributions of the cultural economy to human development, the foundations of the human development and capabilities approach should be taken seriously. In fact, rather than reducing capabilities to a technical issue ('capacities'), we should embrace a more ambitious political agenda by stressing the need to put human rights as a set of non-negotiable principles.

THE 'CULTURAL RIGHT' TO HUMAN DEVELOPMENT?

Rather than go along with the significantly depoliticised mainstream use of the cultural economy in relation to development (Da Costa 2016; Lee 2016), we'd like to return to Mike van Graan's comments about the importance of human rights. There are two important ways in which the links between cultural rights and human development matter, which are rooted in the Universal Declaration of Human Rights:

1   Everyone has the right freely to participate in the cultural life of the community, to enjoy the arts and to share in scientific advancement and its benefits.
2   Everyone has the right to the protection of the moral and material interests resulting from any scientific, literary or artistic production of which he is the author.

Universal Declaration of Human Rights, Article 27

One important connection between human rights and human development is that everyone should be able to partake in cultural life, which includes the freedom of expression to do so without persecution. While not every artist is (or has to be) a rebel, for the cultural economy to contribute to healthy debate and dialogue, it is crucial that artists have the liberty to express their thoughts (and also the ability to materially benefit; see Chapter five). Arterial Network recognised this as a particular difficulty across many African countries and founded Art Watch Africa, which published the report *Monitoring Freedom of Creative Expression* (Art Watch Africa 2013). This report is an overview of the extent to which freedom of expression is protected by law, and the extent to which these laws are upheld, in 47 countries across the continent. While the report is a helpful starting point, it remains limited by its formulaic nature. Due to the wide geographical scope, the country profiles seem to have taken most information at face value, leaving many questions about nuance and contradictions that exist surrounding the protection of artistic expression in these countries.

In 2016, Arterial Network published a very different kind of report: *How Free Is FREE? Reflections on Freedom of Creative Expression in Africa* (Arterial Network 2016). This document presents a range of texts, written by artists, activists, and academics in an attempt to provide greater detail about the issues that exist across the continent, alongside a range of solutions, or attempts to get to solutions.

With reference to the context in Burkina Faso, theatre scholar Mahamadou Mandé, argues that 'beyond the legal and regulatory framework, it should be noted that the vast majority of Burkina Faso's artists have always enjoyed freedom of action and creation due to the lack of official censorship structures' (Mandé 2016, 97–98), but continues to provide a wide array of examples that musicians, journalists, filmmakers, theatre-makers, and writers have been subjected to pressure, exclusion, and harassment under the regime of François Compaoré, the country's President between 1987 and 2014. The paradox is that despite retaliations against, and the exclusion of artists, it was a group of musicians that led the charge against Blaise Compaoré in 2014 (Chouli 2015; Frère and Englebert 2015). Two of the most visible figures of this popular uprising were Sam'k Le Jah and Smockey (a homonym for 'se moquer', 'to poke fun at'). They mobilised the youth of Ouagadougou (and inspired them in other cities), under the name of the Balai Citoyen ('citizen broom') to sweep clean the politics of the country.

One consideration to make here is that the use of music as a political tool in Burkina Faso highlights the paradox of human development: while music was used as a tool to attain greater freedom of expression, musicians in fact really needed that freedom of expression to speak up. Freedom of expression, like capabilities, are not something that a society will maintain once it has been attained. Quite to the contrary, both actually require constant effort and struggle to maintain. We should thus, as Nomi Dave argues, move beyond a mere assumption that music makes a positive contribution to society by exploring what it actually ends up doing in relation and through capabilities (Dave 2015).

Another consideration to bear in mind about the connection between human rights and human development is that everyone has the right to benefit from the revenues ('material interests') that may result from their creations. This means that while everyone can create, those creations that generate revenues should benefit the artist. It does however neither mean that the artist should get *all* revenues, nor that *all* artists should get paid for what they create. Farida Shaheed, a former Special Rapporteur in the field of cultural rights for the United Nations *Human Rights Office of the High Commissioner* (OHCHR), made the case that the economic side of cultural rights (copyright) should not trump the right to participation and access (Shaheed 2013, 2014) – as discussed in Chapter five.

CONCLUSIONS

There are many ways through which the cultural economy could contribute to human development. But human development itself is also a precondition to the effective functioning of the cultural economy. This means that while there is potential to foster human development through the cultural economy, the potential of the cultural economy is often hampered by a lack of human development (De Beukelaer 2015).

The crux here is that the cultural economy is not intrinsically a driver of human development. At least it isn't if we assess the role of the cultural economy against either the philosophical foundations laid out by Amartya Sen and Martha Nussbaum, or the more pragmatic and quantitative approach used by the United Nations Development Programme. However, the cultural economy can be one of the mechanisms that help attaining human development goals by strengthening capabilities if there are explicit provisions in policy and implementation that focus on attaining these specific goals. In this sense, claims about human development outcomes are quite similar to claims about inclusion or sustainable development, which we discuss elsewhere in this book: There is a real potential, but not one that materialises easily or naturally, as the reports and policy documents we have cited suggest.

As ever, both the cultural economy and human development require careful analysis, conceptual precision, and focused strategic action in order to attain the particular outcomes envisaged. More specifically, if the cultural economy is meant to help foster capabilities and human development, these objectives should be made explicit in detail and should come with very specific strategies to attain these goals. In the absence of clear goals, priorities, and targeted interventions, human development is unlikely to materialise through the cultural economy.

NOTES

1   And it is Nollywood that now serves as a success story of the cultural economy on the continent (Witt 2017), even the film industry managed to grow despite difficult trading conditions, including the sale of unauthorised DVDs (Larkin 2008; Lobato 2010).

2   The United Nations Conference on Trade and Development (UNCTAD) was founded in 1964 in an attempt of 'developing' countries to rectify the lack of balance and fairness in global trade streams and regulations. Raúl Prebisch, UNCTAD's first Secretary General, was an Argentine economist and one of the foundational theorists of dependency theory, which significantly influenced the work and stance of the organisation. Since its inception, UNCTAD has been a vocal voice for the interests of 'developing' countries (the Group 77, which founded UNCTAD – and became a formal power block in doing so). See the historical overview of the organisation by Karshenas (2016) for greater detail.

3   The series of *Creative Economy Reports* (2008; 2010; 2013; 2013) has been published by different organisations. This has influenced their tone and message considerably. UNCTAD published the first *Creative Economy Reports* in 2008 and 2010 under the direction of Edna dos Santos-Duisenberg. They focused primarily on international trade, as per the mandate of the organisation, and continued to do so in their 2016 version, led by Carolina Quintana and René Kooyman. UNESCO, however, published the 2013 'special edition' of the report for which Yudhishthir Raj Isar was the principal investigator and lead author, under the direction of Danielle Cliché, Secretary of the 2005 Convention.

4   The United Nations Educational, Scientific and Cultural Organisation was founded in 1945 as a post-war institution 'that would reflect enlightenment values in seeking to end human violence through education' (Singh 2011, 1). The preamble of UNESCO's constitution notes that 'since wars begin in the minds of men [sic], it is in the minds of men [sic] that the defenses of peace must be structured' (UNESCO 1945). The background and programme of the organisation, as articulated by its first Director-General Huxley (1946), evokes Emmanuel Kant's treatise *Perpetual Peace* (1775) as both a guiding principle and a grand objective of the new international organisation.

5   Interestingly, in the report, Cliche (2015, 22) uses the definition of *human development* above in the same text to define *sustainable development*. This illustrates the

conceptual overlaps and lack of precision in debates about both 'human' and 'sustainable' development, as we discuss in Chapter seven.

6 Rudyard Kipling (1899): 'Take up the White Man's burden/The savage wars of peace/Fill full the mouth of famine/And bid the sickness cease'.

7 www.data.worldbank.org/indicator/NY.GDP.PCAP.CD.

8 www.unstats.un.org/unsd/methods/m49/m49regin.htm.

9 www.imf.org/external/pubs/ft/weo/faq.htm.

REFERENCES

Abrahamsen, Rita. 2000. *Disciplining Democracy: Development Discourse and Good Governance in Africa*. London; New York, NY: Zed Books.

Appadurai, Arjun. 2004. "The Capacity to Aspire". In *Culture and Public Action: A Cross-Disciplinary Dialogue on Development Policy*, edited by Vijayendra Rao and Michael Walton, 59–84. Stanford, CA; London: Stanford University Press.

Arizpe, Lourdes. 2004. "The Intellectual History of Culture and Development Institutions". In *Culture and Public Action: A Cross-Disciplinary Dialogue on Development Policy*, edited by Vijayendra Rao and Michael Walton, 163–84. Stanford, CA; London: Stanford University Press.

Art Watch Africa. 2013. "Monitoring Freedom of Creative Expression". *Arterial Network Report*. Cape Town: Arterial Network.

Arterial Network, ed. 2016. *How Free Is Free? Reflections on Freedom of Expression in Africa*. Cape Town: Arterial Network. www.arterialnetwork.org/ckeditor_assets/attachments/332/howfreeisfree-updated_final_31082016.pdf.

Baumann, M.-O. 2017. "Forever North–South? The Political Challenges of Reforming the UN Development System". *Third World Quarterly* 39 (4): 626–41.

Chouli, Lila. 2015. "L'insurrection Populaire et La Transition Au Burkina Faso". *Review of African Political Economy* 42 (143): 148–55.

Cliche, Danielle. 2015. "Introduction". In *Re-Shaping Cultural Policies*, edited by UNESCO. Paris: UNESCO.

Da Costa, Dia. 2016. *Politicizing Creative Economy: Activism and a Hunger Called Theater*. Dissident Feminisms. Urbana, IL: University of Illinois Press.

Dave, Nomi. 2015. "Music and the Myth of Universality: Sounding Human Rights and Capabilities". *Journal of Human Rights Practice* 7 (1): 1–17.

De Beukelaer, Christiaan. 2015. *Developing Cultural Industries: Learning from the Palimpsest of Practice*. Amsterdam: European Cultural Foundation.

De Beukelaer, Christiaan. 2016. "The Social and Built Infrastructure of Cultural Policy: Between Selective Popular Memory and Future Plans". *International Journal of Cultural Policy*, DOI: 10.1080/10286632.2016.1248951.

Easterly, William. 2006. *The White Man's Burden: Why the West's Efforts To Aid the Rest Have Done So Much Ill and So Little Good*. New York, NY: Penguin Press.

Escobar, Arturo. 1995. *Encountering Development: The Making and Unmaking of the Third World*. Princeton, NJ: Princeton University Press.

Fabre, Cécile, and David Miller. 2003. "Justice and Culture: Rawls, Sen, Nussbaum and O'Neill". *Political Studies Review* 1 (1): 4–17.

Fantom, Neil, Tariq Khokhar, and Edie Purdie. 2016. "The 2016 Edition of World Development Indicators Is Out: Three Features You Won't Want to Miss". *The Data Blog.* April 15, 2016. www.blogs.worldbank.org/opendata/2016-edition-world-development-indicators-out-three-features-you-won-t-want-miss.

Ferguson, James. 1990. *The Anti-Politics Machine "Development", Depoliticization and Bureaucratic Power in Lesotho.* Minneapolis, MN: University of Minneapolis Press.

Fioramonti, Lorenzo. 2013. *Gross Domestic Problem: The Politics behind the World's Most Powerful Number.* Economic Controversies. London; New York, NY: Zed Books.

Frère, Marie-Soleil, and Pierre Englebert. 2015. "Briefing: Burkina Faso–the Fall of Blaise Compaoré". *African Affairs* 114 (455): 295–307.

Graan, Mike van. 2011. *The Creative Economy, Development, Culture, Human Rights and Democracy in Africa: Joining the Dots.* Nairobi: Arterial Network.

Hesmondhalgh, David. 2016. "Capitalism and the Media: Moral Economy, Well-Being and Capabilities". *Media, Culture & Society* 39 (2): 202–18.

Huxley, Julian. 1946. *UNESCO: Its Purpose and Its Philosophy/UNESCO: Ses Buts et Sa Philosophie.* Washington, DC: American Council of Public Affairs.

Isar, Yudhishthir Raj. 2015. "Widening Development Pathways: Transformative Visions of Cultural Economy". In *The Routledge Companion to the Cultural Industries,* edited by Kate Oakley and Justin O'Connor, 477–87. London: Routledge.

Karshenas, Massoud. 2016. "Power, Ideology and Global Development: On the Origins, Evolution and Achievements of UNCTAD: Focus: The Origins, Evolution and Achievements of UNCTAD". *Development and Change* 47 (4): 664–85.

Kipling, Rudyard. 1899. "The White Man's Burden: The United States & the Philippine Islands, 1899". *McClure's Magazine,* February 1899.

Larkin, Brian. 2008. *Signal and Noise: Media, Infrastructure, and Urban Culture in Nigeria.* Durham, NC: Duke University Press.

Lee, Hye-Kyung. 2016. "Politics of the 'Creative Industries' Discourse and Its Variants". *International Journal of Cultural Policy* 22 (3): 438–55.

Lobato, Ramon. 2010. "Creative Industries and Informal Economies: Lessons from Nollywood". *International Journal of Cultural Studies* 13 (4): 337–54.

Mandé, Hamadou. 2016. "Artistic Freedom and Cultural Creation in Burkina Faso". In *How Free Is FREE? Reflections on Freedom of Creative Expression in Africa,* edited by Artwatch Africa, Arterial Network, 94–104. Cape Town: Arterial Network.

Moss, Giles. 2018. "Media, Capabilities, and Justification". *Media, Culture and Society* 40 (1): 94–109.

Moyo, Dambisa. 2010. *Dead Aid: Why Aid Is Not Working and How There Is Another Way for Africa.* London: Penguin.

Nederveen Pieterse, Jan. 2010. *Development Theory.* 2nd ed. Los Angeles, CA; London: Sage.

Neuwirth, Rostam Josef. 2013. "Global Governance and the Creative Economy: The Developing versus Developed Country Dichotomy Revisited". *Frontiers of Legal Research* 1 (1): 127–44.

Nussbaum, Martha C. 2003. "Capabilities as Fundamental Entitlements: Sen and Social Justice". *Feminist Economics* 9 (2–3): 33–59.

Nussbaum, Martha C. 2011. *Creating Capabilities: The Human Development Approach.* Cambridge, MA: Belknap Press of Harvard University Press.

Nussbaum, Martha C. 2016. "Introduction: Aspiration and the Capabilities List". *Journal of Human Development and Capabilities* 17 (3): 301–8.

Pratt, Andy C. 2013. "Promoting Sustainable Development through Culture: Current Status, Challenges and Prospects". In *UNESCO at a Glance: 2013 Culture and Development: Unveiling New Prospects for Development through Culture*, edited by Korea National Commission for UNESCO, 47–55. Seoul: Korean National Commission for UNESCO.

Rahnema, Majid, and Victoria Bawtree, eds. 1997. *The Post-Development Reader.* London; Atlantic Highlands, NJ; Dhaka; Halifax, NS: Cape Town: Zed Books; University Press; Fernwood Pub.; David Philip.

Rao, Vijayendra, and Michael Walton. 2004a. *Culture and Public Action: A Cross-Disciplinary Dialogue on Development Policy.* Stanford, CA; London: Stanford University Press.

Rao, Vijayendra, and Michael Walton. 2004b. "Culture and Public Action: Relationality, Equality of Agency, and Development". In *Culture and Public Action: A Cross-Disciplinary Dialogue on Development Policy*, edited by Vijayendra Rao and Michael Walton, 3–36. Stanford, CA; London: Stanford University Press.

Sacco, Pierluigi, Guido Ferilli, and Giorgio Tavano Blessi. 2014. "Understanding Culture-Led Local Development: A Critique of Alternative Theoretical Explanations". *Urban Studies* 51 (13): 2806–21.

Sen, Amartya. 1992. *Inequality Reexamined.* New York, NY: Cambridge, MA: Russell Sage Foundation; Harvard University Press.

Sen, Amartya. 1999. *Development as Freedom.* Oxford; New York, NY: Oxford University Press.

Sen, Amartya. 2009. *The Idea of Justice.* Cambridge, MA: Belknap Press.

Shaheed, Farida. 2013. *Report of the Special Rapporteur in the Field of Cultural Rights, The Right to Freedom of Artistic Expression and Creativity.* A/HRC/23/34. Geneva: UNHCR.

Shaheed, Farida. 2014. "Copyright Policy and the Right to Science and Culture". Human Rights Council, Twenty-eighth session GE.14-24951. New York, NY: United Nations General Assembly.

Singh, J. P. 2011. *United Nations Educational, Scientific, and Cultural Organization (UNESCO): Creating Norms for a Complex World.* Routledge Global Institutions. New York, NY: Routledge.

UNCTAD, and UNDP. 2008. *Creative Economy Report 2008: The Challenge of Assessing the Creative Economy: Towards Informed Policy-Making.* UNCTAD/DITC/2008/2. Geneva: United Nations.

UNCTAD, and UNDP. 2010. *Creative Economy Report 2010: Creative Economy: A Feasible Development Option.* UNCTAD/DITC/TAB/2010/3. Geneva: United Nations.

UNESCO. 1945. *Constitution of the United Nations Educational, Scientific and Cultural Organization.* London: UNESCO.

UNESCO, and UNDP. 2013. *Creative Economy Report.* Paris and New York, NY: UNESCO and UNDP.

Witt, Emily. 2017. *Nollywood: The Making of a Film Empire.* New York, NY: Columbia Global Reports.

7

SUSTAINABILITY

On June 6, 2013, UNESCO published a short video on its YouTube channel titled 'Let's put culture on the agenda now!' This 87 second message includes a few claims and ideas, voiced by Irina Bokova (then the General Director of UNESCO) and Helen Clark (then the Administrator of the United Nations Development Programme, UNDP). The video starts with the following messages:

> Culture: works for development
> Culture: drives development
> Culture: enables development
>
> (UNESCO 2013)

The video then continues with Bokova and Clark taking turns high-lighting connections between culture and (sustainable) development in a variety of ways:

> 'Culture is who we are' (Bokova). 'Culture shapes our identity' (Clark). 'UNESCO and UNDP work across the world to build on culture' (Bokova), 'as a means of fostering respect and tolerance and respect among people' (Clark), 'as a way to create jobs and improve people's

> lives' (Bokova), 'as a way to include others, and understand them'
> (Clark). 'Culture helps preserve our heritage, and make sense of our
> future' (Bokova). 'Culture empowers people' (Clark). 'Let's put culture
> on the agenda now!' (Bokova and Clark).
>
> (UNESCO 2013)

The video ends with a series of words in association with culture, visualised in the same way as the opening sentences. These terms are identity, music, heritage, cinema, inclusion, dance, creativity, festivals, knowledge, arts, dialogue, museums, and diversity. The word diversity stays on screen slightly longer than the other ones. Below, we will explore the significance of this variety of claims and terms being associated with culture. But first we have to ask: which agenda?

From the video, it is not clear on which 'agenda' we should 'put culture now'. But the reason we use it at the start of a chapter on sustainability is of course because that is the 'agenda' they speak of. This raises the question of whom the message is intended for, and what purpose it serves, as this kind of advocacy for an implicit objective assumes great familiarity of the audience. The answer lies in two clues.

First, the end of the video acknowledges that it has been produced 'with the generous support of the Millennium Development Goals Achievement Fund' (MDG-F). The MDG-F was set up in 2006 as a partnership between the United Nations Development Programme (UNDP) and AECID, the Spanish agency for development cooperation. The purpose of the fund was to include 'culture' in the efforts to attain the MDGs, as part of Spain's focus on linking 'culture and development' (Baltà Portolés 2013). This funding and the timing of the video suggests that the message is meant to influence the debate on the 'post-2015 development agenda', the follow-up to the MDGs, even if this remains implicit.

Second, later in 2013, when UNESCO and UNDP jointly published a 'special edition' of the Creative Economy Report, Bokova and Clark clarify the message that also resonates through the video more explicitly in their joint foreword:

> At a time when countries are striving to reach the Millennium
> Development Goals and the world is shaping a new post-2015 global

development agenda, we must recognize the importance and power of the cultural and creative sectors as engines of sustainable human development.

(UNESCO and UNDP 2013, 11)

While these claims are positive and optimistic, they ignore the extent to which the cultural economy is a large polluter, both directly (because cultural products, events, and organisations often have significant carbon footprints) and indirectly (mainly because the ways through which we consume digital culture pollutes through data-centres, device manufacturing, and the planned obsolescence that makes us discard those devices at alarming rates) (Maxwell and Miller 2012). More fundamentally, in her book, *This Changes Everything* ('this' meaning climate change), Naomi Klein stresses that the environmental threat posed by climate change is rooted in a cultural problem:

Contemporary humans are too self-centered, too addicted to gratification to live without the full freedom to satisfy our every whim—or so our culture tells us every day.

(Klein 2015, 17)

The cultural logic of our dominant economic model assumes ever greater productivity and profit, which translates to ever greater economic growth. In order to maintain this kind of production and consumption, many manufactured goods are designed with 'planned obsolescence' in mind: the idea that if products have a short lifespan, consumers will generate more repeat purchases, thereby increasing demand and generating greater profits. This is an issue that has increased significantly since we started consuming electronic devices that facilitate cultural consumption (Maxwell and Miller 2012). Just think of the number of electronic devices you have owned during the past ten years and how many of them have ended up in a landfill or incinerator.

Klein does however stress that we do actually manage to make sacrifices for a range of things that are larger than our individual needs. Many people make significant changes in their consumption patterns in order to curb their carbon footprint. However, she argues, because the technological means to make a transition to a zero-carbon future do actually exist, and the science of the limits of our planetary capacity is almost unanimous, the real challenge to attain the level of sustainability to avert the worst levels of climate change are indeed cultural.

In practice, sustainability is commonly conceptualised as reliant on three pillars: social sustainability (people), environmental sustainability (planet), and economic sustainability (profit). This approach presumes that when the three pillars attain their respective objectives, we can speak of sustainability though a context where only social and economic sustainability is merely *equitable*, a context with only environmental and economic sustainability is merely *viable*, and a context with only environmental and social sustainability is merely *bearable*. All three pillars are essential to make societies *sustainable*. While appealing in its simplicity, we do however believe this approach both downplays the complexity of societies and lacks a cultural dimension (see also Clammer 2012).

This chapter explores the tension between the use of culture as an awareness-raising force towards sustainability and as a sector that puts a strain on the planetary environment itself. It does so by teasing out the paradox of how we can balance the claim that culture is a 'driver of sustainable development' (see details below) and the realisation that cultural production can be a serious threat to a possible transition to such sustainable futures.

Our argument derives its structure from the 'four strategic paths' to linking culture (through cultural policy) and sustainable development proposed by Nancy Duxbury, Anita Kangas, and Christiaan De Beukelaer (2017, 222). First, safeguarding and sustaining cultural practice; second, 'greening' the operations of cultural organisations; third, raising awareness about sustainability and climate change through the arts; and fourth, fostering global citizenship to strengthen political support to tackle the global issue through global measures.

The question remains on what basis they were able to make the above claims about the role of 'culture' and 'cultural and creative sectors' as a 'driver and enabler' or 'sustainable human development'.[1] Before turning to a detailed discussion of these strategic paths, we'll first explore what falls under the different meanings before turning to the roles they might reasonably be expected to play. Is the role of culture merely a positive one? What is 'sustainability'? And what does 'culture' mean in this context? Are we talking about art, culture, 'cultural industries', cultural identity, creativity, or creative economy? Or are we talking about all of it? While these terms are used inter-changeably, particularly in the video message by Irina Bokova and Helen Clark, this raises the question of how and why claims about significantly different things seem to have been lumped together.

WHAT 'SUSTAINABILITY'?

Timothy Morton, who has written extensively about sustainability, calls climate change a 'hyperobject' because it is so complex and vast that we cannot understand it fully; its reach and implications are too far-reaching (Morton 2013). Though it is in response to cli-mate change that we are trying to think of 'sustainable develop-ment' (the *trajectory*) that will lead us to a state of sustainability (the *objective*), which would allow us to inhabit our planet without pillaging it. This is also how the term was defined in the *Brundtland Report*: sustainable development 'meets the needs of the present without compromising the ability of future generations to meet their own needs' (World Commission on Environment and Develop-ment 1987, 42).[2]

This does however raise the question of what would count as 'sustainable'. The general agreement seems to be that we need to curb the increase of the planet's average temperature to 2°C, with the onset of the industrial revolution as a baseline. Although it is much less clear how we will change our lives in order to get there or how we can make that transition. This is why we define 'sustainability' as the preservation of a liveable social, political, economic, and cultural cli-mate on this planet; and 'sustainable development' as the process of transition towards that state.

While Bruntlandt's definition includes intergenerational justice in this conceptualisation, the discussion of 'sustainability' was, at the time, largely preoccupied with the environment, whereas 'development' was mainly preoccupied with the social and economic conditions of people living in 'developing' countries (see Chapter six). With the adoption of the Sustainable Development Goals (SDGs) in 2015, one significant thing has changed. Where the Millennium Development Goals (2000-2015) focused on 'developing' countries, the SDGs now focus on *all* countries. This will hopefully better align the rather different needs and interests of different countries and people around the world. However, despite the various campaigns to 'put culture on the agenda', Antonios Vlassis argues it neither became a 'stand-alone goal' nor a significant part of other goals (2015). The link between culture and sustainability is thus not significantly integrated in thinking about sustainable development. Moreover, while Irina Bokova and Helen Clark argue there *is* indeed a link between cultural and sustainability, it is not an inherently positive one as they suggest.

Sustainability is however far more than a response to the immediate dangers of human-induced climate change alone. The SDGs focus on a definition of 'sustainable development' that is multi-dimensional, by involving education, gender, citizen participation, and so on. It does so not only by merely including reference to these issues, but by stressing they are interconnected. This reinforces the understanding of sustainable development as going beyond climate change. But as much as culture is no panacea for environmental issues, neither does it inherently resolve social issues (Oakley and Ward 2018; see also Chapter two). In sum, while culture can be used to help attain sustainability, it should not be assumed it automatically or intrinsically does so. But that does raise the question of what 'culture' means in this equation.

WHAT 'CULTURE'?

If climate change is a cultural problem (as Naomi Klein argues), and it is a 'hyperobject' that is very difficult to grasp (as Timothy Morton argues), how can we make a straightforward claim that culture 'works for', 'drives', and 'enables' sustainable development (as Irina Bokova and Helen Clark do), which is meant to counter climate change? In order to assess the seeming paradox emanating from these claims, we'll need to unpack what culture *is* and what it *does*.

In 2001, Jon Hawkes, who worked for the Cultural Development Network Victoria in Australia at the time, made the case that the three pillars of sustainability (social, economic, and environmental; or people, planet, profit) are insufficient. He instead proposes a model with

a 'fourth pillar' of sustainability, which builds on the three pillars
common in debates on sustainability, but adds culture:[3]

> Cultural vitality: wellbeing, creativity, diversity and innovation
> Social equity: justice, engagement, cohesion, welfare
> Environmental responsibility: ecological balance
> Economic viability: material prosperity
>
> (Hawkes 2001, 25)

In response to this proposition, Katerina Soini and Joost Dessein
argue that there are more ways to conceptualise the link between
culture and sustainability. They argue that Hawkes' proposal positions
'culture *in* sustainability, and sees cultural sustainability as parallel to
ecological, social, and economic sustainability', while they propose
two more links that are possible: 'culture *for* sustainability, suggests
that both material and immaterial culture are seen as an essential
resource for local and regional economic development' and 'culture *as*
sustainability, encloses the other pillars of sustainability and becomes
an overarching dimension of sustainability' (Soini and Dessein 2016, 3,
emphasis in original).

The ontological reflections Soini and Dessein put forward are
valuable but remain quite abstract when it comes to considering the
practical links between sustainability and the cultural economy. Jon
Hawkes is far more interested in the practical application of his ideas,
in large part because his approach was policy-oriented from the start.
We do however wish to explore which roles the *cultural economy*
could play in relation to sustainability, rather than the role *culture*
could play. We look at how culture functions rather than what culture is.
We do so by teasing out 'four strategic paths' through which culture
(in a variety of clearly defined meanings) can relate to sustainability
(along equally clearly defined meanings), building on the work by
Kangas, Duxbury, and De Beukelaer (2018).

First, we look at 'sustaining practice' in cultural practices and the
production of cultural expressions (including ways of life, tradition,
and living culture). Second, we look at arts and cultural expressions as
a means to 'raise awareness' about both the risks of climate change
and the ways in which we can respond to it. Third, we look at ways in
which the 'cultural industries', comprising those organisations and

companies involved in the production of cultural expressions (including the companies and events that provide the frameworks to produce, distribute, and consumer these expressions) can 'green' (as opposed to greenwash) their operations, because the 'cultural industries' are major polluters too. Fourth, we explore the more fundamental role cultural identity (including who we are as part of the planet and how we humans relate to each other) can play in thinking about climate change as a global issue that requires global commitments and responses.

SUSTAINING PRACTICE

A longstanding concern for the cultural economy has been the need to make sure that existing practices, rooted in long histories, remain viable – both by sustaining cultural relevance and economic tenability. Yet, societal changes and economic pressures often make this difficult. Much like languages and traditions, the creation of cultural expressions occurs in a fragile context where there's a risk of domination by the winners-who-take-it-all (see Caves 2003). In Irina Bokova and Helen Clark's message, this concern is seen as self-evident: 'Culture helps preserve our heritage, and make sense of our future'. This circular argument, where culture is both the past and the future, also serves as the tool in the present to forge this link raises the question of why any action is needed: if culture's role really is self-evident and effective, why do we still need to make a case for it and why would it need support?

In this context, Kirsten Loach, Jennifer Rowley, and Jillian Griffiths (2017) argue that the sustainability of cultural institutions such as libraries and museums (as repositories of cultural knowledge) are not subservient but central to more general sustainability concerns. They stress that while there is some attention for the positive externalities of culture in terms of environmental sustainability, if culture is regarded as the fourth pillar of sustainability, the viability of the sector is an inherent part of sustainability and not a mere external contribution to it.

This chimes with the way UNESCO has included 'sustainability' in its 2005 *Convention on the Protection and Promotion of the Diversity of Cultural Expressions*:

> Cultural diversity is a rich asset for individuals and societies. The protection, promotion and maintenance of cultural diversity are an

essential requirement for sustainable development for the benefit of present and future generations.

(UNESCO 2005, 4)

Here, culture is implicitly compared with biodiversity as an essential component of sustainable development. They go on to explicitly articulate that culture ought to be integrated in 'development' policies, with the objective to ensure a trajectory towards *sustainable* development:

Parties shall endeavour to integrate culture in their development policies at all levels for the creation of conditions conducive to sustainable development and, within this framework, foster aspects relating to the protection and promotion of the diversity of cultural expressions.

(UNESCO 2005, 8)

Though one of the major concerns of this convention, much like the cultural sector as a whole, is to ensure the survival of cultural diversity by ensuring the viability of its institutions (more about this in Chapter three). In this context, Christiaan De Beukelaer and Raquel Freitas (2015) argue that the way in which 'sustainability' is used in the Convention remains rather superficial and dominated by economic concerns, overall lacking a more transformative approach. There is ample possibility for countries or cities to take a more ambitious and transformative angle, as Québec province quickly developed a Sustainable Development Action Plan (in 2009) that integrated culture (Guèvremont 2014), although their Convention remains insufficiently ambitious in terms of connecting the sustainability of the cultural economy (its prime concern) and its role in a broader push towards sustainability. So what can cultural expressions do to articulate the issue more effectively?

RAISING AWARENESS

Accra, like many coastal cities, has a coastline that is both appealing and appalling. The appeal lies in the refreshing breeze, the arts and crafts market, the Kwame Nkrumah Memorial Park, the monumental Independence Square, the fleet of colourful coastal fishing vessels, the James Town Lighthouse, Osu Castle, the James Fort, and many other heritage buildings. Many of these buildings are reminders of the long and brutal colonial history the region has endured. But that does not necessarily make the coastline appalling.

What makes the coast so appalling is the rampant pollution that plagues it. Long stretches of the beach are full of garbage. It also serves both as an open toilet for those residing or working close to the beach and as the place where the open sewers of the sloped city run off into the Gulf of Guinea. As a result, most of the beach in the city centre smells rather unsavourily, as a reminder of the constant flow of pollution. The scale of this pollution means that the closest beaches fit for recreation are Labadi Beach, several kilometres east, and Kokrobite Beach, over ten kilometres west.

In response to this pollution, some musicians have started using their visibility and voice to lament the situation. One such 'artiste' (pronounced as it would be in French, as musicians are called in Ghana), is the rapper *ELi*, short for Edward Elikplim Ayikoe. His song Gold Coast, which also features rapper *Wanlov the Kubolor* (the pseudonym of Emmanuel Owusu-Bonsu, who is part of the duo FOKN Bois, alongside Mensa '*M3nsa*' Ansah), very explicitly addresses the issue of the polluted beach, as Rachel Leah discusses in a new article for Quartz Africa (Leah 2017). While *ELi* does so by standing in plastic waste, *Wanlov* ostensibly defecates on the beach while rapping; with the clumsily cut-out face of former President John Dramani Mahama concealing his genitals. While obviously playful, the song is a strong indictment of the political leadership that has not managed to deal with the increased pollution of the city and its coastline. The music of these Ghanaian rappers thus ties in with artists from around the world who engage with environmental issues. But what does such awareness-raising accomplish?

On December 12, 2015, at the 21st session of the Conference of Parties (COP),[4] the United Nations Climate Conference in the French capital of Paris, adopted the *Paris Agreement*. The main commitment of this agreement was to limit global warming to 'below 2 degrees' Celsius, by the year 2100 and relative to a pre-industrial baseline. This agreement was a significant political accomplishment, for which scientists and environmentalists had been campaigning for years.

In the same year, the United Nations agreed on the 17 Sustainable Development Goals (SDGs) that should be accomplished by 2030. These SDGs replaced the earlier Millennium Development Goals that set the objectives for development policies around the world for the period between 2000 and 2015. And this is the agenda on which Irina Bokova and Helen Clark argued we should put culture now – the message we started this chapter with (UNESCO 2013). This institutional advocacy to give culture a visible role in the SDGs that were at the time under negotiation builds on earlier attempts to connect culture to development in general – rather than 'sustainable' development specifically.

The link between 'culture' and 'development' has its roots in anthropological studies of development interventions, which showed how such interventions were more likely to succeed when they take into account the social and cultural context in which they are proposed. This led to a cultural turn in development studies (see Nederveen Pieterse 1995; Schech and Haggis 2000). In this context, the term 'culture' refers to the ways in which we live together, rather than the cultural and creative expressions that give meaning to our lives. Gradually, claims about culture and (sustainable) development have however conflated these different notions of culture and sustainability (De Beukelaer and Freitas 2015; Isar 2017).

Interestingly, the build-up to the SDGs included ample campaigning about the role culture would be able to play in raising awareness, changing consumption patterns, and working towards much-needed solutions. These campaigns used a range of slogans, including 'the future we want includes culture' (a civil society alliance led by *Culture21*, the *International Federation of Coalitions for Cultural Diversity*, the *International Federation of Arts Councils and Culture Agencies*, and *Culture Action Europe*), there is 'no future without culture' (*ACPCultures+*), and, as we discussed above, 'let's put culture on the agenda now' (UNESCO and UNDP). Despite these efforts, some argue that the campaign failed because some states, such as the USA, refused to integrate culture in the SDGs for fear of this cultural relativism creeping into human rights enforcement (Vlassis 2015).

In the context of COP21, which led to the Paris Agreement, a side-event called *ArtCOP21* aimed to include culture in the conversation about the climate goals that were under negotiation, as highlighted on their website:

> Climate change is often seen through a policy or scientific lens, and solutions are discussed only in political offices, boardrooms and negotiating halls. ArtCOP21 launched ahead of the UN climate talks in Paris, aims to challenge those tropes. Climate is culture. What is required is the active engagement of citizens worldwide in the urgency, value and opportunities of a transition away from fossil fuels and the embracing of a greener, sustainable future economy.
>
> (ArtCOP n.d.)

ArtCOP was a 'global festival of cultural activity on climate change' (ArtCOP n.d.) that took place from September to December 2015, organised by the French organisation *COAL* (the Coalition for Art and Sustainable Development) and UK based *Cape Farewell* (which 'changes the way we think about climate change' by connecting art, science, and activism). The event was primarily a platform for the dozens of organisations that do work related to the theme of the festival to share their interventions and ideas with the vast number of people attending the *COP21* event in their role as government, business, or civil society representatives.

What connects the Ghanaian song and the large-scale action at *COP21* is that they help convey the immediacy and complexity of the issue. First, these artistic interventions help raise awareness about the issues that are readily visible around us. This helps to build the case that urgent action is needed. Whether this is by singing about the polluted beaches in cities that pose health risks as done by *ELi* and *Wanlov*, by writing poetry about the slow inundation of Pacific islands as done by Marshallese poet Kathy Jetñil-Kijiner at *COP21*, or through the visual art of Danish-Icelandic artist Olafur Eliasson, just to name a few. Second, and perhaps more importantly, art can help clarify the scope and importance of the 'hyperobject' that may otherwise be difficult to grasp. The large-scale work done by 'artivist' David Buckland's *Cape Farewell* project is emblematic of such an effort. The project has included expeditions to the Arctic, in which both artists and scientists took part. By bringing together these different people on one ship, *Cape Farewell* managed to push the way in which scientists can communicate the findings of their work through art and the ways in which art can build on a better understanding of the science of climate change in order to raise awareness (Buckland 2012).

The role of art and culture in raising awareness about climate change is promising. Literary scholar Sophia David argues that 'the creativity and experimentation afforded by novels allows us to explore alternative societal and political models, as well as re-imagine a future beyond fossil fuel dependency, and reconfigure our philosophical frameworks to accommodate climate change into our outlook' (David 2016, 65).

While climate change remains an issue that requires scientific study, it also requires engagement beyond science, and the arts are increasingly central to our articulation of the issue as it helps imagine the issue beyond doom scenarios (Robidoux and Kovacs 2018; Yusoff and Gabrys 2011). More importantly, there is also greater acknowledgement that climate change is in fact a cultural issue, precisely because a *cultural change* is needed to attain the sustainability necessary to avert further environmental destruction through climate change (Klein 2015). David Buckland clarifies this:

> Climate change proffers a unique cultural problem: it is a future truth. For both the artists and the climate scientists they have essentially a human story to tell – how feverish and profligate human existence is spoiling our own habitat. Climate change demands that we act now to prevent a catastrophic environment for our children to inhabit.
>
> (Buckland 2012, 3)

The cultural side to climate change is increasingly reflected in the way the issue is communicated. In the fringes of COP23 in Bonn, the *Bundeskunsthalle* organised the exhibition *Wetterbericht* ('weather report'), which combined scientific and artistic depictions of weather, climate, and climate change. Perhaps this approach may help raise awareness and mobilise people to take action. Although the reliance on the arts to accomplish sustainability does raise an important question: If the sector is so useful in raising awareness, does it live up to the principles it preaches?

GREENING THE SECTOR

Agbogbloshie is a former wetland along the Korle Lagoon in Accra. As the city's population rapidly grew over the past decades, the area became an inner-city slum where many domestic migrants ended up. One of the significant economic activities to sustain their livelihoods has been the recuperation of precious metals from discarded electronic devices. Many of these devices were used to listen to music, watch television, play games, and so on. But once discarded, they ended up in the e-waste industry, which has over time heavily polluted the area.

At the same time, the sociologist Andrew Ross points out that how UK policy-makers have framed the core ingredient of the cultural economy ('creativity') as a renewable resource: 'Unlike Bevan's coal and fish, or Thatcher's North Sea oil, creativity was a renewable energy resource, mostly untapped; every citizen had some of it, the cost of extraction was minimal, and it would never run out' (Ross 2007, 17). Some commentators even go as far as arguing that the 'creative industries exhaust almost none of the non-renewable material resources' (Li 2011, 122).

However, the way we transform 'creativity' or 'culture' into commodities relies to a great extent on devices that help produce, distribute, and consume them. The cultural economy thus needs devices to make this work. Our devices may be wireless, but their production requires precious metals and industrial production, and their functioning requires wired networks. There is, simply put, 'no digital without copper' (O'Connor 2016, 1). But also 'pre-digital' cultural production and consumption existed – and continues to exist – in close relation to the manufacturing and short-term use of electronic devices that served to decode the products that contained music and movies (Hesmondhalgh and Meier 2017). The cultural economy does not exist beyond or independently from planned obsolescence that created a gigantic pile of e-waste; the cultural economy is one of its significant causes.

In *Greening the Media*, Maxwell and Miller (2012) make the point that cultural and media industries and devices are not more environmentally friendly than many other industries. While e-books may not use paper, while music and video streaming do not use plastic CDs or DVDs, while smartphones have made a wide range of services easier (and arguably more efficient), these digital innovations rely on two heavily polluting activities: the storage of data and the manufacturing of the devices (which includes mining, shipping, refining, and assembling). Maxwell and Miller indicate that 2.5% to 3% of global carbon emissions result from the energy consumption from the IT industries (2012, 29). This is more than civil aviation, which stands at some 2% of the annual emissions. Surely, there are more people who use computers, cellphones, and rely on digital services than people use airplanes, but the total energy used by digital devices is still staggering.[5]

While major tech firms are investing in renewable energy to power their data centres (Greenpeace 2017), the use of energy is, as Agbogbloshie illustrates, merely part of the issue. The digital devices we use are not durable. In fact, they are largely designed not to be durable. The problem with this 'planned obsolescence' is that we have finite resources. So we are using these valuable resources, including energy, in order to produce devices that have a deliberately short life-span. While some people argue that planned obsolescence drives innovation (Fishman et al. 1993), the main problem is not that products are too durable and thus stifle innovation, but that valuable energy and resources are wasted because the rapid consumption cycles generate massive amounts of waste. A 'circular economy' approach that designs these devices with their re-use, repair, and ultimately recycling in mind would help diminish the environmental damage they create (Webster 2017).

The challenge for the cultural economy, Maxwell and Miller argue, lies in the fact that much of the environmental damage caused by cultural production exists beyond the sector itself. The damage occurs when producing the products and services the sector relies on, but also the ways in which consumers have grown accustomed to engaging with them (through devices and data-centres), which is difficult to impact from the regulatory environment of culture: cultural policy (Maxwell and Miller 2017). Moreover, this wrought relationship extends beyond production and consumption, but also reaches into the legitimation accorded to 'dirty' corporations through their sponsorship of the arts. A prominent example of this is the London museum *Tate Modern* that received sponsorship funding from British Petroleum (BP) until their celebration of that 20-year partnership during BP's disastrous Deepwater Horizon oil spill in the Gulf of

Mexico in 2010 led to significant protests from artists and the arts community (Chong 2015), eventually leading to Tate cancelling their partnership with BP. Protestors stressed that sponsorship by the oil company was a deal that yielded greater benefits to BP than to Tate. They argued that BP was not actually supporting the Tate as much as the public arts institution was legitimising their business (Lam et al. 2013). In this context, the role of arts institutions is thus one that can undermine the environmental awareness-raising that the art they exhibit may seek to accomplish.

Despite this bleak picture, there have been significant efforts to combat the high energy use of arts venues, the gigantic piles of waste created by (music) festivals, and the inefficient touring schedules of artists. The organisation who has spearheaded these efforts is *Julie's Bicycle*. This UK-based NGO has worked with both academics and 'cultural industries' to diminish the carbon footprint and waste generated by the cultural economy. Although it remains difficult to gauge if these efforts manage to counter the environmental damage done elsewhere in the cultural economy.

Given the contradictions between the role cultural expressions can play in raising awareness and the extent to which the cultural economy needs to transform itself, we wonder if the efforts made are sufficient. As the transition to sustainability is not merely a challenge for the cultural economy, but the world more generally, the underlying cultural struggle about responsibility, debt, and ways forward, not to mention the recognition of the issue of climate change in the first place, remains one that will demand greater effort and commitment. So, what kind of social and political community could help us resolve these issues?

FOSTERING GLOBAL ECOLOGICAL CITIZENSHIP

The psychologist Dan Kahan makes two fundamental points regarding our possible responses to climate change. First, that pursuing a trajectory towards sustainability is generally not predicated on facts or data, but on social affiliation. If the group we identify with values the need to adopt such changes, we are likely to go along with that and *vice versa*. Second, the basis on which these differences rest are largely cultural (Kahan 2012).

While culture may for some people indeed be a reason to embrace a shift towards sustainability, the very same cultural basis may be a reason for others to *not* do so. In this context, culture maintains a contradictory relationship to sustainability. Not at least because where one group may see the fragility of the planetary environment, another may prefer looking at the technological mastery we humans (think we) have over it. How can we make sense of these cultural contradictions?

When Kahan mentions that acknowledging climate change as a culturally informed issue, he acknowledges that it is much easier for some than for others to pretend there is no issue at all. When living on an atoll in the Pacific that is slowly submerging, or on the board of the Sahel that is slowly taken over by the Sahara Desert, it is hard to ignore climate change. However, when sufficiently protected by financial resources and insurance to be protected from the immediate effects of climate change, even if struck by increasingly strong hurricanes, floods, or droughts, there is far more leeway to pretend all is fine. To make things worse, Nick Stevenson argues that 'while the responsibility to protect the environment is a global responsibility, it is not the case that those most responsible for environmental harm and those most at risk from the destruction of nature are the same' (Stevenson 2003, 73). The cultural economy may however help move people beyond these issues.

As sustainability is something that has to be global in order to truly exist, how does its attainment chime with the ways in which citizenship is cultivated through culture. Should we address it at a personal, national, or global level? While the contrast Kahan refers to (some people accept the science that there is a problem and others do not) largely aligns with political ideologies, our aim is to shift our attention to the methodological foundations on which cultural expressions are used to build, strengthen, and maintain cultural identities in the form of cultural citizenship. We think the way to move forward in this debate is to reconsider, and possibly redraw, the boundaries of citizenship and belonging towards a notion of global ecological citizenship.

Cultural citizenship is largely based on the difference between cultural communities because cultural expression and policies, through which citizenship is formed and maintained, is based on a methodologically nationalist approach (Beck 2016). This means that identity construction assumes nationality to be the default defining and differentiation factor in identity formation. This – often implicit – starting point has however proven to be ineffective in dealing with the increasing complexity within societies (De Beukelaer 2017), but also calls into question how we ought to think of fundamentally global issues (Stevenson 2003). In response to this, we follow Nancy Duxbury, Anita Kangas, and Christiaan De Beukelaer in arguing that 'we stress the need to foster a cosmopolitan community, that is, a global community that embraces global awareness about a global challenge, beyond merely national or regional interests and priorities' (Duxbury et al. 2017, 224). Sustainability, or preserving a liveable climate on this planet, is a global responsibility that no person nor country can carry alone.

In 2017, the anthropologist Ghassan Hage published the book *Is Racism an Environmental Threat?* In this provocative essay, he explores the ways in which the 'threat' of Muslims uses a language that closely resembles the one we use to discuss environmental waste in relation to climate change. He argues that the way in which racism is an apparatus of domination and exploitation ('general domestica-tion') of people, climate change is the result of a similar dynamic of exploitation of our environment. Here, 'culture' is central to our engagement with climate change, but in a way that radically differs from the positive message Irina Bokova and Helen Clark or the organisations and artists involved in *ArtCOP* conveyed.

Ghassan Hage's critical argument is one that addresses questions of cultural citizenship and environmental citizenship are part of the same concern. Humans should reconsider their presumed 'cultural' superiority in an attempt to reframe their being as part of the broader 'natural' environment. While ensuring that we construct a sustainable world that 'meets the needs of the present without compromising the ability of future generations to meet their own needs' (World Commission on Environment and Development 1987, 42) is a laudable goal, we should not downplay the importance of other living creatures with whom we share the planet. Indeed, 'an ecologically informed citizenship depends not as much upon "nature" as upon the links between "nature" and "culture"' (Stevenson 2003, 70). More specifically,

Green citizenship aims to widen the circle of responsibilities commonly assumed by human beings to include global communities, animals and other 'natural' life forms, all of which may be distant within time and space. Within this, ecological citizenship is necessarily more concerned with obligations than with rights.

(Stevenson 2003, 75)

Reframing citizenship in terms of obligations (what we owe others) in contrast to rights (what others owe us) is helpful, because it opens up to a discussion of the basis on which we decide on the scale and scope of these obligations and responsibilities. In this regard, Kwame Anthony Appiah argues that cosmopolitanism means that,

The idea that we have obligations to others, obligations that stretch beyond those to whom we are related by the ties of kith and kind, or even the more formal ties of a shared citizenship. [At the same time], we take seriously the value not just of human life but of particular human lives, which means taking an interest in the practices and beliefs that lend them significance.

(Appiah 2007, xiii)

This requires a significant cultural and political shift beyond framing sustainability as a contract between countries (such as the *Paris Agreement*, see above). It indeed requires a more fundamental shift that allows us to rethink identity in relation to a global ecosystem that we rely on as much as we are a part of it. While this is perhaps the most significant role the cultural economy can play to attain sustainability, it is also the most difficult to operationalise.

CONCLUSIONS

There are many good reasons to see positive links between culture and sustainability. And we have tried to highlight several of them in this chapter, from the sustainability of cultural practices, to the stories we tell about the environment, and from the way the cultural economy contributes to climate change and may be a part of the solution to the ways in which culture might reshape our identities to foster global environmental citizenship. But there are also good reasons to question the way in which a broad variety of stakeholders in a range of activities related to culture have claimed that link as self-evident.

We would therefore argue there is little reason to join the chorus of cultural advocates who simply argue that culture 'drives' and 'enables' sustainable development. There is simply no evidence of such a self-evident positive correlation. Making such sweeping, imprecise, unsubstantiated claims is therefore counter-productive, as they may backfire, either on conceptual grounds (by pointing out the inconsistent use of both 'culture' and 'sustainability'), on empirical grounds (by presenting evidence to the contrary), or on strategic grounds (by showing how other approaches may be more effective).

While Naomi Klein argues climate change 'changes everything' (2015), Ulrich Beck goes further than that. He argues that what we face is not *change* but *metamorphosis*:

> Metamorphosis is not social change, not transformation, not evolution, not revolution, and not crisis. It is a mode of changing the nature of human existence. It signifies the age of side-effects.
>
> (Beck 2016, 20)

His stance in this regard is however neither a positive nor a negative one, he rather refuses to make a value judgement. But in the light of impending catastrophe and metamorphosis, culture may help guide us through the changes and possibilities that emerge – or need imagination to be crafted.

There are indeed many ways in which positive links between culture and sustainable development can be made. Though these require a great deal of precision and restraint: definitions and demarcation are key, so claims can be precise, while acknowledging both the positive and the negative impacts of culture on sustainable development will help articulate the necessary restraint. In sum, they are not self-evident. So rather than simply repeating buzzwords and largely unsubstantiated claims, clear and precise arguments and evidence for the roles of culture – in all its facets – need articulation for this connection to become convincing to those who are currently indifferent.

NOTES

1   In this chapter, we focus primarily on 'sustainable development' and not on 'human development', even if the terms are often conflated, particularly in UNESCO documents. We engage with the difference between both in Chapter six.

2   *Our Common Future*, the 1987 report of the World Commission on Environment and Development, nicknamed the *Brundtland Report*, after Gro Harlem Brundtland, who chaired the commission (she was also the prime minister of Norway and Director-General of the World Health Organization).

3   Jon Hawkes later expressed some reservations about and criticisms of his own four-pillars model in an interview with Jordi Pascual, as it contributed to a strengthening – rather than the intended contestation – of a 'silo' approach to sustainability (Pascual and Hawkes 2015).

4   The *Conference of the Parties* (COP) refers to parties to the *United Nations Framework Convention on Climate Change*; they have met annually since 1995. The *Meeting of the Parties* (CMP) refers to all parties in the *Kyoto Protocol*; they have met annually in conjunction with the COP since 2005, when the *Kyoto Protocol* took effect. The *Parties to the Paris Agreement* (CMA) refers to all parties in the Paris Agreement; they have met annually in conjunction with COP and CMP meetings since 2016, when the agreement entered into force.

5   The International Telecommunications Union indicated that in 2017, only 48% of the world's population used the internet. In contrast, the International Civil Aviation Organization reported 3.7 billion passengers in 2017, on a global population of 7.4 billion, which amounts to some 50%; although these are total passenger numbers, not unique passenger numbers (World Bank 2017).

REFERENCES

Appiah, Kwame Anthony. 2007. *Cosmopolitanism: Ethics in a World of Strangers*. London: Penguin.

ArtCOP. n.d. "ArtCOP: About". www.artcop21.com/about/.

Baltà Portolés, Jordi. 2013. *Culture and Development: Review of MDG-F Joint Programmes Key Findings and Achievements*. New York, NY: UNDP.

Beck, Ulrich. 2016. *The Metamorphosis of the World*. Cambridge: Malden, MA: Polity.

Buckland, David. 2012. "Climate Is Culture". *Nature Climate Change* 2 (3): 137–40.

Caves, Richard E. 2003. "Contracts between Art and Commerce". *Journal of Economic Perspectives* 17 (2): 73–84.

Chong, Derrick. 2015. "Tate and BP – Oil and Gas as the New Tobacco?: Arts Sponsorship, Branding, and Marketing". In *The International Handbooks of Museum Studies*, edited by Sharon Macdonald and Helen Rees Leahy, 179–201. Oxford: John Wiley & Sons, Ltd.

Clammer, John R. 2012. *Culture, Development and Social Theory: Towards an Integrated Social Development*. London: Zed.

David, Sophia. 2016. "Eco-Fiction: Bringing Climate Change into the Imagination". PhD thesis. Exeter: University of Exeter. www.ore.exeter.ac.uk/repository/bitstream/handle/10871/24331/DavidS.pdf?sequence=1.

De Beukelaer, Christiaan. 2017. "Ordinary Culture in a World of Strangers: Toward Cosmopolitan Cultural Policy". *International Journal of Cultural Policy*, DOI: 10.1080/10286632.2017.1389913.

De Beukelaer, Christiaan, and Raquel Freitas. 2015. "Culture and Sustainable Development: Beyond the Diversity of Cultural Expressions". In *Globalization, Culture and Development: The UNESCO Convention on Cultural Diversity*, edited by Christiaan De Beukelaer, Miikka Pyykkönen, and J. P. Singh, 203–21. Basingstoke: Palgrave Macmillan.

Duxbury, Nancy, Anita Kangas, and Christiaan De Beukelaer. 2017. "Cultural Policies for Sustainable Development: Four Strategic Paths". *International Journal of Cultural Policy* 23 (2): 214–30.

Fishman, Arthur, Neil Gandal, and Oz Shy. 1993. "Planned Obsolescence as an Engine of Technological Progress". *The Journal of Industrial Economics* 41 (4): 361.

Greenpeace. 2017. *Clicking Clean: Who Is Winning the Race to Build a Green Internet?* Washington, DC: Greenpeace.

Guèvremont, Véronique. 2014. "Integrating Culture in Sustainable Development: Québec's Agenda 21, A Model for the Implementation of Article 13". In *Cultural Diversity in International Law: The Effectiveness of the UNESCO Convention on the Protection and Promotion of the Diversity of Cultural Expressions*, edited by Lilian Richieri Hanania, 265–78. Routledge Research in International Law. London; New York, NY: Routledge.

Hawkes, Jon. 2001. *The Fourth Pillar of Sustainability: Culture's Essential Role in Public Planning*. Melbourne: Cultural Development Network: Common Ground.

Hesmondhalgh, David, and Leslie M. Meier. 2017. "What the Digitalisation of Music Tells Us about Capitalism, Culture and the Power of the Information Technology Sector". *Information, Communication & Society*, DOI: 10.1080/1369118X.2017.1340498.

Isar, Yudhishthir Raj. 2017. "'Culture', 'Sustainable Development' and Cultural Policy: A Contrarian View". *International Journal of Cultural Policy* 23 (2): 148–58.

Kahan, Dan. 2012. "Why We Are Poles Apart on Climate Change". *Nature* 488 (7411): 255.

Kangas, Anita, Nancy Duxbury, and Christiaan De Beukelaer, eds. 2018. *Cultural Policies for Sustainable Development*. London: Routledge.

Klein, Naomi. 2015. *This Changes Everything: Capitalism vs. the Climate*. London: Penguin Books.

Lam, Steven, Gabi Ngcobo, Jack Persekian, Nato Thompson, Anne Sophie Witzke, and Liberate Tate. 2013. "Art, Ecology and Institutions: A Conversation with Artists and Curators". *Third Text* 27 (1): 141–50.

Leah, Rachel. 2017. "Forget Bling: Ghana's Rappers Are Putting the Environment Center Stage". *Quartz Africa*, December 19, 2017. www.qz.com/1139821/ghanas-hip-hop-stars-eli-akan-worlasi-azizaa-kwame-write-and-fokn-bois-rap-about-less-common-themes/.

Li, Wuwei. 2011. *How Creativity Is Changing China*. London: Bloomsbury Academic.

Loach, Kirsten, Jennifer Rowley, and Jillian Griffiths. 2017. "Cultural Sustainability as a Strategy for the Survival of Museums and Libraries". *International Journal of Cultural Policy* 23 (2): 186–98.

Maxwell, Richard, and Toby Miller. 2012. *Greening the Media*. New York, NY: Oxford University Press.

Maxwell, Richard, and Toby Miller. 2017. "Greening Cultural Policy". *International Journal of Cultural Policy* 23 (2): 174–85.

Morton, Timothy. 2013. *Hyperobjects: Philosophy and Ecology after the End of the World*. Posthumanities 27. Minneapolis, MN: University of Minnesota Press.

Nederveen Pieterse, Jan. 1995. "The Cultural Turn in Development: Questions of Power". *The European Journal of Development Research* 7 (1): 176–92.

Oakley, Kate, and Jonathan Ward. 2018. "The Art of the Good Life: Culture and Sustainable Prosperity". *Cultural Trends* 27 (1): 4–17.

O'Connor, Justin. 2016. "After the Creative Industries: Cultural Policy in Crisis". *Law, Social Justice & Global Development* 1: 1–18.

Pascual, Jordi, and Jon Hawkes. 2015. "Navigating Through The Pillars: Are We Coming Closer to Culture?" In *Another Europe*, edited by Philipp Dietachmair and Milica Ilić, 416–29. Amsterdam: European Cultural Foundation.

Robidoux, Meghan, and Jason F. Kovacs. 2018. "Public Art as a Tool for Environmental Outreach: Insights on the Challenges of Implementation". *The Journal of Arts Management, Law, and Society*, DOI: 10.1080/10632921.2018.1450315.

Ross, Andrew. 2007. "Nice Work If You Can Get It: The Mercurial Career of Creative Industries Policy". *Work Organisation, Labour & Globalisation* 1 (1): 13–30.

Schech, Susanne, and Jane Haggis. 2000. *Culture and Development: A Critical Introduction*. Oxford; Malden, MA: Blackwell Publishers.

Soini, Katriina, and Joost Dessein. 2016. "Culture-Sustainability Relation: Towards a Conceptual Framework". *Sustainability* 8 (2): 167.

Stevenson, Nick. 2003. *Cultural Citizenship Cosmopolitan Questions*. Maidenhead: Open University Press. www.site.ebrary.com/id/10175205.

UNESCO. 2005. *Convention on the Protection and Promotion of the Diversity of Cultural Expressions*. Paris: UNESCO.

UNESCO. 2013. *Let's Put Culture on the Agenda Now!* Paris: UNESCO. www.youtube.com/watch?v=mWS3UPqm9iU.

UNESCO, and UNDP. 2013. *Creative Economy Report*. Paris and New York, NY: UNESCO and UNDP.

Vlassis, Antonios. 2015. "Culture in the Post-2015 Development Agenda: The Anatomy of an International Mobilisation". *Third World Quarterly* 36 (9): 1649–62.

Webster, Ken. 2017. *The Circular Economy: A Wealth of Flows*. 2nd ed. Cowes, Isle of Wight: Ellen MacArthur Foundation Publishing.

World Bank. 2017. "Air Transport, Passengers Carried". www.data.worldbank.org/indicator/IS.AIR.PSGR.

World Commission on Environment and Development. 1987. *Our Common Future*. Oxford Paperbacks. Oxford; New York, NY: Oxford University Press.

Yusoff, Kathryn, and Jennifer Gabrys. 2011. "Climate Change and the Imagination: Climate Change and the Imagination". *Wiley Interdisciplinary Reviews: Climate Change* 2 (4): 516–34.

INDEX

Note: Page numbers in **bold** refer to tables and page numbers in *italics* refer to figures. Page numbers followed by n indicate end-of-chapter notes.